First World War
and Army of Occupation
War Diary
France, Belgium and Germany

3 DIVISION
7 Infantry Brigade
Prince of Wales's Volunteers (South Lancashire Regiment)
2nd and 1/4th Battalions
4 August 1914 - 31 December 1915

WO95/1414

The Naval & Military Press Ltd
www.nmarchive.com
Published in association with The National Archives

Published by

The Naval & Military Press Ltd

Unit 10 Ridgewood Industrial Park,

Uckfield, East Sussex,

TN22 5QE England

Tel: +44 (0) 1825 749494

www.naval-military-press.com

www.nmarchive.com

This diary has been reprinted in facsimile from the original. Any imperfections are inevitably reproduced and the quality may fall short of modern type and cartographic standards.

© **Crown Copyright**
Images reproduced by permission of The National Archives, London, England, 2015.

Contents

Document type	Place/Title	Date From	Date To
Miscellaneous	2 Battalion South Lancashire Regt. 1914 Aug To 1915 Oct. 4 Bn South Lancs Rgt. 1915 Feb To 1915 Dec.		
Heading	3rd Division 7th Infy Bde. 2nd Battalion South Lancashire Regt. Aug-Dec 1914		
Heading	7th Brigade. 3rd Division. 2nd Battalion South Lancashire Regiment August 1914		
Heading	War Diary 2nd South Lancashire Regt. 7th Brigade. Vol I 4-31.8.14		
War Diary		04/08/1914	31/08/1914
Heading	7th Brigade. 3rd Division. 2nd Battalion South Lancashire Regiment September 1914		
Heading	War Diary 2nd Batt. South Lancashire Rgt. 7th Brigade. Vol II 1-30.9.14		
War Diary		01/09/1914	30/09/1914
Heading	7th Brigade. 3rd Division. 2nd Battalion South Lancashire Regiment October 1914		
War Diary		01/10/1914	31/10/1914
Miscellaneous	2nd Bn South Lancashire Regt.		
Miscellaneous	2nd South Lancashire Regt.		
Heading	7th Brigade. 3rd Division. 2nd Battalion South Lancashire Regiment November 1914		
War Diary		01/11/1914	30/11/1914
Heading	7th Brigade. 3rd Division. 2nd Battalion South Lancashire Regiment December 1914		
Heading	3rd Division. 7th Inf. Bde. War Diary 2nd South Lancashire Regiment December 1914		
War Diary		01/12/1914	31/12/1914
Heading	3rd Division. 7th Infy Bde. 2nd Battalion 8th Lancashire Regt. Jan-Oct 1915		
Heading	7th Inf. Bde. War Diary 2nd Battn. The South Lancashire Regiment January 1915		
War Diary		01/01/1915	31/01/1915
Heading	7th Inf. Bde. War Diary 2nd Battn. The South Lancashire Regiment February 1915		
War Diary		01/02/1915	28/02/1915
Heading	2nd Battn. The South Lancashire Regiment March 1915		
War Diary		01/03/1915	31/03/1915
Heading	7th Inf. Bde. 3rd Div. War Diary 2nd Battn. The South Lancashire Regiment April 1915		
War Diary		01/04/1915	30/04/1915
Heading	7th Inf. Bde. 3rd Div. War Diary 2nd Battn. The South Lancashire Regiment May 1915		
War Diary		01/05/1915	03/05/1915
Miscellaneous	Office of the Deputy Director, Supply and Transport, Base	10/07/1917	10/07/1917
War Diary		03/05/1915	06/05/1915
Miscellaneous	Assistant Director of Supplies.		
War Diary		06/05/1915	08/05/1915
Miscellaneous	D Squadron and Machine Gun Section		
War Diary		08/05/1915	09/05/1915

Miscellaneous	British other ranks.		
War Diary		09/05/1915	10/05/1915
Miscellaneous	Indian other ranks.		
War Diary		10/05/1915	12/05/1915
Miscellaneous	Cavalry Brigade. Appendix I.		
War Diary		12/05/1915	14/05/1915
Miscellaneous	S Battery R.H.A.		
War Diary		14/05/1915	16/05/1915
Miscellaneous	War Diary of "S" Battery, R.H.A.		
War Diary		16/05/1915	18/05/1915
Miscellaneous	Notes from War Diaries, Part CCCXCIV Mesopotamian Expeditionary Force.		
War Diary		18/05/1915	22/05/1915
Miscellaneous	General Staff Branch.		
War Diary		22/05/1915	24/05/1915
Miscellaneous	D.I.W.T., Basrah		
War Diary		24/05/1915	25/05/1915
Miscellaneous			
War Diary		26/05/1915	28/05/1915
Miscellaneous	I am arranging for a sufficiency monthly of superstructure.		
War Diary		28/05/1915	31/05/1915
Miscellaneous	Appendix 35.	21/06/1917	21/06/1917
War Diary		31/05/1915	31/05/1915
Miscellaneous	B.M., R.E., G.H.Q.	21/06/1917	21/06/1917
War Diary		31/05/1915	31/05/1915
Miscellaneous	Appendix 21.	19/06/1917	19/06/1917
Heading	7th Inf. Bde. 3 Div. War Diary 3rd 2nd Battn. The South Lancashire Regiment June 1915		
War Diary		01/06/1915	30/06/1915
Heading	7th Inf. Bde. 3 Div. War Diary 2nd Battn. The South Lancashire Regiment July 1915		
War Diary		01/07/1915	31/07/1915
Heading	7th Inf. Bde. 3 Div War Diary 2nd Battn. The South Lancashire Regiment August 1915		
War Diary		01/08/1915	31/08/1915
Heading	7th Inf. Bde. 3 Div War Diary 2nd Battn. The South Lancashire Regiment September1915		
War Diary		01/09/1915	30/09/1915
Heading	2nd Battn. War Diary The South Lancashire Regiment October 1915		
War Diary		01/10/1915	31/10/1915
Heading	3rd Division 7th Infy Bde. 4th Battalion Sth Lancashire Regt. Feb-Sep 1915 from U K		
Heading	7th Inf Bde 3rd Div Battn Disembarked Havre From England 13.02.15 Battn. Joined Bde. 24.02.15 War Diary 4th Battn. The South Lancashire Regiment February (10.2.15-28.2.15) 1915		
War Diary	Tunbridge Wells	10/02/1915	12/02/1915
War Diary	La Havre	13/02/1915	14/02/1915
War Diary	Bailleul	15/02/1915	18/02/1915
War Diary	La Clytte	21/02/1915	25/02/1915
War Diary	Locre	26/02/1915	28/02/1915
Heading	7th Inf. Bde. 3 Div War Diary 4th Battn. The South Lancashire Regiment March 1915		
War Diary	Locre	01/03/1915	16/03/1915

War Diary	Kemmel	16/03/1915	19/03/1915
War Diary	Laclytte	20/03/1915	20/03/1915
War Diary	Locre	23/03/1915	23/03/1915
War Diary	Westoutre	24/03/1915	24/03/1915
War Diary	Dickebusch	26/03/1915	31/03/1915
Heading	7th Inf. Bde. 3 Div. War Diary 4th Battn. The South Lancashire Regiment April 1915		
War Diary	Dickebusch	01/04/1915	07/04/1915
War Diary	Trenches Dickebusch	08/04/1915	13/04/1915
War Diary	Dickebusch	14/04/1915	19/04/1915
War Diary	Trenches Dickebusch	20/04/1915	25/04/1915
War Diary	Dickebusch	26/04/1915	30/04/1915
Heading	7th Inf. Bde. 3 Div. War Diary 4th Battn. The South Lancashire Regiment May 1915		
War Diary	Elzenwalle	14/05/1915	15/05/1915
War Diary	Dickebusch	16/05/1915	31/05/1915
Heading	7th Inf. Bde. 3 Div. War Diary 4th Battn. The South Lancashire Regiment June 1915		
War Diary	Dickebusch	01/06/1915	03/06/1915
War Diary	Near Hooge	05/06/1915	11/06/1915
War Diary	Busseboom	12/06/1915	16/06/1915
War Diary	N of Hooge	16/06/1915	16/06/1915
War Diary	Busseboom	17/06/1915	21/06/1915
War Diary	Ypres	22/06/1915	24/06/1915
War Diary	Hooge	25/06/1915	30/06/1915
Heading	7th Inf. Bde. 3 Div. War Diary 4th Battn. The South Lancashire Regiment July 1915		
War Diary	W of Ypres	01/07/1915	01/07/1915
War Diary	Ypres	02/07/1915	04/07/1915
War Diary	E of Busseboom	05/07/1915	07/07/1915
War Diary	Sanctuary Wood	08/07/1915	12/07/1915
War Diary	E of Busseboom	13/07/1915	31/07/1915
Heading	7th Inf. Bde. 3 Div. War Diary 4th Battn. The South Lancashire Regiment August 1915		
War Diary	E of Busseboom	01/08/1915	02/08/1915
War Diary	N of Dickebusche	02/08/1915	31/08/1915
Heading	7th Inf. Bde. 3 Div. War Diary 4th Battn. The South Lancashire Regiment September 1915		
War Diary	N of Dickebusch	01/09/1915	30/09/1915
Heading	3rd Division 7 Bde 4th Battalion Sth Lancs Regt. Oct-Dec 1915		
Heading	7th Inf. Bde. 3 Div. War Diary 4th Battn. The South Lancashire Regiment October 1915		
War Diary	N of Dickebusch	01/10/1915	22/10/1915
War Diary	Berthen	23/10/1915	28/10/1915
Heading	Pioneers. 3rd Div. War Diary 4th Battn. The South Lancashire Regiment November 1915		
War Diary	Berthen	29/10/1915	05/11/1915
War Diary	Oudezeele J.14 a. 5.1.	06/11/1915	11/11/1915
War Diary	Oudezeele	12/11/1915	21/11/1915
War Diary	Poperinghe	22/11/1915	22/11/1915
War Diary	Voormezeele	23/11/1915	24/11/1915
War Diary	Renninghelst	25/11/1915	30/11/1915
Heading	Pioneers. 3rd Div. War Diary 4th Battn. The South Lancashire Regiment December 1915		
War Diary	Reninghelst	01/12/1915	31/12/1915

2 BATTALION SOUTH
LANCASHIRE REGT.
1914 AUG TO 1915 OCT.
----
4 BN SOUTH LANCS RGT.
1915 FEB TO 1915 DEC.

1414

3RD DIVISION
7TH INFY BDE

2ND BATTALION

SOUTH LANCASHIRE REGT.

AUG - DEC 1914

7th Brigade.
3rd Division.

2nd BATTALION

SOUTH LANCASHIRE REGIMENT

AUGUST 1914

1·A.
10 sheets

WAR DIARY 121/1063

2nd Lothian and Border Horse.

4th Brigade.

Volume 1.

4 – 31 8.14

2nd Battn. The South Lancashire Regiment.

August 1914

2

Tuesday
4th Aug.   Order to mobilize received

5th Aug.   Mobilization Continued

6th Aug.   Ditto

7th Aug.   Ditto. Capt. Charlton
                2nd Lieut Howitt and 2/Lieut
                Townend dispatched to Depot
                Warrington in pursuance of
                War Office order

8th Aug.   Mobilization Completed

9th Aug.   Sunday

10th Aug.   Training of mobilized
             battalion.

11th Aug.   Ditto

12th Aug.   Ditto

13th Aug.   Battⁿ left Tidworth and
             embarked at SOUTHAMPTON
             and sailed at 5.p.m on S S
             LAPWING.

14th Aug.   At 4.a.m arrived off HAVRE
             and remained at anchor at
             12 noon. Thence proceeded up
             the River SEINE arriving at
             ROUEN about 7.p.m, proceeded
             to rest Camp at MONT ST.
             AGLIN

4

Aug 15ᵗʰ   Remained in rest camp

Aug 16ᵗʰ   Left Camp about 1.45 a.m
            and entrained at ROUEN
            arriving at BUSIGNY about
            6.p.m thence proceeding to
            AULNOYE.

Aug 17ᵗʰ   Left billets about 6.30.a.m
            and marched to MARBAIX
            a distance of nine miles
            arriving about 10.a.m.

Aug 18ᵗʰ   Remained in billets at MARBAIX

Aug 19ᵗʰ   Remained in billets at MARBAIX

Aug 20ᵗʰ   Marched to ST HILAIRE
            arriving about 10.a.m and
            billeted.

Aug 21st. Friday.	Moved about 6.a.m to FEIGNIES where the brigade billeted.
Aug. 22nd. Saturday	Moved about 6.30 a.m with remainder of brigade. During the march the battalion was detached from the Brigade and proceeded to FRAMERIES. where it billeted for the night ne the railway station.
Aug 23rd Sunday.	Batt'n moved at 8.a.m to CIPLY and joined the remainder of the Brigade. About 12 noon the battalion received orders to move to a position about 1 mile North of FRAMERIES and entrench itself there. The Batt'n was in position on the left of the Brigade

Assistance was given in digging trenches by Belgian Civilians. About 5 p.m the enemy fired a few Shrapnel at the working parties. The trenches were immediately resumed and occupied during the night.

Aug 24th
Monday:
At dawn the enemy opened an attack on the trenches at about 5 a.m the troops occupying FRAMERIES on our left were driven back, thus enabling the enemy to eventually enfilade the trenches occupied by C and D Companies who after suffering great loss were compelled to retire covered by A and B Companies. The Battalion eventually succeeded in retiring to SAINT WAAST, and bivouaced for the night about 3 miles to the West of the town.

7

Aug 25th
Tuesday

The Batt'n. hurried off at 2.a.m with the remainder of the Brigade in a S.W direction via Le QUESNO, the Brigade acting as rear guard intending to halt for the night at COWDRAY.

On arrival at SOLESMES about 6 p.m, a vigorous attack was made by the enemy in which the battalion who formed the rear party suffered severely, holding its position until dark. Under cover of darkness the battalion withdrew in small detachments.

8

| Aug 26th Wednesday | Those portions of the Battalion which succeeded in reaching CAMBRAY took part in an action at that place eventually being forced to retire before the superior numbers of the enemy and reached VERMAND that evening. |

Aug 27th — Marched off at 1 a.m. and marched throughout the day.

Aug 28th — Continued marching and eventually reached TARLEFESSE, North East of NOYONS, arriving about 4 p.m. and billeted for the night.

Aug 29th — Battn with remainder of the division moved off about 1 p.m. and marched throughout the night. Major Ashworth assumed command of Battn vice Col. Wanless placed on sick list.

10

Aug 30— Continued marching, arriving at VIC-SUR-AISNE in the evening, where the battalion went into billets.

Aug 31st Marched to COYOLLES arriving there in the evening, where the battalion bivouaced.

7th Brigade.

3rd Division.

2nd BATTALION

SOUTH LANCASHIRE REGIMENT

SEPTEMBER 1 9 1 4:::::

2.A.
13 sheet

$\frac{121}{1082}$

WAR DIARY

2nd Battn South Lancashire Regt
7th Brigade.

Volume II
1 — 30.9.14

2nd Battn. The South Lancashire Regiment.

September 1914

Sept 1st Tuesday.	Continued marching and arrived at VILLERS and went into bivouac.
Sept 2nd Wednesday.	Continued to march with the division and reached PRANGY and went into bivouac.
Sept 3rd Thursday.	Marched to SANCY and went into bivouac.
Sept 4th Friday.	Remained in bivouac at SANCY until about 10.30 A.M. when whole division marched by night via CRECY and CRECY Forest.
Sept 5th Saturday.	Arrived at CHATRES and remained in bivouac throughout the day.

...tere Capt Colville & 85 other ranks, joined battalion as first reinforcement.
Also Sgt Major Roberts and 140 Stragglers etc.

Sept 6th
Sunday.

Division now advanced in a N.E direction through CRECY FOREST, about 5.a.m.
On reaching FAREMOOTIERS. battalion was detailed for outpost duty.
While advancing to take up its position was fired upon, and was unable to take up the allotted line that night.

Sept 7th
Monday.

Battn moved forward about 5.a.m. to endeavour to take up the line VOISINS — MOUROUX.
Several casualties occurred during the day, during wood fighting.
The Battn was withdrawn about 4 p.m. and after a short rest marched with the division to PTS. AULNOYS, where it bivouaced

	Here Lieut Gebbie and about 90 other ranks joined the Battⁿ as 2nd reinforcement.

Sepr 8^t
Tuesday.
Battⁿ marched about 7.a.m in the direction of REBAIS and halted for the night at BUSSIERES.

Sepr 9^t
Wednesday.
Battⁿ moved off with remainder of division about 6.a.m, and during the morning crossed the river MARNE in pursuit of the enemy, and bivouaced that evening in the vicinity of BEZU-le-GUERY

Sepr 10^t
Thursday
Division moved in N.E direction. Battⁿ moved off about 6.a.m. as adv^d guard to 7^t Brigade. and in the evening took up outpost position N of. MONTENHFROY.

Sept 11th Friday	The 7th Infy Brigade formed advanced guard to 3rd Division and moved off about 5.30.a.m Direction of march DAMMARD — NEUILLY. Battn billeted at GRAND-ROZOY
Sept 12th Saturday.	Division moved off at 9.a.m. Progress slow. Brigade billeted that night at CERSEUIL.
Sept 13th Sunday.	Battn moved off about 7.30 a.m to VAILLY, but only reached BRAINE and bivouaced there N of that place
Sept 14th Monday.	Battn moved about 5.a.m towards VAILLY via BRENELLE. Came under heavy shell fire and eventually crossed river AISNE east of VAILLY, and took up a position as reserve to remainder of brigade on high ground about D of St PRECORD

Sep 15th
Tuesday.   Batt. remained in same
position as yesterday under
intermittent shell fire.
Transport, which had not crossed
river was heavily shelled and
eventually, retired in the evening
to BRAINE.

Sep 16th
Wednesday. Situation remained the
same.
Capt Evans and 3 other officers
joined the battalion.

Sep 17th
Thursday.   Situation remains the same
Shelling much heavier
this morning.

Sep 18th
Friday.   Situation remains the same

16

Sept 19th
Saturday.

Situation the same. Enemy made strong attack. Two Companies sent forward to reinforce firing line. Lieut Thorpe and 95 men 3rd reinforcement arrived.

Sept 20th
Sunday.

Very heavy attack made on position by Germans. During the day the Batt'y (less 1 platoon) was sent forward to reinforce various portions of the firing line. The casualties during the day in the battalion were 3 Officers killed 4 Officers wounded 141 other ranks, killed wounded and missing. Of this later number, only a small proportion were missing.
During an advance by the enemy during the evening a few Germans came forward, making signs of surrender.
2/Lt Sutton and 4 men

advanced to meet them, whereupon they were fired on by other Germans concealed behind. 2/Lieut Sutton was wounded and 3 men captured. The names of the Officers killed were 2/Lieut Watson, 2/Lieut Wallace and 2/Lieut Birdwood. Those wounded being Capt Pisani Lieut Gebbie and 2/Lieuts Howitt and Sutton.

Sept 21st Monday.
Batt: (less A Company, under Major Gomer) moved at night from position on N Side of river, the Brigade having been relieved by 16th Brigade.

Sept 22nd Tuesday.
Batt: withdrew to AUGY and occupied billets there, being joined there by the 4th reinforcement. Strength 2 Officers (2/Lieuts McKerrow and 2/Lieut D.S.K. Forgan) and 152 other ranks. On this date the batt: was re equipped with 2 machine guns complete and 10 horses to replace casualties The Officers of the Battalion on this date were.

Major Ashworth Commanding
Major Owen
Capt Ritchie
 "   Colvile
 "   Bagley
 "   Herbert
Lieut Clemens   Adjutant
 "   Fletcher
 "   Salter
2/Lieut Gilmore
 "   Mitchell
 "   Clarke
 "   Thorpe
 "   McKerrow
 "   Forgan
Lieut Boast   Quartermaster
Civil Surgeon L. Gwyn-Davis Medical Officer

It should be noted that the 4th reinforcement consisted mainly of men of the 3rd (Special reserve) Battalion.

Sep 23rd
Wednesday.

A. Company rejoined from the N side of river about 2. a.m. Batt remained at rest in billets at AUGY.

Sep 24th
Thursday.

Batt moved about 2 p.m. and relieved 3rd Worcestershire Regt in vicinity of CHASSEMY. A. B and D Coys occupied positions in woods to the N.W of CHASSEMY watching the Bridge at CONDÉ.
C. Coy & Batt H.Q. remained in reserve at CHASSEMY. Transport parked in small wood about 1 mile S of CHASSEMY.
Major Given assumed Command of 2nd Echelon of 7th Infy Bde Transport; Capt Bagley assuming Command of A. Company

Sept 25th Friday.	No change in situation.
Sept 26th Saturday.	Battn relieved by R. Irish Rifles and withdrew to billets at AUGY. The machine guns were handed over temporarily to R.I.R.
Sept 27th Sunday.	Information received at AUGY about 4.30 a.m. that enemy had attempted to cross the river at CONDÉ. Battn ordered forward at once and left its billets with 3rd Worcestershire Regt about 5 a.m. The alarm proved to be unfounded, and Battn hitchear to AUGY remaining at rest during the remainder of the day.

Sept 28th
Monday.   The Battn remained in billets at
            AUGY.

Sept 29th
Tuesday.   The Battn remained in billets at
            AUGY.

Sept 30th
Wednesday. The Battn remained in billets at
            AUGY.

7th Brigade.
3rd Division.

2nd BATTALION

SOUTH LANCASHIRE REGIMENT

OCTOBER 1 9 1 4

2nd Battalion South Lancashire Regt.
War diary — 1st to 31st Oct. 1914 —

1. Oct. 1914 — Battalion [forming part of 7th Infantry Brigade] moved about 10 pm from AUAY to GRAN-ROZOY [and went into billets there.]

2. Oct. 1914 — Battalion moved at 10 am to BEUGNEUX and remained there until 8.30pm when it moved back to GRAND-ROZOY and joined the Brigade. Brigade moved to NOROY.

3 Oct. 1914 — Brigade arrived at NOROY about 2am [and occupied billets there.] Brigade moved at 7 pm in direction of VAUMOISE.

4 Oct. 1914 — Brigade arrived at VAUMOISE about 3am. Units placed in billets. [Battalion in large farm and mill] — Brigade moved at 6 pm and arrived at SAUNTINE about midnight — [Battalion placed in billets — A & B Coys and Head Quarter details in Match Factory. C & D in main street.]

5 Oct 1914 — Battalion moved [from billets] at 11 pm and marched to LONGUEVIL-St-MARIE arriving there about 1 am

6th Oct. 1914 – Battalion entrained and left 2
   unknown destination at 5.30 am –
7 Oct. 1914 – Arrived RUE about midnight 6th Oct.
   and after detraining moved into bivouac
   about 3 am.
      Moved at 9.30 am to OUVILLE occupying
   billets and bivouac –
8 Oct. 1914 – Battalion left OUVILLE about midnight
   and joined Brigade –
      march continued to REGNEAUVILLE arriving
9 Oct. 1914 about 5.30 am.
      A & B. Coys at once took up outpost position –
   Remainder of Battalion placed in billets.
   Battalion forming part of 7th Infantry
   Brigade. Left billets about 4 pm. and
   marched for about 2 miles N.E, Companies
   on outpost duty joining –
      Brigade moved by motor lorries to PERNES
   arriving between 2 am and 5.30 am on
10 Oct. 1914 and occupied billets –
      Transport marched from REGNEAUVILLE
   about 5 pm 9 Oct arriving at PERNES
   about 3 pm 10 Oct. A hard and trying
   march – completed without casualty –
      Captain Morgan 3rd Battn. and 2nd Lieuts.
   Meredith and Sleigh 4th The Buffs joined
   Battalion at PERNES
11. Oct. 1914 – 3rd Division continued advance in
   N.E direction – Battalion moved off about 9 am.

arrived at HINGES about 7 pm and
in & into billets.

12 Oct. 1914 – Battalion forming part of an
advance guard, left HINGE about 7 am.
By evening the Battalion had taken up an
entrenched position in vicinity of LACOUTRE,
having come into contact with the enemy.
Casualties – a few men wounded.
Captain Melvill N.I.L.F and Captain Andrews
4th The Kings joined the Battalion.

13. Oct. 1914 – Advance made to vicinity of RICHEBOURG
where Battalion entrenched in vicinity of
St. VAAST.
Very wet day. Casualties slight.

14. Oct. 1914 – Practically no change in disposition.
General Hamilton killed between RICHEBOURG
and LACOUTRE. Was buried at night at
LACOUTRE Church. During the ceremony
the firing along the whole line was
exceptionally heavy.
Reinforcement of about 160 other ranks under
Lieut Gibson 3rd Battn and 2nd Lieut S.H.
Taylor and C.J. Woolley 3rd Y & L Regt arrived
at LACOUTRE but did not join Battalion.
Slight advance made.

15. Oct. 1914 – Battalion advanced beyond N end of
RICHEBOURG. Brigade took up position
facing NE.
2nd Lieut McKerron and several men wounded.

16 Oct 1914 – Advance continued in NE direction. 4
At night Battalion was in vicinity of
NEUVE CHAPPELL – 1st Battalion withdrawn
to billets in NEUVE CHAPPELL, being relieved
by 1st Wiltshire Regt.
Reinforcement joined from LACOUTRE.

17 Oct 1914 – About 10am B & D companies moved
forward to reinforce a portion of firing line
supporting 3rd Worcester Regt, and later in
the day remaining 2 companies were
also moved forward.
The object of the portion of the firing
line was directed on to the enemy in the
vicinity of ILLIES, B & D companies being
detailed to fill a gap in the line between
East Surrey and Worcester Regts. Other 2
companies in reserve at HALPEGARBE.
Captain Morgan reported sick.

18 Oct 1914 – Disposition practically unchanged except
that Worcester and Royal Irish Regts had been
relieved by K.O.Y.L.I. and West Kent Regts –
Shine from ILLIES. During the night
trenches extended and improved.

19 Oct 1914 – No change in situation – A & B companies
moved forward in relief of B & D companies.
Trenches further improved.
Captain Ritchie admitted to hospital, sick.
Captain Melvill assumed command of
C company.

5

20 Oct 1914 – Heavy attack made on trenches
 occupied by Battalion – Sin inns heavy losses.
 Captain Bagley wounded. Sin. Holt amongst
 others killed –
   A. & D. Companies sent out to reinforce firing
 line – Lieut. Bleugh wounded – Lieut. Waley
 killed –
21 Oct 1914 – Another heavy attack and considerable
 casualties – Captain Shaw killed –
 Captain Cotale, Lieut. Taylor, Mentieth, Andrews
 Clarke and Thorpe and large number
 of men reported missing –
 Remainder of Battalion withdrawn from
 trenches and placed in billets near
 Western Gate – in BOIS de PLOU
 Heavy attack at night on right on 14th
 Infantry Brigade –
22 Oct 1914 – Heavy firing still continuing on our
 right – Battalion still in billets –
 Battalion mustered today –
   Major Ashworth in command –
   Lieut. Colemans – Adjutant
     "   Entwhistle – Machine guns –
   Captns. Melville & Herbert.
   2nd Lts. Mitchell & Fogan.
   Lieut. Davies (M.O.)
   With 2nd Echelon Transport –
   Major Coen.
   Lieut. Gallie – Transport Officer –
     "   Beast – Quartermaster –

6

Total other ranks about 300 –
I/Spectn recommend that 6 missions have
been granted to CSM Murphy and Sergts.
Byatt and Holden –
During operations on 21st Oct. machine
guns under Lieut. Fulcher did excellent
work. Corpl. Pinnick and Pte. Williams
particularly distinguishing themselves –
Serjt. Winser, machine gun Serjeant killed –
About 10pm 22 Oct. Battalion was ordered
out to assist R.E. in digging trenches and
was withdrawn about 4 am

23 Oct. 1914 – Battalion moved to billets at
RICHEBOURG ST VAAST and remained at
rest all day –
2/Lieut. Forgan reported sick –

24 Oct. 1914 – Battalion remained [at rest in
billets] at RICHEBOURG ST VAAST –

25 Oct. 1914 – Situation practically unchanged –
During afternoon Battalion ordered out to
reinforce Royal Irish Rifles but later
was withdrawn to billets. About 7 pm
a party of 200 under Capt. Melvill
was ordered out to assist R.E. in making
and improving trenches in vicinity of
NEUVE CHAPPELL –
Raining very heavily –
Reinforcement of about 65 Other ranks
joined the Battalion being taken forward

from LACOUTRE by Quartermaster — 7

26 Oct 1914 – Party detailed of fatigue to assist R.E. returned to billets about 4 am. —
About 3 pm Battalion received orders to be in readiness to move out about 4 pm moved in direction of NEUVE CHAPPELL and placed in General Support to the Brigade. —

27 Oct 1914 – Battalion moved forward with Lincoln Regt. and Royal Irish to attack enemy in position in vicinity of NEUVE CHAPPELL. This was not successful and Battalion eventually withdrew and entrenched in new position about 1–00 yards in rear of former one. —
Major & Adjt. Clemens wounded. 2nd Lieut Mitchell killed.
Lieut Davies (R.A.M.O) relieved by Lieut I.M. Pirrie, R.A.M.C. —

28 Oct 1914 – About 1 am Battalion was relieved by Indian Sappers and Miners and withdrew after dawn to billets at RICHEBOURG. —
About 3 pm orders received for Battalion to move out in direction of NEUVE CHAPPELL to support dismounted Cavalry. Remained in support until dawn 29th.

29 Oct 1914 – Battalion withdrew at dawn to original billets at RICHEBOURG.
About 4 pm village heavily shelled by enemy

large guns and all units in billets. 8
is forced to retire to LACOUTRE.
During the shelling the house occupied by
Battalion Head Quarters was struck.
Major Ashworth and Capt. Melville rendered
unfit for duty by severe concussion.
On arrival at LACOUTRE Capt. Melville
was sent to hospital and Major
Ashworth accommodated at Head Quarters
3rd Division.
The Battalion now numbers –
Captain Herbert in command
Lieut. Fulcher – Adjutant & machine guns
    "   Verrier M.O.
With 2nd Echelon –
Major Gour.
Lieut. Salter. Transport Officer.
       Boot. Quartermaster
Total other ranks about 330 –
All placed in billets at South end
of village of LACOUTRE.
Shelling of RICHEBOURG continued
practically all night.

Friday 30 Oct. About 2.30pm whole Brigade
moved in a N direction, arriving at
DOULIEU about 6.30pm
Major Ashworth admitted to hospital.
Captain L.W. Herbert assumes command
of the Battalion –

31. Oct. 1914 – Brigade moved at 9 a.m. & arrived at MERRIS but now occupying billets there –

W. F. Sweeny Major
for O.C. 2nd South Lancs Regt

The Diary up to end of Sept has already been submitted.

This month's diary is entirely due to the careful record kept by Lt. & Quartermaster S. T. Boast who is the only officer of this Battalion now serving in the field – notwithstanding the paucity of officers & all the extra responsibilities thrown on his shoulders this officer has found time to keep things going at "all times" & I consider deserves the greatest credit.

W. F. Sweeny Major
Comdg 2nd South Lancs Regt

29/11/14
Continued on page 16 –

Continued from page 9 —

On 31st Oct. 1914 the Battalion mustered as follows:—

Major B. K. Green — S. Lan. R. Commanding Bryan Transport.
Capt. S. W. Herbert S. S. Lan R. Commdg. Coy.
Lieut. B. V. Pulchin S. Lan R. Acting adjt.
  "   W. C. Salter   "   Transport Officer
  "   S. J. Boast   "   Quartermaster
  "   J. M. Power R.A.M.C. Medical Officer

and about 330 Other ranks.

At this time the Battalion was divided into two Companies. These were commanded as under, there being no Company Officers:—

A + B formed No. I under Coy. Sgt. Major W. Bulger.
C + D   "   No. II   "   "   "   "   J. Brannigan.

These were the only 2 remaining senior non-commissioned officers — with the exception of Battalion Staff —

W F Sweeny Major
Comg 2nd S Lancashire R.

6

2nd South Lancashire Regt.

Date	Officers				Other Ranks		
	Killed	Wounded	Missing		Killed	Wounded	Missing
Bt. fwd	1	3	4		3	63	+ 550
			2/Lt Waldegr(4th Fus?)				
			Thorpe				
			Meredith (6 Fus?)				
22.10.14							
27.10.14	Lt A Mitchell	Lt L.A. Clemens			5	9	11
28.10.14						1	
29.10.14		Major S Ashworth			-	1	-
		Capt. G W Melvill					

7th Brigade.
3rd Division.

2nd BATTALION

SOUTH LANCASHIRE REGIMENT

NOVEMBER 1 9 1 4

82nd   10

2nd Battalion South Lancashire Regt

War Diary.   1st to 30th November 1914.

1 Nov. 1914 - [Sudden orders received for Brigade to move and] left MERRIS about 1 pm, marching [in a] N.E [direction]. Halted at LOCRE about 5 pm and went into billets there.

2 Nov. 1914 - Battalion remained at rest at LOCRE. Orders received for Major Green to be held in readiness to proceed to Base.

3 Nov. 1914 - Captain B. Denison and 2 Lt. J. Gore 3rd Gloucester Regt reported for duty with the Battalion about 1 pm. Major Green proceeds to Base. Battalion still at rest at LOCRE.

4 Nov. 1914 - No change. Still at LOCRE.

5 Nov. 1914 - Brigade moves forward in direction of YPRES marching from LOCRE about 8 am.
Halted about noon about 2½ miles South of YPRES. About 4 pm. 2 Battalions, Gordons and Wiltshires, moved forward to a position in vicinity of HOOGE and shortly afterwards the Battalion and Royal Irish Rifles followed to take up a position in reserve in same vicinity.

11

6. Nov. 1914 - Battalion in & out trenches
in vicinity of HOOGE
Nothing important to record.

7. Nov. 1914 - Battalion in reserve trenches
until about 4 pm when it moved forward
in relief of Royal Irish Rifles.
Suffered severe casualties and getting into
up to Battalion owing to town of YPRES
through which transport had to pass, being
continually shelled and on fire in
several places.

8. Nov. 1914 - Battalion in firing line.
Considerable damage to trenches by
enemy guns - not much rifle fire.
Casualties 3 killed 10 wounded.

9. Nov. 1914 - Battalion withdrew at night to
reserve trenches being relieved by Royal
Irish Rifles. General situation unchanged.
Casualties. 1 killed 3 wounded.

10. Nov. 1914 - Battalion still in reserve trenches.
Capt. Bulger and 5 men wounded.
Situation unchanged.

11. Nov. 1914 - Very heavy shelling all day.
½ Company sent forward during the day
to strengthen firing line - Remainder of
Battalion remained in reserve until
night when whole moved forward to
relieve Royal Irish Rifles who withdrew
to reserve trenches. Weather very bad.

Heavy rain storms. Heavy
shelling and rifle fire.
Casualties. 5 men wounded.

12 Nov. 1914. Continuous heavy rain.
Heavy shelling all day.
Casualties. 1 man killed. 2 or 3
wounded. 2 horses killed.
Captain L.W. Herbert reported sick
and removed to Field Ambulance.
Captain Duncan assumed command of
the Battalion.

13 Nov. 1914. No change in local situation.
Considerable rain all day.
Captain Duncan killed. Captain Gore
wounded. Several other casualties.
Lt. Colonel W.G.A. Green arrived from
England and assumed command of the
Battalion.
Only other officers now are Lieuts. Fulcher,
Salter and Boast (Quartermaster.)

14 Nov. 1914. Position very difficult but everyone
holding on. Continuous heavy rain
has made trenches almost impossible.
Battalion now in Brigade reserve
trenches. All trenches heavily shelled.
Several casualties. Getting forward supplies
very difficult owing to shelling and
bad state of roads.
2nd Lieut. G.T. Spendlove joined the Battalion.

13

15 Nov 1914 - Weather still very bad.
Rain and sleet, very cold.
No change in local situation. "B3"

16 Nov 1914 - Weather still bad.
Battalion still in Bougie avenue
trenches. No change in local situation.

17 Nov 1914 - Weather still wet and cold.
Battalion in trenches in support in
rear of firing line. Shelled heavily
all day by enemy. About 3 am large
shell dropped in "dug out" occupied by
Lt. Col. Green and Lieut. Fulcher, both of
whom were killed. Another shell
seriously wounded 2nd Lieut. Spendlove.
Battalion now left with only two officers -
Lieut. Braun (Quartermaster) and Lieut.
Salter.
Captain G.F. Whelan Royal Irish Rifles
detailed to command the Battalion and
assumed that duty.

18 Nov 1914 - Very cold. Heavy frost. No
change in local situation.

19 Nov 1914 - Still very cold and frosty. Some
snow and rain. Local situation
practically unchanged.

20 Nov - Very cold. Considerable frost and snow.
During the evening the Battalion withdrew
from trenches and marched to
WESTOUTRE occupying billets there.
The Division relieved by French troops.

14

The move was a difficult one owing to the large number of troops and quantity of transport on the roads.

2nd Lieut J. Martin 2. K.S. Rifles attached to the Battalion for duty.

21 Nov 1914 - Still very cold and frosty. Roads difficult for traffic.
Battalion at rest at WESTOUTRE.
Reinforcement of 90 men under Lieut W. P. Carter Thomas 4th S. Staffs Regt. joined the Battalion at WESTOUTRE.

22 Nov 1914 - Battalion still at rest. Quiet day. Lieut. Balter granted leave until 6 pm 29th Nov.
2nd Lieut. J. Martin appointed Acting Adjutant.

23 Nov 1914 - No change [in dispositions].

24 Nov 1914 - 2nd Lieut A. D. M Brown 3rd King's Own Rgt. reported for duty with the Battalion.
Local situation quiet. Fur waistcoats issued.

25 Nov 1914 - Major W. F. Sweeny 4th Royal Fusiliers detailed to command the Battalion, arrived and assumed command on relief of Captn J. P. whelan Royal Irish Rifles who returned to his own Unit.
Battalion at rest in billets at WESTOUTRE.

26 Nov 1914 - Still in billets at WESTOUTRE.
Captain E. Robson and 2nd Lieut W. G. M Boulton joined the Battalion.

27 Nov. 1914 – Brigade moved to LOCRE and occupied billets there.

28 Nov 1914 – Battalion at rest [in billets] at LOCRE. [Situation quiet]

29 Nov 1914 – Still at LOCRE. Local situation quiet.
Company Commanders inspected line of trenches to be occupied by Battn tomorrow.

30 Nov. 1914 – Brigade moved forward and occupied trenches East of KEMMEL, leaving LOCRE about 4 p.m.
Battalion took over position occupied by Liverpool Scottish who withdrew to billets at WESTOUTRE.

W. Flaveny Major
O.C. 2nd South Lancashire Regt.

On this date Battalion mustered as follows:—
Major W. F. Flaveny, Royal Fusiliers – Commanding
Captain E. Nilson – South Lancashire Regt.
Lieut. W. F. P. Thomas – 4. B. Staff. Regt.
  "   W. C. M. Buitton – South Lancashire Regt
2nd "   A. J. M. Brown – 3rd King's Own.
     R. C. Salter – South Lancashire Regt. (on leave)
2nd "   J. Martin – K. J. Rifles – Acting Adjutant
     "   S. J. Boast – South Lancashire Regt. Quartermaster
     "   J. M. Perrie – R.A.M.C. Medical Officer
9 officers and about 340 other ranks. W.F.S.
82 NCO

7th Brigade.

3rd Division.

2nd BATTALION

SOUTH LANCASHIRE REGIMENT

DECEMBER 1 9 1 4

3rd Division
7th Inf. Bde.

WAR DIARY

2nd SOUTH LANCASHIRE REGIMENT

DECEMBER

1914

2nd Battalion South Lancashire Regt 38

War diary —— 1st to 31st December 1914 —

1st. Battalion in trenches in position East of KEMMEL.
2nd Lieut. M.J. O'Shaughnessy joined Battalion [at this position and proceeded to fire trenches]
Two signallers - [Ptes. Atkins and Lloyd] sent with message from support trenches to fire trenches during the night, not having returned, were reported missing.
During the morning volunteers were asked for from men in support trenches to take water to men in fire trenches. Privates Knowles and Wolfe volunteered and performed the duty successfully. They also brought back Sergeant Regan who had been wounded the previous evening. Both these men were brought to notice by the Commanding Officer in a special report to Brigade Head Quarters.
Sergeant [Stephenson] and three other men were wounded during the day.
Very heavy rifle fire commenced about 6pm and continued for some time.

2nd. Battalion still in same position. Local situation unchanged. Usual continuous sniping. About 3 pm two bombs were

division of enemy into centre of our
right trench in addition from rear.
The first one damaged the trench and
injured Lieut. Thomas and a man, all
of whom were rendered unfit for duty.
The second bomb, thrown within a few
seconds of the first and dropping about
five yards to the right, damaged the
corner of the trench and injured one
other man.

During the day the enemy's trenches were
shelled by our Artillery as a result of
a telephone message, and apparently a
reinforcement of the enemy was dispersed
in consequence.

About 9 p.m. a regrettable incident occurred
in our fire trench. A hand grenade
which it was intended should be thrown
into enemy's trench, after being prepared, was
dropped by accident. Captain Robson,
2nd Lieut. O'Shaughnessy and Corporal Smith
being wounded, and Corporal McIlwain
killed. The first named officer who was
in command of the fire trench was
very severely wounded and died shortly
afterwards.

Lieut. Bullton assumes command of fire
trenches.

3rd — No change in situation but during the

evening the Battalion was relieved by 4th Middlesex Regt and withdrew to billets at WESTOUTRE without further casualty.

4th - Reinforcement of 129 other ranks with 4 [Following] Officers (SR on attd) joined the Battalion -
Lieut. W. J. Meredith - 3rd R. Mun. Fus.
2nd " J. W. Quinkey - 3rd R. Lan. Reg
 " W. T. Stamer - N. Staffs. Reg.
 " J. K. Schooling - 5th Middlesex Regt.

The party included several regular Sergeants and a number of old soldiers who had specially re-enlisted.

About 11 a.m. Battalion moved from billets in WESTOUTRE to farms about 1½ miles West owing to accommodation in WESTOUTRE being insufficient.

5th - Very heavy rain. Battalion at rest. Billet occupied by Regimental Transport was burnt down. Cause of fire not known.

6th - Battalion moved to billets at LOCRE. [Following] 3 officers joined for duty:- (SR other regts)
Captain J. F. B. Costin - Y & L Reg
2nd Lieut. A. B. Cowan - Royal Scots
 " J. O. B. Cowan - " "

7th - Battalion at rest in billets at LOCRE.
8th - Battalion moved to billets at BAILLEUL and assumed duty as Corps Troops.
9th - In billets at BAILLEUL refitting and cleaning

41

up for billets -
Several officers who recently joined the
Battalion proceeded to trenches for 24
hours instruction -

10th - No change in situation - Battalion
employed on Corps duties -

11th - 500 other ranks under Captain N.L.
Ballard 3rd Battalion, joined -
This reinforcement includes a very large
number of old time experienced soldiers, who
had specially enlisted -
Battalion still at BAILLEUL and now
commenced to reorganize into four
companies -
Captain Bostin reported as having sprained
his ankle in trenches and sent to Field
Hospital -

12th - No change in situation - Battalion now
reorganized into 4 companies -
A Company commanded by Lieut. J.H. Scholding
B   "   "   "   "   W.J. Meredith
C   "   "   "   Capt. N.L. Ballard
D   "   "   "   Lieut. W.M. Bruilton

13th - No change - Quiet day - Battalion attended
Divine Service parade - first since commencement
of the war -

14th - Refitting continued - Officers and selected
N.C.O's instructed in preparation and
throwing of improvised hand grenades -

15th - Quiet day in billets at Bailleul.
16th -⎫
17th - ⎬ Battalion fully occupied in refitting
18th -⎭ and re-organising in billets at Bailleul.

18th - Reinforcement of 45 men under Lieut R.B. Brankshaw, 3rd Dorsets and 2nd Lieut C.H.S. Duncan, 3rd Royal Scots joined the Battalion.

19th -⎫
20th - ⎬ Refitting and re-organising continued.
21st -⎭ Weather very bad - considerable rain.

22nd - Re-organisation of Battalion into four companies completed and inspected by Brigadier General Ballard, commanding 7th Infantry Brigade, [who in an address to the Battalion expressed his great satisfaction at the appearance of the men] Total strength 16 Officers 979 other ranks. Orders received for Battalion to be held in readiness to rejoin the Brigade. Very wet and cold day. (See also page 50)

23rd - Battalion at rest at Bailleul. Still very wet and cold with snow. Orders received for Battalion to move tomorrow and occupy part of position allotted to 7th Infantry Brigade.

24th - Battalion moved from billets about 12 noon en route for trenches & [and was drawn up just outside the town]

22nd. With a view to ascertaining how many Lancashire men were serving in the Battalion on this date, statements were obtained from Officers commanding companies which gave the following information:-

Blackburn	-	13
Burnley	-	9
Leigh	-	3
Liverpool	-	291
Manchester	-	79
Preston	-	17
Prescott	-	2
Rochdale	-	3
St. Helens	-	168
Warrington	-	47
Wigan	-	83
Widnes	-	47
Southport	-	17

Total = 779.

Birmingham	-	32
London	-	35
Other towns	-	133

= 200.

for an inspection by General Sir Horace
Smith-Dorrien, Commanding 2nd Corps -
After the inspection the General addressed
the Battalion, roughly as follows :-
"Major Sweeny, Officers, non-commissioned
officers and men, 2nd Battalion South
Lancashire Regiment, it has given me
great pleasure to make this inspection
of you after having completed your
reorganisation and as you are now on
your way to rejoin your Brigade in
the actual firing line - I must congratulate
you all on your steadiness, turn out and
general appearance and also express my
admiration of the large number of old
soldiers who I see in the ranks and
who have rejoined their old Regiment at
a time of such great need. I wish to
take this opportunity of speaking to you,
especially those of you who have recently
joined, of the splendid work done by the
Battalion from the commencement of this
campaign, as I feel sure that many of
you may not fully realise all that has
been done by your comrades, many of whom
lost their lives in doing their duty - The
great majority of the original Battalion have
left it in consequence of wounds and
other causes, but it is some satisfaction to

know that many of them will rejoin at the end of the war. I must refer to what is now history when our Army held up at least four times their number at Mons and when this Battalion lost a large number of Officers and men. Then again the various events of that arduous retirement, which was only possible by the determination of all to do their duty — also the great effort of the advance which commenced in the early days of September — and during which the Battalion did so well. Again the splendid work of the Battalion on the Aisne where it distinguished itself at the expense of further heavy losses and lastly, when, although opposed to enormous odds, the great effort of the Battalion in assisting to hold the position at Ypres, where your losses were again considerable — All this has lead to the splendid response from old soldiers, so many of whom I see before me, having set such an excellent example to the younger men of the country, which I hope will be followed by those still at home —
I must remind you that discipline is

a & ? element in this modern fighting. It is the one which helps you to endure the hardships which you will be called upon to face. Many of you have been away for some time, but I feel, that having once again put your shoulder to the wheel, you will do your duty cheerfully and give that obedience to discipline which is so essential to success. It now rests with you to carry on the splendid record which your Regiment has earned in the past and I wish you all the very best of luck."

At the conclusion of the address General Smith-Dorrien was heartily cheered by the Battalion which filed past him on leaving the ground.
Battalion moved forward and took up positions in vicinity East of LINDENHOEK relieving 1st Devons who withdrew.

Just before leaving Bailleul a reinforcement of 1 Sergeant, 1 Corporal and 38 men with 5 [the following] officers 4 S.R. arrived —
Dec 29/15

Captain Thomas James Barron Roberts 3.R.9.F.
"   Evans Smith   3.S.L.I.
2nd Lieut. Christopher Robert Whitaker 3. Dorsets

2nd Lt. Andrew Wentworth King. 3 y. L46
" Joseph Henry Kelly. 3. S. Lan.
This party proceeded to the position
with the Battalion.
Position satisfactorily taken over and
relief completed by about 6.30pm.
D Coy. under Lieut. Bastow in fire trenches.
Quiet night. Very cold and frosty.

25th — Still very cold and freezing hard.
General situation quiet. A Company
relieved D in fire trenches.
Casualties since last night. 3 men
killed. 3 wounded.
Special Christmas card from King and
Queen received and distributed.
Special gifts of sweets for men in
fire trenches received from General
Haldane and distributed.
2nd Lieut. Duncan reported sick and
removed to Field Ambulance.
2nd Lieut. Kelly and 50 men assisting
R.E. in preparing situation for building
redoubt in rear of fire trenches.

26th — Very cold with snow. Sergeants Hayes
and Cross killed in fire trenches.
No other casualties. C Company took
over fire trenches in relief of A.
Lieut. Whitaker and 100 men employed
in assisting R.E. Local situation

47

27th — Wet and very cold. Local situation quiet. Enemy's trenches shelled by our Artillery apparently with satisfactory result. One man - Pte. Whatten - wounded during the day near machine gun trench.
Battalion relieved at night by Gordon Highlanders. Relief completed successfully by about 9 pm, without casualties. Battalion marched to WESTOUTRE and occupied billets there by about 11 pm. A number of men suffering from frost bite in feet but all very cheerful.

28th — Still wet and cold. At rest in billets. 26 men sent to Field Ambulance suffering with feet.

29th — Very stormy and wet. Still in billets at Westoutre. 30 men sent to Field Ambulance. General overhaul and refitting under Officers Commanding Companies.
2nd Lieut. [Cedrails Frederick Burkitt] Wyatt, 3rd S. Lan R, joined.

30th — Very cold but fine. Still at rest in billets. Local situation quiet.

31st — Brigade moves from Westoutre to Dovre. Battalion marching about 10 pm.

occupied billets at Siege. These
were very scattered and generally
unsatisfactory. Considerable difficulty
experienced in obtaining sufficient
accommodation. Very wet and cold.
Captain Roberts, Lieuts. Pirie (M.O) and
Schooling reported sick and were sent
to Field Ambulance.
Lieut. [Arthur Edward] Brown. R.A.M.C.
attached from 7th Field Ambulance.
Battalion now in support with
remainder of Brigade to 9th Brigade
in position at Lindenhoek.
7th Infantry Brigade now made up
as follows:—
H.A.C. Infantry Battalion.
3rd Battn Worcestershire Rgt.
2nd ,, S. Lancashire ,,
1st ,, Wiltshire ,,
2nd ,, Royal Irish Rifles.
On this date the Battalion
mustered as under.

18 Officers Major W. F. Sweeny. R. Fus. Commanding.
(only 4 Coys 2nd Lieut. J. Martin. R.I.R. acting Adjt.
of HAC Bn.   Lieut. S. J. Boast. S. Lank. Quartermaster
O attached   L. C. F. Salter.   ,,   Transport.
from 7th)   2nd ,, A. E. Brown.   R.A.M.C. M.O.
             2nd ,, J. W. Quartley. Kings own. M. Gun.
                  ,, A. W. Pirie.   9 S.R. A. Coy.
                  ,, E. F. B. Wyatt. 3 S. Lank B.

			49
2nd Lieut	A. N. Brown	Kings Own	D.
Captain	E. Smith	2. K. S. I.	B
Lieut	W. J. Meredith	Kings Own	B
2nd "	A. C. Rowan	2. R. Scots	B
Captain	N. S. Ballard	2. S. Lan R	C
Lieut	W. J. Warner	N. Staff. R	C
"	R. S. Crankshaw	2. Dorsets	C
"	W. C. N. Bulton	S. Lan R	D
2nd "	J. O. C. Rowan	2. R. Scots	D
"	C. P. Whitaker	2. Dorsets	D
"	J. H. Kelly	2. S. Lan R	C

and 894 other ranks.

The following officers were temporarily detained in Field ambulance —
Captn. J. J. Cannon-Roberts   2. R. I. F.
Lieut. J. M. Pirries   Kings Own
  "   J. H. Schooling   5 Middlesex
2nd " C. H. S. Duncan   2. R. Scots

J.R. Draper.
Lieut. Colonel
Commdg. 2nd S. Lan R.

3RD DIVISION
7TH INFY BDE

2ND BATTALION
STH LANCASHIRE REGT.
JAN - OCT 1915

To 25 DIVISION
75 BRIGADE

7th Inf.Bde.
3rd Div.

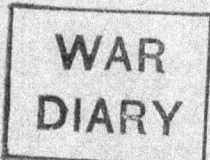

2nd BATTN. THE SOUTH LANCASHIRE REGIMENT.

J A N U A R Y

1 9 1 5

2nd Battalion South Lancashire Regt 51

War diary — 1st to 31st January 1915 —

<u>Friday 1st</u> — Battalion in support and in billets at LOCRE. Very wet and cold — nothing unusual in local situation — Captain Walter Vernon Hume joined the Battalion. No. 9226 Private Thomas Henry Lague 2nd East Lancashire Regiment groom to Captain Hume and one horse arrived.

<u>Saturday 2nd</u> — Still very wet and cold — No change in disposition of Battalion — 2nd Lieut. Duncan rejoined from Field hospital.

<u>Sunday 3rd</u> — Weather conditions bad — wet and cold — no change in local situation — Orders received for Battalion to be prepared to move forward tomorrow to occupy part of position allotted to 7th Infantry Brigade — 2nd Lieuts. Brown & A. S. Brown placed on sick list and sent to Field Ambulance —

<u>Monday 4th</u> — Still very wet and cold — Lieuts. Stamer and Crankshaw placed on sick list and sent to Field Ambulance — Battalion left LOCRE about 4.45 pm and advanced to part of position East of LINDENHOEK allotted to 7th Infantry Brigade, taking over from Royal Scots Fusiliers,

52

who withdrew.
Relief carried out successfully but was
not completed till about 11p.m. This
was in consequence of the disposition
of units being relieved being slightly
different to that occupied by the 6th
Battalion on relief by Gordon Highlanders
on 27th December. This caused some
confusion and delay.
D Company under Lieut Burton in fire
trenches. A in local support. C in
general support. B in reserve at Kemmel
cross roads.

Tuesday 5th. Continuous rain. Trenches in a
very bad state. In some cases full
of water and mud. Men standing
over knee deep. Every effort made
to bail out and improve trenches.
Company relief carried out at night.
B to fire trenches under Captain Smith.
Other companies changing position.
Casualties during the day. 3 men killed.
1 wounded.
Lieut. Pearse (M.O) rejoined from sick list.
Lieut Albert Edward Brown, on relief
returned to Field Ambulance.

Wednesday 6th. Captain Charles Norman Wheeler
3rd Battalion with 33 other ranks,
arrived at LOCRE. Men unwounded

were in billets but Captain Wheeler proceeded to join the Battalion in the evening.
Battalion still in same positions. Companies relieved as follows — A. under Captains Dunne and Wheeler to fire trenches. B. to reserve at Lindenhoek Cross roads. C. local support. D. general support.
Very stormy and wet night.
Casualties during the day — 4 killed. 3 wounded.

Thursday 7th — Still very stormy and wet. Battalion in same position — Companies relieved in the evening. C Company under Captain Ballard to fire trenches. Other companies changing. Casualties during the day — Captain Wheeler and 2 privates killed — one man wounded.

Friday 8th. Very wet day. Battalion withdrew during the evening, from positions on relief by Scots Fusiliers and marched to billets at LOCRE arriving about 11 p.m. Casualties during the day. 2 men killed. 1 wounded.

Saturday 9th. Pouring with rain all day. Worse than ever. In billets at LOCRE. Quiet day. Captain Mark Philips Rathbone, 3rd

Battalion and 2nd Lieut. Thomas
Knox-Shaw, 3rd Q.O.L. Regt. joining the
Battalion.

Sunday 10th – Battalion at rest in billets at
LOCRE – Local situation quiet –
Captain Roberts rejoined from Field hospital.
Captain Smith and 2nd Lieut. Kelly reported
sick and removed to Field ambulance –
2nd Lieut. Wyatt and Corpl. Wilkins proceeded
to St Omer for course of instruction in
machine gun –

Monday 11th – Still in billets at LOCRE. No change
in local situation. Orders received for
Battalion to be in readiness to move
forward tomorrow –
Very wet and cold day –
Lieut. Balter reported sick and removed to
Field Ambulance –

Tuesday 12th – Still wet and very cold – Battalion left
billets at LOCRE about 4 pm and
proceeded to position East of Kemmelhoek,
relieving Royal Scots Fusiliers. Position
occupied was more than that occupied
on 4th January. "A" Company under
Captain Hume and "B" Company under Captain
Ballard, occupied fire trenches, furnishing their
own supports. This arrangement differs
from that adopted on previous occasions, the
intention being for the two companies to

54

remain in position for 48 hours, reliefs being arranged by Officers Commanding Companies.

Battalion took over the positions successfully by about 8pm and Royal Scots Fusiliers withdrew without casualties.

Before being relieved the Royal Scots Fusiliers reported that it was thought the enemy's snipers were in our lines in a farm known as "Tobacco Farm", as a working party had been fired on apparently from this farm.

Lieut. Whitaker, no. ... and no. ... volunteered to reconnoitre the farm and vicinity. This they accomplished successfully but found nothing.

Wednesday 13th. Raining heavily all day. Local situation fairly quiet. Disposition of Battalion unchanged. D Company under Lieut. Boulton in support, B Company under Captain Roberts, in reserve at LINDENHOEK Cross Roads.

Trenches in a very bad state. Every effort made to improve them but very difficult owing to continuous rain.

Shelling by ourselves and enemy during the day. Casualties today. 3 men wounded.

56

On this night we made an attempt to place a machine gun in rear of E. trench but this did not prove a success.

<u>Thursday 14th</u> Considerable sniping during the day. 2nd Lieut. Huartly, M.G. officer and three men killed.

The loss of 2nd Lieut. Huartly was very much felt as this young officer had shown distinct keenness and energy which rendered him an officer of unusual worth.

General disposition of Battalion unchanged but during the evening B Company under Captain Roberts and D Company under Lieut. Burton, relieved 'a' and 'b' in fire trenches and supports under the arrangements adopted on 12th.

On relief 'a' Company withdrew to LINDEN-HOEK Cross roads and 'b' Company to Supports.

During the night Lieut. Whitaker placed No. 2092 Pte. T. Medlicot and 6795 Pte. J. Farr D Company in a position which they occupied alone until 16th, during which period they caused the enemy considerable annoyance and, possibly, casualties. Both these men had volunteered for this special duty.

An extract from Lond. Gazette 57
dated 5th Jan. mentions 1st Jan, describes
the introduction of a new decoration
called the "Military Cross" for Officers
not above the rank of Captain, and
Warrant Officers.

Amongst the list of individuals to
whom the decoration was awarded the
undernamed appeared:—
Lieut. B. T. Fulcher. South Lancashire Regt. (deceased).
Sergeant Major T. V. Roberts. South Lancashire Regt.

Friday 15th — Very windy day but fairly fine.
Some improvements made in trenches.
Battalion disposition unchanged. Local
situation fairly quiet. Enemy's position
heavily shelled by our artillery during
the day with apparent satisfactory results.
Casualties during the day – 1 man killed.

Saturday 16th — No change in disposition of Battalion
during day but was relieved by 4th Royal
Fusiliers during the evening. Relief was
considerably delayed and not completed till
about 11 p.m. when Battalion withdrew to
billets at LOORE.
Casualties during the day – 1 man killed.
1 man wounded.
Local situation unchanged. Weather wet
and cold.
A reinforcement of 60 other ranks, under

2nd Lieut. Williams Laws, 5th Battalion, joined the Battalion at LOCRE.
2nd Lieuts. Randolph Gomer Culmow and Eric Graham Fletcher 3rd Battalion, also reported their arrival.

__Sunday 17th__ Battalion at rest in billets at LOCRE. Local situation quiet. Considerable rain.
Captain Ballard reported sick and removed to Field Ambulance.
Captain Rathbone assumed command of "C" Company.

__Monday 18th__ Weather very bad - snowing and raining. Battalion at rest in billets. No change in local situation but considerable artillery fire heard during the day and evening, some distance N.E. of LOCRE.

__Tuesday 19th__ Very wet day - Battalion still in billets at LOCRE. Local situation quiet.
2nd Lieut. Duncan reported sick and sent to Field Ambulance.

__Wednesday 20th__ The following 2nd Lieuts. on probation joined the Battalion from H.Q. 6 -
Elveny Ashton Dothie.
Ismair Malcolm Eldridge.
Cyril Oliver Ellis
Douglas Harrison Layton
Hugh Lloyd Owen

59

Arthur Joseph Samut
Samuel Stansfield-Smith

Battalion moved from billets at LOCRE
about 4 pm and proceeded to position
allotted to 7th Infantry Brigade, east of
LINDENHOEK, relieving 4th Royal Fusiliers.
Actual relief took place without
casualty but one man, 7500 Pte.
Leyden, was wounded on road from
Lindenhoek cross roads to Battalion Head
Quarter position.
Relief completed by about 9 pm and
Royal Fusiliers withdrew. "B" & "D" in fire
trenches, "A" in support, "C" in reserve at Cross Roads.
As Battalion arrived in position rain
commenced and continued heavily all
night. 2nd Lieut. Kelly rejoined from Field Hospital.

Thursday 21st — Disposition of Battalion unchanged.
Local situation fairly quiet. No casualties.
Raining heavily all day.
"C" Company moved from Lindenhoek Cross
Roads to support with "A" Company.

Friday 22nd — Fine bright day but very cold. Heavy
frost at night.
Very heavy fire by our artillery from
vicinity of KEMMEL and LOCRE, most of the
day on enemy positions East of those
places.
Very heavy rifle and artillery fire from
position north of LOCRE, during the evening

and practically all night.
Casualties during the day – 2nd Lieut.
Ellis severely wounded. L.786 Serjt. S.
Stanley killed, apparently through his
standing up in his trench to look at
an aeroplane overhead – 4 others wounded.
"A" and "B" Companies went forward to
fire trenches, relieving "C" and "D"
Companies who withdrew to support
position – 3 horses to F.1 Mobile Veterinary Hospital.

Saturday 23rd. Fine and bright day but very cold
and frosty.
No change in disposition of Battalion.
Casualties during the day – 4 men
wounded – Lieut. Leaventhorpe R.E. in charge of
working party in C1 trench at night, killed.
Captain Ballard rejoined from Field
hospital.

Sunday 24th. Fine but dull day – no rain – Heavy
shelling by enemy's artillery of right and
left of section occupied by Battalion, –
at least 3 shells nearly found our
supports but no casualties during the
day.
2nd Lieut. Douglas Alfred Hann 3rd Battn.
arrived at LOCRE.
Battalion relieved by 4th Royal Fusiliers
and withdrew to billets at LOCRE,
arriving about 11 p.m.
Relief carried out very satisfactorily and

without casualty.
During this tour of duty the trenches were much improved by the Battalion, and by working parties under Major Nation and Lieut. Seventhorpe. R.E.
A party of 50 men of the Battalion, billeted at KEMMEL, came forward each night under Lieut. Maudsitt, to fire trenches, and carried out some good work.
These parties brought up sand bags filled with bricks, which were taken to the trenches for improving parapets and proved very successful.
The Battalion lost a number of men who were sent to Field Ambulance suffering from swollen feet.

Monday 25th - Dull and very cold. Battalion at rest in billets at LOCRE. Heavy Artillery fire in positions NE of LOCRE.
Local situation quiet.

Tuesday 26th - Fine day but cold. Battalion still in billets at LOCRE. Local situation quiet but continuous heavy firing NE of LOCRE.
Captain Roberts reported sick and sent to Field hospital.
Captain Hatchbone assumes command of B Company.
2nd Lieut. Wyatt rejoined from machine gun course.

Wednesday 27th. Very cold and frosty. Battalion still at rest. Medal for distinguished conduct in the field, presented to Corporal Windle, machine gun section, by General Haldane, Commanding 3rd Division.
The incident in connection with which Corporal Windle was awarded this medal was briefly as follows:-
"On 20th October 1914 the machine guns of the Battalion under the command of Lieut. B.W. Tulleken, had been placed in a commanding position on the second floor of a cottage some distance East of NEUVE CHAPPELL and in the vicinity of which the Battalion was entrenched. During the day the guns did some very excellent work and this was continued next morning until about 10.30 am when it was found that the enemy, who had attacked this part of the line in force, had broken through, and the teams were obliged to leave the guns.
Corporal Windle, Lance Corporal Millward and Pte. Newbold however returned and succeeded in working a gun which prevented the enemy from getting forward."
A reinforcement of 120 men under Captain Frederick Alexander Brunt, Gloucester Regt, and 2nd Lieut. John Bogle Gunn, 3rd S. Lan.

63

Regt. arrived –
Lieut. Meredith reported sick and sent to Field hospital –

Thursday 28th. Very cold – freezing hard – Battalion moved forward, leaving LOCRE about 4.30pm and took over position occupied by Royal Scots Fusiliers East of KEMMEL – B and D Companies in fire trenches. Relief completed by about 6 pm. – casualty – one man wounded – and Royal Scots Fusiliers withdrew to billets at LOCRE –
Fine clear frosty night. During the relief enemy showed some activity by continuous rifle fire – road leading from village to trenches being particularly marked –
The positions taken over were much better than those on the right and which the Battalion had occupied on the last few tours –

Friday 29th – Fine, clear and frosty. General disposition of Battalion unchanged – A and C Companies moved forward to fire trenches. B and D withdrew to support –
Between 2.30 am 3pm enemy aeroplane was noticed above fire trenches and support lines – Shortly afterwards the village of KEMMEL was heavily shelled at Eastern end. Enger heavy shelled pitched in vicinity of houses in which companies in support – A and C – were accommodated – The companies

turned out but were caught by shells as they vacated the buildings, 4 men being killed and 14 wounded.
During the evening B and D companies moved forward to fire trenches in relief of A and C who withdrew to support.
The relief was rendered difficult by the bright moonlight, 2 men being wounded. One man who was carrying supplies to the position "Q2" was also wounded by a sniper.
A corner of the road between F8 and F7 and 500 yards West of G1 was much marked.

Saturday 30th. Still very cold. Some snow. Local situation fairly quiet. General disposition of Battalion unchanged. B and D companies, ——— by 25% from A and C, in fire trenches, remainder in support.
Casualties - 1 man killed.

Sunday 31st. Fine day, but cold. Heavy rifle fire by units on left at enemy's position. Reason unknown by us. During day thaw set in causing trenches to become very muddy. Battalion general disposition unchanged. Local situation quiet.
During improvement of G1 trench the body of a French soldier was discovered. It was removed and properly buried by a

Colonel H. A. Dudgeon commanding 1st Battalion arrived from hdqrs a.a.g. 3rd October, & H.Q. to take command of 2nd Battalion from major R. Inab.

party of "B" Company, under Captain
Rathbone. Documents found on the
body were forwarded to Head Quarters 7th
Infantry Brigade.

On this date the undermentioned
officers were actually present with
the Battalion —

Major W. F. Sweeny. R. Fus. ~~Commanding~~
Lieut. C. S. Boast. D. Sanff Quartermaster.
"   J. Martin   R. I. R. Acting Adjt.
Captain W. F. Hume D. Sanff comdg A Coy
   "   M. P. Rathbone   "   "   B.
   "   N. L. Ballard   "   "   C.
Lieut. W. C. W. Sutton   "   "   D.
2nd Lieut. J. O. C. Cowan   D. R. Brds.
   "   C. P. Whitaker   3. Dorsets
   "   H. B. Gemmen   S. Lan.
   "   J. H. Kelly   3. L Lan
   "   D. A. Hann   "
   "   J. B. Gunn   "
   "   E. G. Fletcher   "
   "   C. F. B. Wyatt   "
   "   W. Laws   "
   "   A. W. Ping   3 gds.
Tem.   C. A. Dobie   It. A Co
   "   H. M. Eldridge   "
   "   D. H. Layton   "
   "   H. L. Owen   "
   "   A. J. Samms   "
Lieut. I. M. Pirie   R. A. M. C. M. O.

Jemdr. St. L. Stanfield-Smith, H.a.c.
Captain F.a. Bruce, Gloster Rgt.
Colonel F.a. Dudgeon, D.S.O, Commdg. Malta
and about 600 other ranks

66

F.a. Dudgeon Lt Colonel.
Commdg 2. S. Lanc

7th Inf.Bde.
3rd Div.

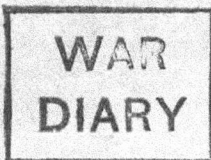

WAR DIARY

2nd BATTN. THE SOUTH LANCASHIRE REGIMENT.

F E B R U A R Y

1 9 1 5

2nd Battalion South Lancashire Regt.

War diary - 1st to 26th Feb. 1915.

Monday 1st - General disposition of Battalion unchanged. Local situation quiet. Very muddy in consequence of continued thaw. Battalion relieved in F Section by Royal Scots Fusiliers and in G Section by Lincoln Regt. First reliefs completed by about 7.40pm, but latter reliefs very slow and relief not completed till about 10 pm. 2nd casualties during relief. 3 men slightly wounded. Rifle carrier by one man broken in two by bullet from enemy's trenches. No other casualties during day.
Battalion withdrew to billets at WESTOUTRE, arriving there about midnight.

Tuesday 2nd Wet day. Battalion at rest in billets at WESTOUTRE. Local situation quiet.
A reinforcement of 50 men under 2nd Lieut. Thomas Rich Bivet-Escott, 3rd Battn, which arrived at WESTOUTRE yesterday evening was distributed amongst companies.
Two additional machine guns - Maxims - received.
Temporary 2nd Lieuts. Bennett and Eldridge joined Bader school, BAILLEUL, for instruction. Lieut. F. A. Sutton and 2nd Lieut J. S. Boast, S. Lan Regt. joined the Battalion.

68

Wednesday 3rd – Fine day but very cold.
Disposition of Battalion unchanged. Local
Situation very quiet.
Battalion paraded at 10.30am for inspection by
Lieut. General Sir. C. Fergusson Bt. C.B. M.V.O. D.S.O.
Commanding 2nd Corps.
2nd Lieut. Boast assumed duties of Battalion
Transport Officer.

Thursday 4th – Fine day – cold wind – no change in
disposition of Battalion. Local Situation quiet.
Two wagons limbered, G.S, 8 horses and 4 pack
Saddles r.f received from 3rd Divisional Train.

Friday 5th – Very fine day – Bright sunshine.
Battalion moved from billets at WESTOUTRE about
5pm and proceeded via LOCRE to position East
of KEMMEL, taking over same section as on
last occasion, relieving 1st Royal Scots Fusiliers
and Lincoln Regt [who withdrew to billets at
LOCRE.] Relief completed by about 10.30pm.
1 man slightly wounded during relief.
A and B Companies in fire trenches. B and
D in support at KEMMEL.
Lieut. Boulton accidentally wounded in the
hand by a "Very" light while instructing Officers
of his company newly joined – 2nd Lieut. Whitaker
assumed command of D Company.

Saturday 6th – Very wet day – General disposition of
Battalion unchanged. B and D companies
relieved A and C in fire trenches, latter being
withdrawn to support in KEMMEL.

During the day the Western side of
KEMMEL was heavily shelled. Few
shells pitched in vicinity of our trenches.
One man killed in machine gun trench.
One wagon G.S. and 2 horses handed over to
3rd Divisional Train in consequence of the
Battalion being in possession of full
establishment of four travelling kitchens.

Sunday 7th. Dull day and inclined to rain.
Considerable shelling by our artillery from
positions West of KEMMEL on to enemy's positions.
Local situation in position occupied by
Battalion fairly quiet.
A and C Companies relieved B and D in
fire trenches, latter withdrawing to support.
During the day a periscope being used by
2nd Lieut. Gunn was struck by a bullet from
enemy trenches, wounding him slightly.
No other casualties during the day.
At night red and green lights were seen
in enemy's trenches.

Monday 8th. Fine bright day. Staff Sergeant Thomas
Henry Murray, Indian S.&T. Corps arrived
and was attached to the Battalion on
probation with a view to being recommended
for a commission.
General disposition of Battalion unchanged.
B and D Companies relieved A and C in
fire trenches, latter withdrawing to support.

70

During the afternoon enemys artillery was in action and shelled our trenches. 2nd Lieut. Pring and 3 men wounded. Several shells pitched on to KEMMEL-LOCRE road damaging the road and delaying transport with rations. Transport nearly caught on road.

Tuesday 9th Wet day - Fine by evening - Fairly quiet day - Our artillery very active in position West of KEMMEL - Battalion relieved in I Section by Royal Scots Fusiliers by about 9 pm - and in G Section by Lincoln Regt by about 11 pm - Very dark night - no casualties - On relief Battalion withdrew to billets at LOCRE - Major Sweeny proceeded to 28th Division to take over command of 2nd Battalion East Yorkshire Regiment -

Wednesday 10th Fine bright day - many aeroplanes about. Battalion at rest in billets. Local situation quiet but our artillery East of Locre very active all day. 2nd Lieut. [Talbot Grove-Lescott] 3rd Battalion and 105 other ranks joined -

Thursday 11th Fine day - Battalion still in billets at Locre - Situation generally quiet -

Friday 12th Dull day - rather cold - snowing part of the day followed by rain in the evening.

71

No change in disposition of Battalion.
Local situation quiet.
Major [Harold Temple] Cotton joined the
Battalion.

Saturday 13th. Very wet and squally. Battalion moved
forward from Locre at 6 pm and proceeded
to Kemmel occupying original positions East
of that village, relieving Royal Scots Fusiliers
in F Section 5 and 6 and Lincoln Regiment
in G Section 1, 2 and 3 and D 3.
Relief completed by about 10 pm (when
relieved units withdrew from the positions.)
Casualties during relief - 1 man killed and
2 wounded - B and D Companies in fire trenches.
Major Cotton visited all positions occupied
by the Battalion.
Quiet night generally.

Sunday 14th. Very wet day. Captain [Francis William
Massy-Drew] joined the Battalion and
assumed command of D Company.
Local situation quiet - Casualties - 1 man
killed and 1 wounded.
Heavy artillery fire on our left about 10 pm
and continued practically all night, by 27th
Division.
General disposition of Battalion unchanged.
A and C Companies relieved B and D in
fire trenches. Later withdrawing to support
in Kemmel village.

72

Monday 15th Very wet day. Cold. Local
situation quiet. General disposition of
Battalion unchanged. B and D Companies
to fire trenches. A and C withdrawing to
bivouac at Kemmel.
Casualties - 2 wounded.
Quiet night. Heavy artillery fire on our
left about 8pm.
Notification received that 4th Battalion had
arrived at BAILLEUL and were to join 7th
Infantry Brigade.
Temporary 2nd Lieuts. Dobbie and Owen proceeded
to Cadre School BAILLEUL.

Tuesday 16th. Very fine and bright day but cold.
Considerable number of aeroplanes about.
No change in general disposition of Battalion.
A and C Companies to fire trenches in relief
of B and D.
Casualties - 2 wounded.

Wednesday 17th Very wet. Quiet in our immediate front.
2nd Lieuts. [Island Ernest] Thompson and [William]
Kissere joined the Battalion.
About noon 9th Infantry Brigade which was at
rest in billets at Locre and should have
relieved the Battalion tonight, was suddenly
ordered out and proceeded to position North of
Locre in vicinity of YPRES apparently to
reinforce troops there.
Orders received for 7th Infantry Brigade to

73

remain in position till further orders.
2nd Lieut Hann reported sick & sent
to Field Ambulance - Bronchitis - 5 wounded -

Thursday 18th Squally and cold - Local situation
quiet but enemy's artillery very active,
apparently searching for our guns - many
shells pitched on to ground West of Kemmel
village and hills.

Four men down with scurvy for water from
G2 trench. Ground near pump is apparently
watched and snipers are very active.

Total casualties during the day - 5 men
wounded.

Battalion disposition unchanged.

A and C Companies to fire trenches in
relief of B and D who withdraw to support.

Friday 19th Very windy and squally. Lieut. Salter
rejoined from sick leave and joined 'A'
Company for duty.

Battalion still in trenches. 75 inch shells
for about an hour during afternoon and
a breach made which was repaired after
dark.

Enemy reported to have occupied an old
trench in front of F5 during the day but
a reconnaissance made during the night
did not discover any change in their
disposition -

Saturday 20th Fine day - milder - Information

74

reached the Battalion that the un mentioned had been mentioned in despatches dated 14th Jan. 1915, from the Field Marshall Commanding-in-Chief, British Forces in the Field —

Captain S. C. Clemens.   I. Irish
Lieut. B. T. Fletcher (killed).   "
Lieut + Qm. S. J. Boast.   "
Lieut. J. M. Pirie. R.A.M.C. attd.   "
2nd Lieut J. Martin. K.R. Rifles   "
3162 Sgt. J. Stephenson.   S. Lan R
4124 Pte. J. Coady   "
6679 "   C. Knowles   "
7712 "   O. Wolff   "

also that the following awards had been granted for good service in the field —
D.S.O. — Captain W. B. Ritchie
Mil. Cross — Captain L. A. Clemens.
Hon. Captain — Lieut + Qm S. J. Boast.
2nd Lieut. J. Martin, K.R. Rifles, acting Adjutant to the Battalion was also promoted to the rank of Captain.

No change in general disposition of Battalion —
Local situation fairly quiet.
A and C companies to fire trenches relieving B and D.
Total casualties today — Lieut. Meredith

Severely wounded.
2nd Lnt. T. R. Sweet-Escott severly
wounded.
1 man killed. 4 wounded.
5 Officers of 4th Battalion were taken
round positions occupied by Battalion,
for instruction.

Sunday 21st Fine day but misty. Battalion in
same position. During the afternoon
F5 trench occupied by D Company
was heavily shelled by the enemy.
The parapet being blown in and
2 men slightly wounded.
B and D Companies to fire trenches.
A and C to supports.
Casualties - total for the day. 2 men
referred to above.
Quiet night. Bright moonlight.
7 Officers, 4 Company Sergeant Majors
and 4 Company Quartermaster Sergeants
of 4th Battalion visited the positions
occupied by the 2nd Battalion and
received instruction in their duties in
connection with the positions generally.
Report received that Lieut. Meredith
had died of wounds at Loire.

Monday 22nd. Fine day but misty. This
increased by evening.
Quiet day generally. No casualties

76

during the day. Good work
done by D Company under the
command of Captain Drew, in
repairing parapet, draining trench
and improving details in 75.
This was possible by the Company
taking advantage of the heavy
mist.
In the evening the Battalion was
relieved as follows:-
75. 7. 83 by Liverpool Scottish.
G.1. 2.   by Liverpool Scottish
Northern end of 92 was taken over by
the 2nd Battalion The Buffs, also 93.
Relief completed by about 10.30pm
when Battalion withdrew to billets at
Locre.
Casualties during relief: 3 men
slightly wounded.
This completed a tour of 9
successive nights in the trenches by
the Battalion and although this was
twice the normal period during
which the weather conditions had
been very trying, all ranks showed
remarkable cheerfulness, many men
singing and playing "mouth-organs"
on the march to billets.
As the Battalion arrived in Kemmel

village they were supplied with **77**
hot tea before leaving Locre.

Tuesday 23rd Fine bright day. Battalion at
rest in billets at Locre.
Local situation very quiet.
The G.O.C. 7th Infantry Brigade,
Brigadier General C. Ballard, visited
Battalion Head Quarters and the
Commanding Officer took this
opportunity to introduce all Officers
present with the Battalion.
A most successful concert, organised
by Captain J Martin Acting Adjutant,
and Regimental Sergeant Major T.V.
Roberts, was held in a large school
house in which a portion of the
Battalion was billeted.
The Commanding Officer and all
the officers of the Battalion were
present.

Wednesday 24th Snow, sleet, very cold. Battalion
still in billets at Locre. Local
situation quiet, but considerable
Artillery fire all day from our
positions East of Locre.
2nd Lieut. Humphrey Kitson Thomas, 3rd
D. Can? and 22 other ranks
joined the Battalion.

Thursday 25th Heavy fall of snow. Very cold.

No change in disposition of Batt'n - Local situation unchanged. Considerable artillery fire heard from vicinity of Kemmel.

Friday 26- Bright clear cold day. Enemy's artillery very active East of Kemmel. Battalion left Locre at 6.15pm and proceeded to position allotted to 7th Infantry Brigade, taking over G3 and part of G2 from The Buffs. Part of G2. G1. G6. 75. 57 and S3 from Liverpool Scottish and 74. 76 and S2 from H.A.C.

Casualties during relief - 1 man killed. Bright moonlight night. Relief completed by about 10.30pm [when relieved units withdrew.]

B and D companies under Captains Rathbone and Drew respectively in fire trenches - A and C companies under Captains Hume and Bond in Support at Kemmel.

Quiet night generally -

On this occasion a portion of 4th Battalion, as shown below, was attached for instruction, on joining 7th Infantry Brigade, and companies were divided amongst our companies in the various positions allotted to us.

79

Head Quarters. Major C. Crofield
      Captain. Izzard adjt.
A. Company under Major C. F. Harvey
B " " Captain G. L. Roberts
Machine guns. Lieut. L. S. Henshall.
Stretcher bearers.   C. S. Law. R.A.M.C (T.F).
Signallers.
On this date, Lieut. S. M. Lewis, L.ame,
attached to the Battalion proceeded on
leave and Lieut. Alexander Duncan
Shrews, R.A.M.C. was attached for
temporary duty.

Saturday 27th. Very idle day, some sleet. General
disposition of Battalion unchanged.
Trenches shelled on and off, by
enemy artillery throughout whole day.
F.5 and 6 heavily shelled about 6 a.m.
About 10 shells from German howitzers
dropped near east end of Femme
about 4 p.m. but did no damage.
Companies in support were obliged to
vacate, temporarily, the billets occupied
by them and occupy "dug outs".
Several buildings were hit but there
were no casualties.
Lieut. F.A. Sutton was killed in G1 trench.
One man wounded in F.7.
Very quiet night.
Companies in support relieved those in

fire trenches, latter withdrawing to support.

Sunday 28. Bright clear and very fine day but very cold.
Disposition of Battalion unchanged.
Local situation fairly quiet.
A farm house "Peckham" in vicinity of enemy's trenches East of Kemmel, and which it was thought gave cover to their snipers, was successfully shelled by our howitzers about 11 am.
Casualties during the day – 1 man killed.
Companies in fire trenches relieved by those in support.
On this date the Battalion mustered as follows —

Lieut. Colonel F. A. Dudgeon – Commanding. x
Major H. J. Cotton. x
Captn. J. Martin – K. I. Rifles. Acting Adjt x
" L. J. Boast. L. San. Quartermaster x
2nd Lieut. E. F. N. Wyatt " Machine guns x
" J. L. Boast " Transport
Lieut. J. M. Sivric. R.a.m.c. M.O. on leave
" A. B. Shires
Captn. W. V. Hume L. San. "A" Coy. x
" M. P. Rathbone " B x
" N. S. Ballard " C (on leave) x
" F. W. M. Drew " D x

81

Captain E. A. Brunt — R. of Offrs. — "C" Coy.
Lieut. C. T. Salter — Yorks Regt. — S. Sam.
2nd Lieut. W. Laws
    "   J. A. C. Cowan — R. Scots. (on leave)
    "   C. P. Whitaker — Dorsets
    "   J. H. Kelly — S. Sam.
    "   L. Sweet-Escott
    "   R. B. Gilmore
    "   C. G. Fletcher
    "   C. H. R. Thomas
    "   C. E. Thompson
    "   W. Roscoe
Acting " C. A. Dobbie   H. A. C. ⎫ ex Cadet School
   "   " H. M. Eldridge   "   ⎬ Bailleul
   "   " H. L. Owen   "   ⎭
   "   " A. J. Sanner   "
   "   " F. A. Layton   "
   "   " L. Mansfield-Smith "
   "   " J. H. Murray — J.S. + J.C.

and 955 other ranks —

                    † A. Scudamore, Lt. Colonel.
Commdg. 2. S. Bank.

7th Inf.Bde.
3rd Div.

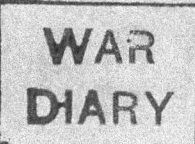

2nd BATTN. THE SOUTH LANCASHIRE REGIMENT.

M A R C H

1 9 1 5

2nd Battalion South Lancashire Regiment 82

War diary. — 1st to 31st March 1915.

Monday 1st Very cold - icy wind - Blizzard during the morning -

No change in general disposition of the Battalion -

Quiet day in trenches -

Kemmel shelled about 12.30pm by enemy's howitzers and again in the afternoon with shrapnel - No damage done -

Orders received for Battalion to remain in position until 4th March - two additional days -

Companies in support carried out usual relief of those in fire trenches - latter withdrawing to support -

Casualties during the day - 2 men killed - 3 wounded -

Tuesday 2nd Fine and clear but very cold -

Disposition of Battalion unchanged -

Several shells from enemy's position pitched in Kemmel and vicinity during the day - Very little damage done and no casualties amongst companies in support there -

Fairly quiet day in trenches -

Usual relief carried out during the

March -

evening -
Casualties during the day - 1 man killed 3 wounded.

Wednesday 3rd. Very wet day. No change in
situation. Rather quiet generally -
Usual reliefs carried out during the evening -
Casualties during the day. 1 man killed, 4 wounded.

Thursday 4th. Very wet night and morning -
Quiet day generally -
During morning our Artillery shelled enemy
fire trenches in front of our F4 and 5,
Also on F6 & 7 -
Battalion relieved as follows -
E 1. 2. 3. 6 by The Buffs.
E 4. 5. 6. 7 by R. A. 6.
S. 2. 3. by R. A. 6.
Relief was very slow and not completed
until after midnight -
Various parties withdrew as relieved, to
billets at Locre - last party arriving there
about 1.30 am 5th. Very dark night -
Two companies of 4th Battalion on relief
withdrew to Locre and joined remainder
of Battalion billeted there -
Casualties during day - 2 men killed -
5 wounded - 2 of latter during relief -

Friday 5th. Fine mild day. Battalion at rest
in billets at Locre. [Local situation
quiet. Heavy artillery fire took place
all night N.E. of Locre.]

- March -

Saturday 6th - Heavy artillery fire continued during morning N.E. of Locre.
Fine morning - wet afternoon and night.
Battalion still at rest in billets.
Local situation quiet.

Sunday 7th. Very wet morning - Showery afternoon and evening.
Battalion at rest in billets at Locre.
Local situation quiet. Heavy firing by our Artillery East of the village during the afternoon.
Battalion ordered to furnish 600 men to form a digging party which left Locre at 6 pm returning shortly after midnight.
One man wounded during progress of work.

Monday 8th. Very cold day - East wind.
No change in disposition of Battalion.
At rest in billets.
Local situation quiet.

Tuesday 9th. Very cold day - Easterly wind until evening when fall of snow commenced.
Disposition of Battalion unchanged. Still at rest in billets.
Local situation quiet but heavy shelling by our artillery took place on line East of Locre.
Bursts of enemy shells could be heard from direction of Kemmel.

March — 2nd Lieut. Hann rejoined from hospital.
The ft[?] entry is extracted from supplement
to London Gazette, 6th March, published on 8th
March 1915 —
3rd Battalion — Second Lieut. to be Lieut —
W. Laws from Gen. Reserve of officers — of 26 Dec 1914.
T. A. Hann
Both these officers are now serving with 2nd
Battalion —

Information received this evening that all
units of 7th Infantry [Brigade?] [will?] remain
at Locre until probably 12th March, the
85th Infantry Brigade remaining in the position
at present occupied by them —

Wednesday 10th. Dull and inclined to rain.
Our artillery east of Locre very active
during early morning —
Local Situation generally quiet —
No change in disposition of Battalion —

Thursday 11th. Dull and misty — clear later —
No change in disposition of Battalion —
Local Situation very quiet.
News received of success by 1st Army
and communicated to all ranks.
Orders received for 7th Infantry Brigade to be
prepared to move forward early tomorrow
morning to attack part of enemy's position.

Friday 12th — Orders received for 7th Infantry
Brigade to attack SPANBROEK MOLEN HILL.

March -

3rd Worcester. 1st Wilts and 2nd S. Lan. R. were 87 ordered to occupy assembly trenches as it had been previously prepared, the 2nd Royal Irish Rifles being in reserve.

The Battalion marched from billets at Locre at 3 am moving via Kemmel and Lindenhoek. The march was delayed in consequence of the road being blocked by 2nd S. Lan. R. which was returning from carrying stores to Kemmel and by working parties of the 85th Brigade.

It was nearly broad daylight when the Battalion moved into position. Cover was taken behind a small wood and in folds of the ground. The assembly trenches being fully occupied by Worcesters and Wilts.

The attack was to have taken place at 8.30 am but was delayed until 4.10 pm owing to a thick mist which prevented Artillery Observation.

The actual attack was made by two companies each of Worcesters and Wilts - the 2nd S. Lan. remaining in support - but it did not succeed.

After it had failed the Battalion was heavily shelled for about 1½ hours.

A great many shells went just over the Battalion, but the men were absolutely steady and owing to the good dispositions made by Company Commanders, those that

march.

burst near did not do much damage.
At 6 pm orders were received for the Battalion
to march back to billets at Locre.
Two platoons of 'C' Company were left in
occupation of a supporting trench, until
relieved by East Surrey Regt.
The Battalion arrived at Locre about midnight
and occupied billets there.
Casualties during the day were 15 men
wounded, 3 of whom subsequently died of their
wounds.

Saturday 13th Very fine clear day — Battalion at
rest at Locre.
Local situation quiet. Considerable
artillery fire in position N.E. of Locre.
51 N.C.O. & men joined the Battalion.
Staff Sergt. J. H. Murray, I.S. & I.C, returned
to his own unit.
C.S.M. J. W. Webster sent to base en route for
England, under War Office authority, as being
unsuitable for the duties of his rank in
the field, but suitable for clerical duties at home.

Sunday 14th Orders received for the Battalion 7th
Infantry Brigade — 2nd S. Lan. R. & 2nd Royal
Irish Rifles — to proceed to position in vicinity of
WULVERGHEM and relief of other Units there.
Battalion left Locre about 5 pm marching via
DRANOUTRE.
Shortly after Battalion moved off enemy made

March –

a violent attack in vicinity of ST. ELOI and a very fierce bombardment by enemy but our guns answered.

Battalion moving forward from Locre in direction of Kemmel to relieve 85th Infantry Brigade in that vicinity, were ordered to "Stand fast", and 2nd S. Lan. and 2nd K.I.R. were halted a short distance from Westoutre [under same orders.]

About 9 pm all relieving units were ordered to return to their billets except 2nd R.I.R. which were ordered to billets at Dranoutre.

Later orders were issued that no reliefs were to take place tonight.

Battalion arrived at Locre about midnight, occupied billets there and was warned as "Battalion on duty". The 7th Infantry Brigade being held as "Army Reserve".

Heavy artillery and rifle fire continued practically all night along the line — WULVERGHEM — WYTSCHAETE — ST. ELOI — and apparently also further North in direction of YPRES. Captn. Shuna sick and sent to F.A.

Monday 15th. Very misty morning – clear by noon –
Battalion still at Locre. Heavy firing which had continued all night, much reduced by about 5 am but occasional outbursts took place and continued throughout the day, until evening when the local situation became exceptionally quiet.
Battalion completed tour of "Battalion on duty" at 5pm.

March.
90

Orders received that 7th Infantry Brigade would still remain as "Army Reserve" and be prepared to move at one hours notice.
Orders also received that no reliefs would take place tonight.
Quiet night.

Tuesday 16th. Fine day but inclined to be misty.
Battalion still at Locre. During the morning orders were received to be prepared to move this evening to positions in vicinity of Wulverghem under same arrangements as for 14th. Later in the day this was cancelled and Battalion ordered to remain at Locre.
Three Battalions of 7th Infantry Brigade – 3rd Worcesters, 1st Wilts and 4th S. Lan – moved from Locre during the evening to positions East of Kemmel relieving Units of 85th Infantry Brigade, who withdrew from the positions.
2nd S. Lan and 2nd R.I. Rifles remaining at Locre.
Local situation quiet. During the night occasional bursts of artillery and rifle fire could be heard from positions East, North East and South East of Locre.

Wednesday 17th. Fine morning. Frequent bursts of fire continued during early morning.
Local situation quiet.
Orders received about noon for Battalion to be prepared to move forward to

March.
positions East of Kemmel to relieve Units
of 8th Infantry Brigade.
Battalion left billets at Locre at 6 p.m.
Relieved 4th S. Lan. R. and a Bott. line of
8th Infantry Brigade in J5. B.3. G.1.2.3.4 & 6.
Relief completed by about 10 p.m. No casualties.
'A' and 'C' Companies [under Captains Brent
and Callard] in fire trenches. Remaining
two companies in support at Kemmel.
Quiet night.

Thursday 18th. Fine day. General disposition of
Battalion unchanged. Enemy shelled vicinity
of G6 with howitzers and the supports in
position there were moved forward to fire
trenches. No damage done. Otherwise a
very quiet day.
2 men killed in G2.
Very dark night. B and D Companies
[under Captains Rathbone and Drew] relieve
'A' and 'C' in fire trenches. [latter withdrew
to support at Kemmel.]

Friday 19th. Cold winds and considerable snow.
No change in general disposition of the
Battalion. Very quiet day. Usual relief
took place during the evening.
Casualties during the day. 1 Sergeant
and 1 man wounded.
During the evening two Battalions of 7th
Infantry Brigade. 3rd Worcesters and 4th S.

March.

8. San. K were withdrawn from part of
the position allotted to the Bde, i.e., on
relief by two battalions of 4th Infantry Brigade.
The two battalions on relief withdrew to
billets at La Clytte.

Saturday 20th. Fine and bright but rather cold.
Captain [Richard Arthur Ogden] Taylor and
2nd Lieut. [William Roscoe] Gaskell 3rd Battalion,
and 40 other ranks arrived at Socre and
proceeded, in the evening, to join the Battalion
at Kemmel.

No change in general disposition of the
Battalion. Usual reliefs took place in
the evening.

Local situation generally quiet. G4 trench
was shelled by enemy during the day.
No damage done although one shell
actually pitched into our part of the
trench, fortunately all men were clear.
Casualties during the day were four
men wounded.

An incident which occurred yesterday
may be of some interest and is recorded
briefly as follows:

2nd Lieut. Thompson who recently went through
a short course of instruction in the
working of trench mortars, had been
operating with one in G1 trench and
had apparently given the enemy some

annoyance during yesterday. In the
evening, who from the enemy trench
were pitched at G. Three of these
dropped in the parapet doing no
damage. A fourth pitched into the
trench without exploding and on 2nd Lieut
Thompson's attention being drawn to this
he immediately went to it, picked it
up and threw it clear of the trench.
As he did so another bomb was
pitched into the trench, hitting him on
the arm and falling without exploding.
Lieut. Thompson picked this up also
and threw it clear.
The incident is noted to record the
coolness displayed by this officer in a
situation which might have been a
serious one.

Sunday 21st. Very fine bright day. Many
aeroplanes about. Quiet day in trenches.
Usual company reliefs carried out during
the evening. General disposition of Battalion
unchanged.
Casualties during the day 1 man wounded.
During the night frequent bursts of
rifle fire from enemys trenches took place.
No damage done.

Monday 22nd. Fine day. Local situation
quiet during the day. Usual reliefs during

March.
the evening.
Quiet n.w. Casualties during the day 3 men wounded.

Tuesday 23rd. Dull day. Showery by evening. Heavy rifle fire from enemy trenches from about 3.30 a.m. to 4 a.m. After our reply situation became quiet and remained so generally throughout the day until about 6 p.m. when enemy commenced to shell the area between Kemmel Cross Roads and Lindenhoek Cross Roads with shrapnel — no damage done.

Quiet day in trenches. Casualties during the day — one man wounded. Battalion relieved during the evening by Devon Regiment, [a unit of] 14th Infantry Brigade.

Relief successfully carried out without casualties and was completed shortly after midnight.

On relief the Battalion withdrew to billets (huts) in vicinity of LA CLYTTE. Wet night — heavy showers.

Wednesday 24th. Dull and showery. Orders received during the morning for Battalion to move to DICKEBUSCH this evening. Battalion left LA CLYTTE about 7.30 p.m. and moved forward to DICKEBUSCH arriving

there about 2.30pm. Occupied bivouac shelters 96
in a small wood about one mile West of
the town. Battalion settled down by about
11 pm. [Captn Rathbone reported sick & sent to F.A.]
Very wet night.

Thursday 25th. Still very wet. Battalion disposition
unchanged. Bivouac very uncomfortable with
rain and mud.
Captain Ballard and 2nd Lieut Hain reported
sick and sent to Field Ambulance.
2nd Lieut. [Raymond Savage] 3rd D. San. R. and
16 other ranks joined the Battalion.
Very heavy artillery and rifle fire commenced
during the evening along the line –
WYTSCHAETE – ST. ELOI. and extending NORTH.
This continued practically all night.
Artillery fire in frequent bursts – rifle and
machine gun fire continuous. Cold night.

Friday 26th. Very cold and wet.
Disposition of battalion unchanged. Orders
received to be prepared to move this
evening.
Battalion moved from bivouac shelters to billets
North and South of village of DICKEBUSCH
vacated by 4th D. San. R. who took up position
in trenches N.E. of village – move completed by
about 6.30pm. Transport remained in bivouac
shelters.
1st Wilts R. moved into shelters vacated by

March:
Battalion:-
2nd Lieut. [Duncan Williams] "B" month,
3rd S. San. K and one Private joins the
Battalion.
Very heavy rifle fire commences about 8pm
East of Dickebusch and continues for
some time.
Very cold clear night. Bright moonlight.
Two companies of the Battalion - A
and B. detailed to carry miscellaneous
stores, obstacles &c to position taken over by
1st S. San. K.

Saturday 27th - Bright day but very cold.
No change in disposition of Battalion.
Considerable artillery fire East and
North East of Dickebusch practically
all day.
Heavy rifle fire commences at dusk
and continues in frequent bursts
throughout the whole night.
Cold frosty night.

Sunday 28th - Bright day - very cold winds.
No change in Battalion disposition. Still
at rest in Dickebusch. Local situation
generally quiet. Occasionally small
bursts of artillery fire East and North
East.
Usual rifle fire during the evening and
night but not nearly so heavy as

March
last night.
2nd Lieut. [William Edward] S-ber, 3rd
S. San. N. arrived.
Ribbon of Military Cross presented to
Regimental Sergeant Major J. T. Roberts, by
G.O.C. 3rd Division - Major General
Haldane.

Monday 29th. Fine bright day - cold winds.
Battalion still in billets at Dickebusch.
100 men detailed to assist in road
making.
A and B companies detailed to improve
trenches in position to be occupied
by Battalion. Moved off about 6.30pm
and worked from 7.30pm to 12 midnight.
Local situation generally quiet.
2nd Lieut. [William Everard] Dickson
4th Lancashire Regiment, joined the
Battalion for duty.

Tuesday 30th. Bright day, Cold wind.
No change in disposition of Battalion.
100 men employed in road making.
B and D companies continued work
commenced by A and C last night, working
from about 7.30 to 11.30pm.
Casualties - 1 man wounded.
Considerable rifle fire during the night.

Wednesday 31st. Very fine day. No change
in disposition of Battalion.

March.

"A" and "B" Companies continued work of
improving trenches, working from
about 7.30 pm to midnight.
No casualties.
Orders received for Battalion to be in
readiness to move forward in relief
of 1st Battalion.
Very quiet night.
Information received that 2nd Lieut. J.O.C. Cowan
3rd R. Scots R. was promoted to Lieut.

On 31st March the Battalion mustered as
follows:—
Lieut. Col. F.A. Dudgeon, L. San. Commanding Battn.
Major H.J. Carton.   "   Senior Major
Captain J. Martin.   R.S.R. Acting Adjutant
   "   S.J. Boast.   L. San. Quartermaster
Lieut.   A.B. Chewe. 1st R.W.K. Medical Officer
2nd "   E.F.B. Wyatt. L. San. Machine Guns
  " "   J.S. Boast.   "   Transport Officer
Captain F.W.M. Shew   "   Comdg. F. Coy.
   "   F.A. Brent.   Yorks R.   "   A "
   "   A.O. Taylor.   L. San.   "   B "
Lieut.   R.L.F. Balter   "   "   D "
2nd "   W. Dawe
  " "   J.O.C. Cowan , 3. R. Scots.
2nd "   C.V. Whitaker , 3. Yorks.
  " "   J.H. Kelly , 3. L. San
  " "   J. Sweet-Escott   "
5 Captains (2 attd), 18 subalterns (9 S.R., 3 attd)

March.
2nd Lieut. N. B. Glendyne & den
"   "   S. W. [illegible] S. b. [illegible]
"   "   Q. B. Sletcher
"   "   R. [illegible]
Lt. G. Taylor
Lt. H. C. Thomas
Lt. G. Stalker
Lt. G. Thompson & den
Lt. Vickers
Lt. G. Leetham   to hôp. T.

and 292 other ranks

The undermentioned officers borne on the
strength of the Battalion were in
hospital -

3 Captain [Lt. T. Hume   & den K
           [M. L. Ballard   "
           [M. V. Rashbone   "
1 Lieut   [D. A. Hann   "

7th Inf.Bde.
3rd Div.

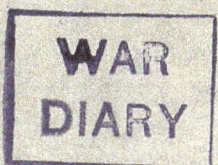

2nd BATTN. THE SOUTH LANCASHIRE REGIMENT.

A P R I L

1 9 1 5

2nd Battalion South Lancashire Regt.

War diary – 1st to 30th April 1915.

Thursday 1st. Very fine bright day – Bright sunshine and very warm.
Local situation quiet.
Battalion moved from Dickibusch during the evening – companies moving independently between 7 and 7.30pm to position East of the town relieving 4th South Lancashire Regt.
Relief completed in excellent order by about 10.30pm when relieved unit withdrew to billets at Dickebusch.
No casualties.
Fine mild night. Local situation fairly quiet.
"B" Company under Lieut. Balfour and "D" Company with half to under Captain Drew in fire trenches.
Remainder of Battalion in support in vicinity of "Cross Roads, B.W. corner Square N6.a. Sheet 28 Belgium".

Friday 2nd. Dull and inclined to rain all day. No change in disposition of the Battalion. Local situation generally quiet. Casualties during the day – two men wounded.

April.

__Friday 2nd__ Continued - Rain commenced about 6pm and continued all night.

__Saturday 3rd__ Very dull day - Occasional showers - Heavy rain commenced about 9 pm and continued all night.
No change in general disposition of Battalion.
'B' Company relieved by 'A' Company in fire trenches during the evening.
No other reliefs.
Local situation generally quiet.
Casualties during the day one man killed and one man wounded.

__Sunday 4th__ Dull cold day, bold winds.
Lieut Cowan wounded slightly, a few minutes while superintending placing of obstacles in front of trenches. No other casualties.
No change in front trenches of Battalion.
A slight change in disposition of Brigade took place in consequence of which the Battalion sector was increased from 2½ to 3 companies.
'D' Company withdrew to Supports.
Remaining half of 'B' Company moved forward to fire trenches which tonight are occupied by A, B and C Companies under the command of Captain Brady, Lieut Battis and Captain Taylor respectively.

April

<u>Sunday 4th</u> continued. Local situation
remarkably quiet.
During the day it was noticed that
the enemy was apparently mining in
the direction of the trenches held by
the Battalion. This was duly reported
and steps taken to deal with the
matter.

<u>Monday 5th</u>. Very wet miserable day.
No change in disposition of Battalion.
Companies disposed as last night.
No casualties during the day.
Sergt. Millwood killed in fire trenches
about 10.30pm. This N.C.O. had
performed very good work throughout
the campaign both as a machine
gun and company N.C.O. and his
loss is much regretted by all ranks.
One other man wounded during the
evening.

<u>Tuesday 6th</u>. Very boisterous dull day – cold winds.
No change in general disposition of
Battalion.
"D" Company under Captain Drew and
one platoon of "C" Company moved
forward to fire trenches in relief of
portions of A. B. & C. Companies, who
withdrew to supports.
Heavy rain commenced about 9 pm

April -
Tuesday 6th Continues and intense all night - 8
no Co. officers during the day.
2nd Lieut. [Crafford] Leigh-Smith, 4th
San. Fus. joined the Battalion.

Wednesday 7th Bitterns cold and very showery.
No change in disposition of Battalion
until evening when relieved by 4th
Battalion.
No casualties during the day [but two]
men wounded during relief. 4th Battalion
also sustained five men wounded.
Companies on relief withdrew to
billets in Dickebusch, last party
arriving about midnight.
Local situation fairly quiet, although
area North and South of Dickebusch
was shelled by enemy during the
day. One billet about 1000 yards
South of town, allotted to "B" Company
4th Battalion, was slightly damaged, one
man being killed and one man
wounded.

Thursday 8th. Very cold ground. Heavy
showers. Battalion at rest in billets
at Dickebusch.
Local situation very quiet.
About 6 p.m. heavy bombardment
commenced in area North of Ypres
and caused a certain amount of

April —
Thursday 8th continued —
concern amongst troops at rest in
Dickebush.
Bombardment continued very heavy
until about 11 p.m. From about this
hour till about dawn on 9th, firing
by Artillery North of Ypres continued but
not nearly so heavy.

Friday 9th. Fine bright day with occasional
rain. Very cold winds.
Battalion still in billets at Dickebush.
"A" and "B" companies detailed for
work in improving trenches, working
from 4 p.m. to midnight.
A special party of 2 Officers and 30
Other ranks worked from 8 p.m. till
dawn 10th in making a drain in
communication trench.
All these working parties were under
the immediate command of Major
Cotton.
No casualties.
Heavy bombardment again took place
North of Ypres from about 8 p.m. to
some time after midnight.

Saturday 10th. Fine and bright. Rather
cold winds. Battalion still in billets.
During the morning enemy

April -   10

Saturday 10th Continued - Pitched several
    shells on to area South of Dickebusch,
    apparently searching the road.
    Two shells pitched near the billet
    occupied by Officers of 'B' Company.
    Severely wounding one man who was
    outside the billet. No other damage.
    Otherwise local situation quiet.
    Heavy Artillery fire throughout whole day
    north of Ypres.
    B and D Companies employed in
    improving trenches, working from 8 pm
    till about 2 am, 11th.
    Casualties - Two Sergeants and three men
    wounded.

Sunday 11th - Fine bright day. No change in
    disposition of Battalion. Still at rest
    in Dickebusch. During the morning
    enemy pitched several high shrapnel
    shells over centre of town but
    without doing any damage.
    Otherwise local situation quiet.
    A and B Companies again employed
    in improving trenches working from about
    8 pm to 1 am, 12th.
    One man wounded.

Monday 12th - Fine day but inclined to be
    hazy.

April.   11
Monday 12th continued - No change in disposition
of Battalion. Local situation quiet.
D Company detailed to continue work of
improving trenches, working from about 8pm
to 2 am 13th. No casualties.
About 11.30pm the noise of aircraft overhead was heard in the vicinity of the
Battalion transport about 3 miles West of
Dickebusch and a hostile airship of the
"Zeppelin" type was seen to pass over,
travelling in a Southerly direction.
Several bombs were dropped from the
airship but beyond making a number
of large holes in the ground no damage
was done in this area.
About midnight the airship returned,
shaping a Northerly course and
flying practically over the town of
Dickebusch. The night was very clear
and starry and the airship could be
easily seen.
Tuesday 13th. Mild day - rather day.
Local situation quiet. Battalion moved
from Dickebusch and took over position East
of town occupied by 4th Battalion.
Companies moved off independently between
7.15 and 7.45 pm.
a. b. and 3 Platoons of D Company in

April.
Tuesday 13th continued -
fire trenches. D and 1 Platoon of B in support.
Relief carried out in excellent order and completed by about 10 pm when relieved Battalion returned to billets -
Casualties during relief - two men wounded.
Rainy night -

Wednesday 14th - Dull, showery and rather cold day. No change in disposition of Battalion.
Reinforcement of 1 Sergeant and 24 other ranks arrive [at Dickebusch and proceeded to join the Battalion during the evening.]
Very quiet in sector occupied by the Battalion but about 11.45pm some unusual disturbance was caused in the sector on the left of that occupied by units of 9th Infantry Brigade. [It appears that the enemy had succeeded in sapping in the direction of a house held in the vicinity of the fire trenches occupied by a unit of 9th Infantry Brigade and in addition to blowing up the house they bombarded a portion of the fire trenches with grenades and trench mortars. Our artillery in the vicinity of Dickebusch were immediately warned and at once opened a very heavy fire on the enemy's

April. 13
Wednesday 14th Continued.

position East of that town and north of the Sector held by 7th Infantry Brigade.

This apparently caused confusion and loss in the enemy's lines as from reports received from deserters in our lines, our artillery fire was well directed and most effective.

The situation quieted down soon after midnight and the night passed without further incident.

Casualties during the day - one man wounded.

Thursday 15th - Fine bright day. Local situation very quiet.

No change in general disposition of Battalion.

D Company and 1 Platoon of C to fire trenches in relief of A and 1 Platoon of B who withdrew to support.

Quiet night. Three men wounded.

Friday 16th. Fine day. During the day the enemy pitched a number of shells in the vicinity of Battalion Head Quarters, apparently searching for our guns. No damage was done and beyond this the local situation was quiet.

April 5th
Friday 16th continued.   14

No change in general disposition of the
Battalion.
"A" Coy and 1 Platoon of "B" to fire
trenches in relief of "B" and 1 Platoon
of "B" who withdrew to support.
Casualty during the day - one man
wounded.
2nd Lieut. [Frederick William] Partington,
3rd Battalion and one man joined at
Dickebusch and proceeded to join the
Battalion in the evening.
Still night.
Three other men wounded during the
night.

Saturday 17th. Fine bright day. No change in
general disposition of the Battalion.
1 Platoon of "B" Company to fire trenches
in relief of another of same company.
Local situation quiet.
Hostile aeroplane dropped two bombs in
field occupied by transport of R.A.C.
about ½ mile from Battalion transport.
No damage done as the bombs did
not explode. This incident occurred about
6 pm.
About 7 pm our artillery in the area
North of Dickebusch opened a heavy

April.   15
Saturday 17th Continued.
fire on enemy position, in connection with
an attack being made by 5th Division.
Later on, received information that a mine
had been exploded and enemy trench
captured at 7.10pm, one Officer and three
men of 106th Regiment being also captured.
A later report stated that 9 more prisoners
had been brought in, including 2 Artillery
Officers.
Our artillery fire, although much decreased,
continued practically all night.
The attack did not affect the disposition
of the Battalion, and so far as our
Sector was concerned the night was quiet.

Sunday 18th. Very fine bright day.
General disposition of Battalion unchanged.
2 Companys and 1 Platoon of "B" to fire
trenches in relief of "A" and 1 Platoon of
"B". Latter withdrawn to Support.
Casualties during the day - one man
killed and one man wounded.
Local situation quiet.
Our Artillery in vicinity of YPRES opened
heavy fire about 6 pm, and was
very active during the whole of the
evening.
Quiet night in Battalion Sector.

April -

Monday 19th - Very fine warm day - Bright Sunshine - Very quiet in Battalion Sector. About 12.30pm enemy succeeded in pitching several shells into village of Dickebusch after shelling in that vicinity practically all morning - One shell struck a billet occupied by 'B' Company with 2 H.Q. and demolished nearly all the roof - injuring two men - Some consternation was caused amongst the inhabitants but beyond the breaking of glass in a few houses no other damage was done -
During the evening the Battalion was relieved by 4th Battalion -
Relief was well carried out and completed by about 10pm when the Battalion withdrew to billets at Dickebusch -
One man slightly wounded during relief -
Local situation remarkably quiet -

Tuesday 20th - Fine bright warm day - Battalion at rest in billets and huts at Dickebusch - Local situation quiet -
Our artillery North of Dickebusch was very active during the evening and practically all night -

April.
Tuesday 2nd Continued.
Battalion furnished Special working party of 1 Officer and 30 men to carry out Special work in trenches - working from 8pm to about midnight.

Wednesday 21st. Fine day. Battalion still at rest. Local situation quiet.
Artillery North of Dickebusch very active. 250 men from Bn and 2 companies detailed for Special work, and carrying stores, in connection with trench position, working from about 8pm to shortly after midnight 22nd. Casualty - one man wounded.

Lt Luitt, Bain, Nigalls Bush and sent to BHQ

Thursday 22nd. - Fine day - No change in disposition of Battalion - Local situation unchanged.
Very heavy firing commenced during the afternoon and continued all evening and night, North of Dickebusch. The firing was much heavier than usual.
The Battalion received the following message about 11 pm. "All troops in billets should be ready to move at a half hours notice".
In consequence of this all companies "stood by" all night.
Very cold night - Very clear.

April.

Friday 23rd. Bright day. Strong W. winds.
Very heavy firing all day North of
Dickebusch. Battalion "standing by" all day
in billets.
Local situation unchanged.
Whole Battalion detailed for special work
in Section East of Dickebusch, working from
about 9 pm to about midnight.
The amount of work performed by the
Battalion was very satisfactory, a Staff
Officer being sent to the Commanding Officer
to express the appreciation of the G.O.C.
No casualties. Very clear night.

Saturday 24th. Fine day. Cold winds.
Artillery still very active. Local situation
unchanged.
Battalion still in billets. "Standing by" as
Divisional reserve.
Considerable activity between Dickebusch
and Ypres.
Heavy rain during night.

Sunday 25th. Fine day. No change in local
situation or disposition of Battalion during
the day.
Very considerable activity North of Dickebusch.
In the evening Battalion moved out to
relieve 10th Battalion, Companies marching
independently between 7.45 pm and 8 pm.

April.

Sunday 25th continued.

19

Relief well carried out and completed about 10.45 p.m. when relieved Battalion withdrew to billets at Dickebusch.

No casualties during relief = during the night, one man wounded.

Road along which transport was moving shelled by enemy - one shot about every 15 minutes.

No damage to transport which completed its work and was back in bivouac before midnight.

Monday 26th. - Heavy artillery fire from our guns apparently along whole line north of Dickebusch, practically continuous all last night and today.

Very fine bright day. Enemy aeroplanes very active, but good shooting by our anti-aircraft guns compelled them to fly very high, making their observations difficult.

In consequence of the enemy using obnoxious gas, which were directed towards our trenches, the troops were provided with improvised gauze masks, which were impregnated with a special solution to assist in counteracting the effects of the gas.

April -
Monday 2ⁿᵈ continued.

During the day some of the trenches
occupied by the Battalion were shelled by
enemy guns and slightly damaged.
Casualties during the day three men
wounded.

About 7 pm a number of high explosive
shells were pitched by enemy over centre of
Dickebusch. Several civilians and soldiers
being hit. One civilian and one soldier
killed.

Road along which transport was moving
with supplies was shelled continuously
during the evening and night. This
caused some annoyance but no damage
was done.

No change in general disposition of the
Battalion.

One platoon of "B" Coy relieved another of
same company in fire trenches. No other
reliefs.

Tuesday 27ᵗʰ. Fine day. Heavy artillery fire
heard all night and continued
throughout the day.

During the morning Dickebusch was again
shelled from enemy position East of the
village. Between 2 and 4 pm a number
of shells were again pitched into the

April 27th
Tuesday 27th. continued -
village but these came from guns which
were apparently operating north west of
Ypres - quite a new direction.
The shelling caused troops to vacate their
billets temporarily but no damage was done
to the village. Two or three men of other
units and several horses were killed.
No change in general disposition of
Battalion and very little excitement in
trenches occupied by the Battalion -
'D' Company to fire trenches in relief of
'A' Company. 1 Platoon of 'B' exchanged.
Casualty during the day - one man killed.
Enemy again shelled road used by
transport. No damage done.

2 A. & S. H. arrived at Dickebusch
this evening and billeted there for the night.
Situation quiet in Battalion Sector.

Wednesday 28th. Very bright fine day -
very warm. General situation much
quieter. Some activity amongst our
artillery in positions N. W. of Dickebusch
during the morning and evening and
about midnight but nothing like the
heavy bombardment of yesterday.
A little shelling by enemy in Battalion
Sector took place during the day, but

22

April -
Wednesday 28th continued -
The local situation generally was quiet -
General disposition of Battalion unchanged -
'A' Company to fire trenches in relief
of 'B' - 1 Platoon of 'B' exchanged -
Draft which arrived yesterday was taken
forward and joined companies - A 23 -
B 18 - C 26 - D 22 = 89.
Very bright moonlight night -
Road used by transport taking supplies
to Battalion again shelled at regular
intervals by enemy - no damage done -
Casualties during the day - four men
wounded -

Thursday 29th - Very fine warm day -
2nd Lieut. [John Edward French] Strickland, J.
San R. joined at Dickebusch and proceeded
to join Battalion in the evening -
Some artillery fire heard frequently during
the day from area N.W. of Ypres -
Situation in vicinity of Dickebusch generally
quiet -
During the night enemy in front of
Battalion sector showed some unrest as
rifle fire was heavier than usual -
Casualties during the day - one man
killed, three wounded.
Very bright moonlight night - One platoon
'B' Coy exchanged in fire trenches. No other relief -

23

April -
Friday 30th - ditto - Very fine and light -
No change in general disposition of the
Battalion. D company and 1 platoon of B
Coy have traveled in relief of A and 1
platoon of B.
Situation in Battalion Sector unchanged -
Roads leading from Dickebusch to position
shelled by enemy all evening and
night, causing some annoyance to transport.
Casualties during the day, 2nd Lieut Wyatt
and one man wounded - both died of
wounds in dressing station -
2nd Lieut Roscoe assumed charge of machine
guns in relief of 2nd Lt Wyatt wounded.
and sent to field ambulance -

On this date the Battalion mustered as
follows -

1   Lt.Colonel F. A. Dudgeon   D.San. Commanding Battn.
1   Major   H. J. Cotter   "   Senior Major
5   Captains   L. S. R. Acting Adjt
            L. G. Craik   D. San. Quartermaster
    Lieut   A. B. Chivers   R.A.M.C Medical Officer
16 2nd .   J. L. Brost   D. San. Transport Officer
            Lt Roscoe   "   Machine gun
    Captn. F. W. McIver   "   Commdg D Coy
        "   F. A. Brent   Gloster R " A "
        "   A. O Taylor   D. San.   " C "
2   Lieut   R. C. F. Battie   "   " B "

April -
Friday 30th interned.

Lieut. C. P. Whitaker. 3 Dorsets.
2nd " J. A. Kelly. S. Lan.
" " J. Sweet-Escott "
" " R. S. Gilmour "
" " T. W. Goldsmith "
" " C. G. Fletcher "
" " R. Sodge "
" " W. R. Gaskell "
" " C. H. R. Thomas "
" " W. C. Sadler "
" " C. E. Thompson "
" " W. C. Dickson Lan. 7
" " T. A. Mallory "
" " T. W. Partington S. Lan
" " J. C. T. Stricklands " (On Field Ambulance)
Lieut. W. Laws.
and about 1100 other ranks.

Cas. month.
K.3. W.1 + 24

Hodgson L/Pl
Commander 2/S Lan Reft.

7th Inf.Bde.
3rd Div.

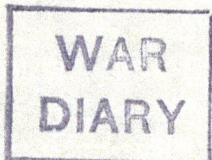

2nd BATTN. THE SOUTH LANCASHIRE REGIMENT.

M A Y

1915

2nd Battalion South Lancashire Regt.

War Diary — 1st to 31st May 1915.

Saturday 1st. — Grey sharp in morning dull and rather cold day. — Rain in evening. — Front of Ridgewood & River Yser swamp. No damage done to Battalion below River. Relief of 4th Battalion during the night. Relief was slow and not completed till about midnight. On Ridgewood Battalion withdrew and was ordered to muster in rear of A and 'B' Coys and a that shrapnel burst in rear of Ridgewood. — A that shrapnel burst in rear of where reserve [one] Company Regiment in Billets at Sunbrush. Three Platoons of B Company proceeded on Lancashire Hill & the main body C to own disposition in reserve to remainder of those in Billets in Sunbrush and to those supporting hands in case of emergency. No casualties during relief. 2 casualties during the day — one Sergeant and one man wounded.

May —
Sunday 2nd. — Still out rather cold of no shower in general inspection of the Battalion. May bottom seemed known to improve of Ridgewood Survey the day went on & southern Sunbrush were districted and no casualties & few heavy setting fire commenced in vicinity of Ypres and West of the town. Early though men moving from the direction and careful in distant house of German. Some were quite noticeable near Sunbrush Evening comparatively quiet, also not settling in vicinity of Sunbrush we came upon before Ypres appeared this evening. The disturbance this evening Silver machine gun assumed command of Company.

Monday 3rd. — Rather dull, quiet day. — No shower in disposition of Battalion. — Sunbrush & houses continued during the day. — no damage done — Heavy rain during evening and night.

No. 1768.

OFFICE OF THE DEPUTY DIRECTOR, SUPPLY AND TRANSPORT, BASE,

Basrah, *10th July 1917.*

To Inspector General of Communications, Basrah.

MEMORANDUM.

1. I would like to draw your attention to the following figures anent the tonnage which is now required for the monthly maintenance of the army in Mesopotamia.

The total monthly tonnage required to *maintain* the army is 48,120 tons made up as follows :—

							Tons.
British	...	Troops.	...	...	...	Supplies.	5340
Indian	...	„	...	...	...	„	10305
British	...	Troops.	...	...	...	Fuel.	4005
Indian	...	„	...	...	...	„	6870
Animals.	...	Grain	...	...	...		10800
„	...	Fodder	...	...	...		10800
						Total	48120

I notice that the numbers of the Force, both in men and animals, still show a practically steady increase of 10 per cent per month. Adding then 10 percent to my total of 48,120 tons, the total tonnage required to *maintain* the Force for the month of August would be 52,932 tons.

2. To set against this we have a total figure of 8,307 tons obtained by local purchase monthly, and deducting this figure from the grand total of 52,932 tons we get the net quantity of 44,125 tons monthly which has to be imported from outside this country in order to *maintain* the Force in Mesopotamia.

3. You know of course that at the present moment we have not succeeded in reaching our ideal of a reserve of 60 days of supplies, fuel and forage for the army in Mesopotamia, though, with the exception of hay stuffs, the position is, I think, very favourable and taking the whole of the rest of the items into consideration we might say that we have arrived at the figure of 45 days instead of the 60 days aimed at.

4. You are only able for the present to allot us 38,000 tons for supplies, fuel and forage monthly, thus leaving a deficit of 6,000 tons monthly on the requisite *maintenance* figures.

5. I understand that from August onwards the D. D. L. R. hopes to obtain 11,000 tons per month from this country, so this being obtained would make the deficit only 3,000 tons per month. You have given authority for all animals on the L. of C. to be placed on three-quarter forage ration and this practically for the time being balances the deficit against us, so on the whole the general situation may be considered quite favourable.

6. I am of course aware of the circummstances which necessitate an allotment of tonage to us from India which does not at present quite cover our monthly maintenance, but I feel it my duty to place these facts and figures in front of you in order that you may, in weighing and balancing the various opposing factors in the demand for tonnage on India, be able to judge from the Supply and Transport point of view the relative urgency of our need for increased tonnage.

The figures I have given you are actuals, and I have nothing left up my sleeve which I have not placed before you.

(Signed) W. PARKER, *Colonel*,

D. D. S. & T., Base.

28

May -
Monday 3rd Berlin.

Most of Battalion employed during the night as working parties in carrying out improvements in Company areas. One man killed - one other man wounded in Ridgewood.

Tuesday 4th - Fine morning and afternoon. Stormy wet night. Local situation generally quiet. During the morning B and D Companies moved forward to Ridgewood in relief of A and C Companies who returned to Scherpenberg. No casualties.

Wednesday 5th - Still and very close day. Disposition of Battalion unchanged. About 2 pm orders were received for Battalion to be prepared to move at 15 mins notice, much 2, a & b am 1st N.Z. Rifle to support to Brits of 5th Division as necessary. Battalion "Standing by" until further orders until about 7 pm when further orders were received for whole Battalion to form a special working party and proceed to Bellegoed Farm N & E of Kruisstraathoek on the night of which place they were to continue work already commenced — Companies moved

May -
Wednesday 5th 10 an —
from Bivouacs and billets at 7.30 pm leaving Scherpenberg about 8 pm. After this have the Battalion the enemy opened fire which was apparently directed towards hill 60, and continued for some time.

Thursday 6. Whole of whole Battalion area engaged upon completed about 2 am an companies marched back to Bivouacs and billets. No casualties in Companies. Shells from our own and enemy's guns passed over the Battalion continuously from the while time they were at work. One man of Battalion Supplies wounded in St Eloi. At 10 pm orders were received for Battalion to be prepared to move at short notice to support Brigade area No. 6 of Scherpenbergh. During the morning enemy fired several large shells into Vierstraat and Scherpenbergh but no slight damage was done, there were no casualties. About a few more Companies & & and A withdrawn from Bivouac in Ridgewood to Scherpenbergh in reserve to support mortar

Date.	Place.	Extract.

Assistant Director of Supplies.
Base I. E. F. " D."
July 1917.

14-7-17	......	*Salt.*—I raised the question of importing this from India again in lieu of local purchase and Colonel Parker told Fitzgerald, A.D.L.R., to go into matter of prices and amount purchased.
		India gives us Rupees 1·9 as the price per maund to pay, but would appear to lose sight of the fact that Rupees 1·4 of this is excise and goes back to Government. From my own knowledge I know salt only actually costs Government two to four annas per maund in the end.
22-7-17	......	*Forage.*—We have only eight days at and *en route* to Baghdad and the situation is serious. Suptrans Army has wired us to do all we can and Colonel Parker has gone over to see the Inspector General of Communications. The D. A. C. is 250 tons, of which about 100 tons is being obtained locally, though of this we only know by surmise. Here we are hampered as usual by loading and other difficulties and shortage of despatch from India.
		Despatches from India.—India is ignoring our order of urgency and has already this month sent 2,000 tons of unwanted stores (milk, etc.) whilst refusing to send us badly wanted forage.

May -
Thursday 6th 1901 [?]

During the afternoon Major H.J. Ofton and Captain J.T. Boast proceeded to 15th Infantry Brigade automatic machine to be occupied by Battalion - Battalion moved from Stapshorst at 8.30pm marching in a north Easterly direction -

Friday 7th -
Battalion arrived about 4.30am at a point on African-Bommes railway South East of Zillebeke and occupied machine entrenchment - the mount was much detached by various units carrying out relief movements very slowly - Had the next few clear the mount would have been completed by about moonrise - Shortly after arrival at front, machine about the Battalion was disposed as follows -

Headqrs. Companies and two companies "A" and "B" in line on railway embankment to in north bank of railway West of hill 60.
"C" and another S.M. of Essex of Etang de Zillebeke as "D" company moved into position. Bay were heavily shelled by enemy, two men being killed and ten others wounded -

May -
Friday 8th 1901 [?]
Battalion remained in these positions during movements of day.
During the enemy shelled severely the Battalion in new position and occupied trenches on Hill 60 - moving about 8.15pm
15th Infantry Brigade relieved by 13th Infantry Brigade Battalion attached to 13th Brigade -

Saturday 8th
About 10.30am Battalion completed by march from the command of Bompaine myrs the command to Bompaine myrs Battalion. Lieut Ball and Captain Logie respectively been somehow turned into two of S.O. 6 & J. Johnson. May who withdrew and who Deys who withdrew from the position or relief - "B" Company action on railway embankment on way of trenches following a front of Q.O. Rifles who also withdrew - During the relief Lieutenant J.H. Kelly was wounded and removed to Field Ambulance -

During the night officers of the Battalion were fully occupied in

Date.	Place.	Extract.
		"D" Squadron and Machine Gun Section **32nd Lancers.** **June 1917.**
8-6-17	……	Reports received from Beled Ruz——Escort of 15 rifles to empty cart convoy proceeding from Mahrut to Beled Ruz encountered 300 mounted and 100 dismounted Arabs, Beni-Tamin, near bridge on main road 4 miles south west of Beled Ruz at 6 A.M. 28th and opened fire on Arabs who lined nullah north of road. About same time convoy of 9 Fiat lorries with escort of 18 rifles arrived from Mahrut; this caused Arabs to retire and both escorts held up Arabs at range of 1200 yds. till arrival of 2 L.A.M. cars from Beled Ruz. Shortly after 2 troops 32nd Lancers followed L.A.M. cars. Cavalry who were without B.O. were commanded by Lieut. Graham 67th Punjabis, ground north of road was unsuitable for L.A.M. cars which therefore escorted convoy on its way to Mahrut. Cavalry then swung right and drove Arabs from two successive positions on Khaiyat Lamloon hills, On reaching Abu Dehan Canal Lieut. Graham ordered a retirement. Time 10-30 A.M. During the operation he with 3 sowars as right flank guard were taken in flank by dismounted Arabs who had worked round by a parallel nullah, and came under heavy fire at close range as result of which they were all killed, Lieutenant Graham reported killed outright. Our cavalry now reduced in strength from 38 to 32, with 10 horses killed or wounded, retired in good order to main Beled Ruz road, where they halted till 1 P.M. in hopes of regaining nullah where casualties occurred. Owing however to large number of Arabs who followed them up they were unable to do so, and returned to Beled Ruz. Arabs report that Shaikh Hamid of Beni-Tamin was killed during the fighting. This however requires confirmation, 12 Arabs also killed reported and certain numbers men and horses wounded by our M. G. fire. *Casualties.* Nos. Lance Dafadar Abdul Rahman … … 3445 Sowar Nial Muhammad … … 4029 Acting Lance Dafadar Abdul Rahman … 3452 Sowar Fazar Ali Khan … … 3825 *Wounded.* Sowar Sali Muhammad … … 1685 Sowar Sultan Khan … … 3783
		Director of Works. **Force " D."** **July 1917.**

Date.	Place.	Extract.
-7-17	BAGHDAD	A large deposit of bitumen having been located near Kuweit, arrangements are being made for an officer to visit and report upon its possibilities, as regards cost at seashore, etc. Bitumen is successfully used as a road surface in Baghdad and makes a good water proofing for the sides of tanks.

May.
Saturday 8th cont.

reconnoitring the positions held by the
Battalion, which owing to the maze of
trenches was very difficult.
Throughout the whole night the enemy
fire was very heavy and continuous.
On daybreak all ranks immediately
commenced much an improving the positions
and this continued all day with great
success.
She whole sector occupied by the
Battalion was strewn with a large number
of dead Germans - both British and German -
A special party were detailed to bury the
dead.
It was observed that a large number
of dead Germans had suffered severely
from the effect of their own rifle fire
a number were found shot through the
back of the head - these men having
apparently taken refuge in shelters, having been
for the purpose of harassing advancing
troops, as many of them were found
near these bodies, and they had been
shot in attempting to retire.
All surrounded both the men attacks
and sent to 13th Hussar rear guarding, as
were also several shorter stages with

May.
Sunday 9th cont.

numbers 105, 117, 137, and 53, were there
arms heavy - especially the late bombing-
bombardment from 10 noon yesterday 12 12
noon today was 17 their ranks
movements.
She night of improving the position
continued all night and as now
found most of our men the sector
became available from having been
partially on the position all night,
and to the positions are improved
supplies are increasingly easier
from Suchebruck when transport
was accomplished.

Sunday 9th. Fine bright day - No incidents.
No change in general dispositions -
the Battalion during the day "B" and
"D" companies exchanged places. This
not a minor to give B company who
has moved in today the last two
days a chance of obtaining cover -
their number of improvement continues -
Fully the largest dust and continues
this work.

Special thanks for me in drawing 6th
out of trenches when easier is the
Battalion, together with a special solution.

British other ranks.

Killed	27
Died of wounds	7
Wounded	119
Prisoners of war	2
Missing	3
Total	158

Indian officers.

Killed	5
Wounded	5
Total	10

Indian other ranks.

Killed	18
Wounded	116
Missing	1
Total	135

Mon.
Sunday 9th Coul. 15 —
During the day some excellent work
was carried out by a party under
Regimental Sergeant Major S. F. Roberts.
This drew the arms, Nursing stumps
this sector, consumed latrines and prepared
a spare water supply, collected a
large quantity of tools, ammo, equipment
and miscellaneous stores — All this work
made a great improvement in the sector.
Heavy shelling by enemy all day, during
an occurrence of officers — many part of
which from 13 am Relieve 6/13.
Many — 2nd Lt. W. 6. Sadler killed —
2nd Lt. W. 6. Stevens and 2nd Lieut. Fletcher
wounded. The losses were all to casualty
on their duties —
Other ranks. Nine killed. At wounded —
6 of the losses were all to carry on
their duties —
At Supplies successfully taken forward under
some arrangements as yesterday —

Monday 10th — Quiet night day. N.G. work —
No change in disposition of the Battalion —
Enemy opened a very heavy rifle and
machine gun fire on Battalion trenches
about 3 am — daybreak — on which time all

Mon.
Monday 10th Coul. 15 —
ranks were "standing to arms" and bombarding
officers present in trenches. Our artillery at
once opened a heavy bombardment on
enemy trenches and the Battalion kept up
no every disturbed — the bombardment
shook any action by enemy
The work of improving the position and
burying the dead progressed throughout
the day —
About noon enemy bombarded the means of
his artillery, the rifle & arms of our
advances the trenches and their in a
very short time & the rest on
There seemed to be transport men in position
the trenches to the right and left of
the trench. Orders had previously been
issued in the event of this particular
Kinds being experienced we was to be blown
up from the new by means of a mine
which had obviously been laid under it.
The movement of the men so experienced
officers was watched by the N.C.O. in charge
of the mine, as an examination of the
trench and arrangement, were made to
fire the mine. Fortunately the fear did
not ignite properly and upon any
further action was taken the situation
was explained — And the fuse was

Indian other ranks.

Killed	6
Wounded	63
Missing	1
Total	70

14th Lancers.

British officers.

Killed.—Captain P. D. C. Eliot.
Wounded.—Captain I. G. Gibson.
　　　　　Lieutenant E. McK. Nicholl.

Indian officers.

Killed.—Jemadar Atar Singh.
　　　　　Jemadar Ramji Lal.
　　　　　Jemadar Amir Singh.
　　　　　Jemadar Daryao Singh.
Wounded.—Risaldar Sarwar Singh.

Indian other ranks.

Killed	12
Wounded	42
Total	54

16th Squadron Machine Gun Corps.

British officers.

Killed.—2nd-Lieutenant J. O. P. Clarkson (13th Lancers).

British other ranks.

Killed	3
Died of wounds	2
Wounded	17
Total	22

Indian other ranks.

Wounded	11

Grand Total.

British officers.

Killed	6
Died of wounds	1
Wounded	16
Prisoner of war	1
Total	24

May—
Monday 10th Cont:—

regrets the consequences would have been
very serious as the sources of the trench
never have suffered heavy loss —
Since this incident orders have been
issued that only written orders from the
Officer Commanding the Particular trench,
to expedite the running are to be acted on —
Casualties from noon yesterday to noon
today — 4 other ranks killed — 14 wounded —
2 of the latter continuous duty —
Supplies again successfully taken forward —
Enemy's shelling of Ypres continues during
the day and night. The fires in this
town continue fiercely —

Tuesday 11th. Fine and bright. N.E. wind —
No change in the general disposition of
the battalion. 16 Company relieves 'C'
Company in advanced fire trenches.
Work of entrenching positions and improving
dead still continued —
Much annoyance was caused by a light
field gun which enemy had brought up
into this line and by machine guns and
snipers. These were all hunted out and
willing fire directed on them —
During the day sounds of mining
were heard in the vicinity of our

May—
Tuesday 11th Cont:—
advanced fire trench — The N.E. on our
extreme left — and discovered that
the enemy were running under our own
fire in the direction of our fly trenches —
The N.E. immediately commenced to counter-
mine —
Casualties from 13 noon yesterday to 12
noon today: Other ranks — 1 killed — 4
wounded — two of the latter were able to
carry on their duties —

Wednesday 12 —
Rather dull day — S.W. wind —
Sustained of hostile aeroplanes -
About 5am enemy again bombarded our
advanced fire trenches disabling one machine
gun — the situation during the day
was much quieter than usual —
Casualties 15 noon yesterday — Other ranks
one killed — 9 wounded — 5 of whom were
able to carry on their duties —
About 6 pm the artillery on our sector
suddenly opened a heavy fire on
the enemy's position in front. This continued
for about 10 minutes and then slowed —
the battalion on our own commenced rapid
rifle fire and kept this up with a
view to causing the enemy to advance
to his front line — after about 15 minutes

CAVALRY BRIGADE.

May 1917.

APPENDIX I.

List of battle casualties of 7th Cavalry Brigade from 13th December 1916 to 31st May 1917 (both dates inclusive).

13th Hussars.

Officers.

Killed.—Captain W. H. Eve.
  2nd-Lieutenant J. F. Munster.
  2nd-Lieutenant G. Lynch-Staunton.
  2nd-Lieutenant E. V. Rolfe.
Wounded.—Lieutenant-Colonel I. I. Richardson.
  Major E. F. Twist.
  Captain S. O. Robinson.
  Lieutenant J. V. Dawson.
  2nd-Lieutenant G. R. Pedder.
  2nd-Lieutenant G. L. Welstead.
  2nd-Lieutenant I. A. Lord.
  2nd-Lieutenant T. Williams-Taylor.
  2nd-Lieutenant H. C. D. FitzGibbon.
Prisoner of War.—2nd-Lieutenant E. F. Pennington.

Other ranks.

Killed	24
Died of wounds	5
Wounded	102
Prisoners of war	2
Missing	3
Total	136

13TH LANCERS (WATSON'S HORSE).

British officers.

Wounded.—Captain F. H. Moody, M. C.
  Major I. H. Watson.
  Lieutenant G. R. Murray (died of wounds).
  Captain G. N. Watson.
  Major A. McC. Jameson.
  Captain A. G. O. M. Mayne.

Indian officers.

Killed.—Risaldar-Major Abdur Rahman Khan.
Wounded.—Risaldar Ranjor Singh.
  Risaldar Bhola Singh.
  Jemadar Hakim Singh.
  Jemadar Jaimal Singh.

May -
Wednesday 12 to next -
The Artillery opened fire on to the enemy's trenches - This was all done with a view to disturbing any preparations by enemy -
The Battalion was relieved during the evening by 1st London Highlanders - Relief completed very successfully by about 11.30 pm -
One man slightly wounded during relief -
On next Battalion withdrew to billets at Sheikhbagh.
The Commanding Officer before leaving the positions sent his report on the ranks of the G.O.C. 13th Infantry Brigade s who remarks him to convey to all ranks of the Battalion his sense of deep & sincere appreciation of the Battalion during its short tour of duty with the Brigade -
The final remarks of the G.O.C. 13th Brigade were "Your men have motion like lions and you have in Togn into Battalion" -
It may here be placed on record that whilst the Battalion was ordered to proceed to Ypres to the spirit shown

May -
Wednesday 12 to next -
by all ranks was excellent and shewn great keenness to maintain its reputation already earned by the Battalion.
The 800 wounds have been the enemy in the little break by the Battalion hit most remarkable effects, the faces of the dead soldiers who were known by dark and muster were quite expressionless by our men were quite free of all muster work of heavy enemy artillery. They forst known to the fact intensity of the exces men of the enemy trenches &
Thursday 13 [Battalion looks in billets at about 8 am and remained at not - Manufact the day - Very dark and warm night.
Several situation Spies - Several the night enemy futched some known shells into village of Sheikhbagh - no damage done -
Friday 14 - Very wet morning - B.H.Q. inspection & Battalion workshops - Gross situation quiet -
Same afternoon - Village of Sheikhbagh again shelled by enemy about 6 pm -

"S" Battery R. H. A.—contd.
April 1917.

Date.	Place.	Extract.
19-20-4-17	......	Remained in camp.
21-4-17	......	Left 3-30 a.m., crossed river Tigris 3 miles below Khan Duluyiah, trotted up to Cobbe's column (1st Corps), reached them near Al Khubn at 8 a.m. Left at 4-30 p.m., did a left flank stunt but did not come into action. Were shelled by a field battery but had no casualties. Camped at Al Khubn at 9-30 p.m. Horses really worse than I have ever seen them. Everywhere very stony and as many horses had no shoes by this time their feet were in a pretty bad state. Over 10 miles trotting (25 miles).
22-4-17	......	Left 6-30 a.m., left flank of VII Division, were joined at 8-30 a.m. by C-56 Bty. R.F.A. Came into action in Ajali Canal, had good trench target and few parties moving in the open. One horse hit (D-66 who were alongside had 8 hit), 32nd Lancers did reconnaissance and returned reporting strongly held and 2 machine guns. Later in the day 32nd Lancers charged this trench supported by guns and 4 L.A.M.'s. Col. Griffiths, Capts. Hogg and Hunter (Adjt.) missing and trench not taken. Trench was reached and jumped by many who were practically all killed. Fired over 200 rounds, 8 miles trot. Camped at Police Post at 10-40 p.m. (19 miles) L A M'.s report shooting excellent.
23-4-17	......	Left at 7-5 a.m., (C-56 left us) crossed railway and followed Ajali Canal and eventually the railway line to Samarrah Railway Station. Found about 16 engines (all slightly damaged) and 250 trucks (in good order). Passed over yesterday's fight and found bodies of 32nd officers. Camped at 7 p.m., about 2½ miles S. of Samarrah on right bank (13 miles).

"S" Battery, R. H. A.
May 1917.

Date.	Place.	Extract.
18-5-17	ABU SAKHAR	Marched at 11 P.M. due west into desert to co-operate with column from Sumaikchah against Khasraj Arabs.
19-5-17	......	Halted at 2 A.M., till 4 A.M., advanced through encampments sending flocks to rear. Were fired on from main encampments and saw Arabs fleeing. Fired 38 rounds: Armoured cars killed 25 Arabs. Cavalry burnt encampment, 2000 cattle brought in and more prisoners. About 60 or 70 Arabs killed. Leading shaikh and 2 others picked up dead with shrapnel in them. Returned to bivouac at noon. Operations considered successful.

May -
Friday 14th continued.

no damage done. 3 horses wounded. During the afternoon the Bishop of Pretoria visited the area in which the Battalion was billeted and delivered a very interesting address to the men. The G.O.C. 7th Infantry Brigade and many officers were present and the remnants of the Bishop were much appreciated by all ranks.
Quiet night.

Saturday 15th. This day. Battalion remained at rest during the day. Enemy shelling quiet.
During the day the commanding officer was informed by G.O.C. 7th Infantry Brigade, that the Battalion had been selected to carry out certain special improvements on the line of the allotted to the Brigade. The shelling was known on the first report received from B.G.C. 13th Infantry Brigade on the night down by the Battalion while in the trench till 6 to no the area allotted to our Brigade, and also on the nature of work of different times by the W.O. when the Battalion has been employed few work in improving the line when not actually

May-
Saturday 15 continued.

in the firing line. It was also directed that during the time the Battalion was employed on this special work, the men would not be detailed for trench duty.
B.G. and 2 companies, formerly protecting Works Howard about Thom and Nugh Hill about 2 am an

Sunday 16th.
When the Battalion returned to billets during the night were one man killed and one man wounded. 2nd Lieut. Entsworth was also slightly wounded but was able to continue his duties.
During the night, Saturday-Sunday, Shrapnel was thrown by enemy but no damage done. Battalion at rest during the day.
During the morning the commanding officer inspected the work done by the Battalion last night. Most of yesterdays extension to Switzerland trench shelter during the

2

Date.	Place.	Extract.
		War Diary of **"S" BATTERY, R. H. A.** April 1917.
6-4-17	......	Joined Cassels' Bde. at Jisani. Brigade consisted of 1 section "S" Battery, R.H.A., 1 section D-66th Battery, R.F.A., 21st Cavalry, 2 squadrons 32nd Lancers. Followed XIII Division to Kuwar Reach. (22 miles).
7-4-17	......	Active reconnaissance up to the Shatt-el-Adhaim. Came into action against trenches and observation ladder. Were very heavily enfiladed by two 5-9" and four field guns. Bombr. Corbett killed. Was relieved at dusk by XIII Division. Returned to Kuwar Reach. 1 horse killed, 2 badly hit about legs. Fired about 60 rounds (16 miles).
8-4-17	......	Remained in camp.
9-4-17	......	Aeroplane reports Turks advancing from Deli-Abbas and Cavalry Division was likely to be surrounded. Marched *via* Ruins to Chaliyah (Shiala) on the Nahr Khalis. (18 miles.) Enemy turned out to be Cav. Div. transport.
10-4-17	......	Returned to Kuwar Reach. Left camp at 9 p.m., marched E. in front of XIII Division to the Deli-Abbas—Sindiyah road (36 miles) about 5 miles N. W. Chaliyah. (Shiala).
11-4-17	......	About 7-30 a.m., the Cavalry Division were seen retiring. Came into action 500 yards W. of road and had the target of a lifetime. Turks advancing line after line in the open. When firing at 1600 yards the XIII Division marched through the guns. Bombr. Miller and Gunr. Warren wounded by rifle fire and 3 horses and 1 mule hit by shrapnel. Came into action behind Grace's Hill and had some good dismounted cavalry targets. Were pretty continuously shelled by 2 field guns. About 11 a.m., our 60 pdrs. started to shell us with H. E. and shrapnel. About 4 H. E. and 6 or 8 shrapnel were fired. Major Fergusson-Pollok, 32nd Lancers, Bombadier Hart, 5 cavalry horseholders and 10 horses were killed. Capt. Brook, Capt. MacDonald and 5 others were wounded by one 60 pdr. H. E. We retired ½ mile. Reached camp 11 p.m. at XIII Division Hd. Qrs., 9 miles from water. Fired about 200 rounds. (16 miles) Turks acknowledge 1000 casualties on 11th.
18-4-17	......	Left Kuwar at 5 a.m., did a chukkur and a demonstration 5 miles up the Adhaim, stayed there about ½ hour and returned to Tigris 2 miles S. of Adhiam. At 1-45 p.m., crossed the Adhaim bridge and after 10 miles trot saw the Turks in small groups all over the country. After a few rounds at each group they started to come in, one group after another. Kept coming into action for a few minutes and then advancing. This went on until everyone we could see had surrendered except about 100 infantry with 2 field guns who limbered up at first round and got away in the dusk. The Turks at first attempted to hold us up but as there was very little cover, and they seemed pretty exhausted from want of water, they started to come in very soon after the guns came into action. Total capture was 900 infantry, 3 machine guns complete on mules and many transport ponies and mules. Reached camp at Khan Duluyiah about 11-15 p.m., fired about 120 rounds, 18 miles trotting (36 miles).

May.
Sunday 16th continued –
afternoon but no damage done –
A, B, and C Companies forming working parties paraded at 8 pm and returned to billets about 2 am 17th – 1 man wounded. Wires mended. Was quite satisfactory –
Several situation quiet –

Monday 17th – About 3 am Northern end of Sickhuck was shelled – about six shells – slight damage done to two buildings –
Still day with some rain –
Battalion on rest during the day –
Strong rain during the evening and all night – Owing to this the Battalion could not carry on its work of improving the trenches always in hand. A, B, and C Companies were employed in carrying stores to men in Brigade Sector paraded about 7 pm and returned to billets about after midnight –
Again men billets – Three men wounded –
Several situation during the day was quiet but about midnight the village of Sickhuck was again shelled by many – about eight shells were scattered about the village but no damage done –

May –
Monday 17th continued –
whilst was returning from its nightly supplies were shelled –

Tuesday 18th – Army duty non day and heavy rain. Battalion as not during the day met. During the afternoon General Stockwell commanding 137 Division visited the Battalion and expressed his great satisfaction with the excellent report which he had received from S.O.b. 5th Division on the good work done by the Battalion during the time it was attached to that Division for duty with 13th Infantry Brigade on fell 60 and also with the 2nd Infantry Brigade the Battalion had generally during its time he had been extremely fortunate in that it was owing to this that the Battalion had been attached to the 1st Division for the important work on which it was now employed –
An observance with the instructions from S.O.b. 3rd Division the others was duly promulgated to all ranks of the Battalion – Owing to the continuous rain the Battalion had a few men at the Battalion transport

CONFIDENTIAL.

Serial Number. $\frac{7}{1052}$.

Notes from War Diaries, Part CCCXCIV.
MESOPOTAMIAN EXPEDITIONARY FORCE.
(FORCE " D.")
GENERAL STAFF.
ARMY HEADQUARTERS, INDIA.

October 1917.

Assistant Director of Veterinary Services, Cavalry Division.
March 1917.

A few notes on the cavalry operations to date.

22nd March 1917.—The main point which strikes one when viewing the cavalry operations, starting from, say the 14th December and culminating with the advance on and capture of Baghdad on March 11th is the extraordinary amount of work a horse will stand. In connection with this point it must be taken into consideration that the cavalry horse both British and Indian, carries an average weight of 2¼ stone, and also the very indifferent feeding it received during most of this period. With regard to the latter point it should be borne in mind that during the advance of Baghdad most of the horses' rations consisted of rice, which I do not consider of much feeding value, a very small amount of hay, with an insufficiency of water. During this period the British cavalry lost an extraordinary few horses from exhaustion.

The first horses to be evacuated for debility were the small, light boned country breeds, of which several of the Indian cavalry regiments have a good number; also most of the cases of exhaustion occurred among this class. In my opinion this campaign has proved the uselessness of mounting the Indian cavalry on the small, light boned underbred horses which are generally issued to them; they require just as big a horse as is issued to the British cavalry.

I consider the best horse for cavalry work is a well bred Waler or English horse standing about 15 hands. Coarse bred horses will not stand the work.

Our rather heavy losses from exhaustion were caused by the very long tiring days (although the actual distances covered when measured by map, were not great), the bad grain the horses received—a large percentage of rice which a large number of tired horses will not eat—and the shortage of hay and bhoosa. Hay and bhoosa were often provided, but the horses did not have time to eat it. Scarcity of water also contributed to the losses from exhaustion.

With regard to veterinary organisation it should be remembered that the amount of veterinary aid it is possible to render in a hostile country is very limited, therefore all horses which cannot continue the march with their unit should be shot, as if these are left otherwise they might fall into the enemy's hands.

Mobile Veterinary Sections on the march should consist entirely of mounted men, although syces are quite good enough for work in a standing camp.

May.
Tuesday 18. continues

Men engaged and not in forward with.
300 men were employed in carrying miscellaneous stores, providing about 7 hrs and returning to billets soon after midnight.
No casualties.
Local situation very quiet.
Very dark and dull night.
2nd Suss. Zillebeke & Railway dugouts sick. Battery sent to ? Company
Australian workers in 8 Irish Australian
Silver Officers that dame, MONT NOIR —

Wednesday 19th:— Battalion resting and doing the usual in disposition of the
No change in the Battalion.
Local situation very quiet.
Owing to very bad weather conditions the Battalion was unable to carry out any work.
Very fine warm day.

Thursday 20th:— No change in general disposition of Battalion.
Companies as having up to noon.
Rested during the afternoon.
2nd Suss.[Edward Percy Widdowson] 3rd S. Sam R. and 2m Suss.[Alan Bayning Wilson]

May.
Thursday 20. continues

4. Lieut Suss. joined the Battalion.
Whole Battalion engaged in special work from about 8pm to 2am 21st.
A, B, & D Companies.
'C' Company company machine—
Total Casualties — 9 men wounded.
Fine day. Battalion at rest.

Friday 21st:—
During the day.
1m Suss. George Renale Ashburner (one)
3. 2. Sam R. joined the Battalion.
Local situation quiet.
A, B and D Companies forming a working party moved off to ? Position about 6 pm.
Working Party Martin reports Buick and Lorimer sent to S[?] Rest Station, MONT NOIR.

Saturday 22nd:— Companies arrived back about 3am after a good night work.
3 men wounded during the night 21-22.
Very fine warm day.
Battalion on rest during the day.
Local situation quiet.
Working Party of 550 men furnished by A, B and C Companies moved off to position about 8pm.
One man wounded during the night. —

GENERAL STAFF BRANCH.

Notes from War Diaries, Part CCCXCIII, Mesopotamian Expeditionary Force, (FORCE "D"), June 1917.

Copies circulated to the following Branches, Army Headquarters, etc :—

1. Secretary, Army Department.
2. General Staff Branch.
3. Adjutant General's Branch.
4. Quartermaster-General's Branch.
5. Ordnance Branch.
6. Military Works Branch.
7. Medical Services Branch.
8. Military Secretary's Branch.
9. Financial Adviser.

Simla, the 31st October 1917.

May –
Saturday 22nd Continued —
About 10.30 pm. shelling in area north of
office commenced heavy fire on enemy
trenches, which continued for some time –
Sunday 23rd – Working parties arrived back
in billets about 2 a.m.
Fine bright day – Battalion at rest during
the day.
Large situation quiet –
2nd Lieut. Thompson assumed duty as
acting adjutant of the Battalion –
Lieut. Roland Gudgeon Proceeds to England
on special leave on medical grounds –
Major Paton assumes command of the
Battalion –
10.10 a.m. 2 companies forming a working
party from left about 8pm. billets
about 2.30 a.m. Battalion returned to billets –
Monday 24th – Battalion at rest. a man
wounded –
the work on which the Battalion was
engaged on this occasion was on
support trench in the vicinity of
OOSTHOEK, between the village of ST. ELOI
and ELLUSE (SLUICE) NO. 7 on YPRES–COMINES
Canal – Obst – Obst 26– BELGIUM –
The actual situation was rather an
anxious one on the night of the

May –
Monday 24th Continued –
surprise by 5 o'clock – Sunday – During the
progress of the work much annoyance
was caused by enemy rifle fire but in
spite of this, very good progress
was made and the work put in
showing the value of the bright Sunday –

Monday – a very heavy Artillery
bombardment took place from our
north of YPRES and about 3 am.
there was practically every sort it
was reported that our line in that
vicinity was being attacked by the
enemy.
About 3 am. troops all not in vicinity of
DICKEBUSCH were noticed to stray gaze
coming by NE. wind blowing from
direction of enemy trenches – Sentries and
others with were actually in the open
were particularly affected by the gas which
caused them to feel sick and then
into a most dreadful –– the gas
having about the [?] for several
hours – From this, some idea of the
eminence of the gas being used by the
enemy, can be gathered, as DICKEBUSCH
is quite 4 miles from enemy position
South & of YPRES.

D. I. W. T., Basrah.

Forwarded. Please let me know when you can commence the work of closing the gap referred to in this memorandum.

The present water level of the Euphrates is 127 feet and low water level is 125 feet.

It is very desirable from the point of view of irrigation that the breach should be closed as soon as possible.

(Sd.) J. C. RIMINGTON, *Major-General,*

Engineer-in-Chief, G. H. Q.,

Mesopotamian Expeditionary Force.

APPENDIX 53.

No. E.-298-14.

Engineer-in-Chief's Office.

General Headquarters.

30th June 1917.

Chief Engineer, 1st Corps.
Chief Engineer, 3rd Corps.

After consultation with Engineer Field Park please submit an estimate of your average monthly requirements of tools, noting especially any in regard to which your requirements are likely to be very intermittent and temporary.

2. This is not to include possible requirements of Field units, but only of Field Engineers.

There is a severe shortage of tools and to promote economy the Ordnance Department have ordered the E. F. Park only to stock enough for local works requirements (and have hitherto failed to supply even this).

I had hoped E. F. Park would be able to meet the local needs of Field Engineers by loan from this stock, when they get it, but E. F. P. say special provision will be necessary, and to decide this I wish to know as exactly as possible the probable nature of your requirements.

(Sd.) J. C. RIMINGTON, *Major-General,*

Engineer-in-Chief, G. H. Q.,

Mesopotamian Expeditionary Force.

May -
Monday 24th Continued -
Fine bright day. Very warm -
All ranks in Bivouacs & men were
withdrawn and returned to Endroave
Supp WESTOUTRE.
Battalion on rest during the day. In
much activity throughout whole day in
area North of YPRES -
Southern entrance to DICKEBUSCH shelled
by enemy Howitzers during the day. -
Several buildings hit - no casualties in
Battalion but several in other units -
2nd Lieut Gaspell reports sick and sent
to Hpers not home MONT NOIR.
O.C. and 3 Companies firing working
party moved out about 6 pm and
proceeded to same area as last night to
complete work already commenced -

Tuesday 25th - Task on which Battalion was
engaged, completed and Companies return
to Bivouacs about 2 am. The marchs
carried out from first satisfactorily and
during the moving the following shewn
message was received though about.
"Quartin 7th Infantry Brigade -
"To O.C. 2.B.I.R. -
Bgm. 567. 26th -
The Division commander has heard

48

May -
Sunday 26th Continued.
with great satisfaction of the extremely
good work done by your Regiment during
the past few days -"
B. M. 7th Inft Bde. 9.5 am.
The 13.14.15. & 16. of Infantry Brigade also
sent a message thanking Regiment for
the day he was highly gratified with
work done by the Battalion on 24th
Infantry Brigade area -
The Co. R.E. C. Division also expressed
satisfaction with work done by the
Battalion -
Casualties during the night were 2nd Lieut.
Brownes and 6 other ranks wounded -
The Hpers returned and to other parties
more able to continue their duties after
having their wounds dressed -
Battalion at rest during the day -
Very few from enemy drag-
Enemy Shelling much greater during the
day - Various enemies in the Artillery
North of YPRES became very active
and continued to the extreme trench -
a very few enemy aeroplanes about -
Machine hostile consisting of On 13 am
3 Companies proceeded about 6 pm

47

It is thought that the present stock will be sufficient for the needs of the Army at present, but that a small reserve is necessary to meet casualties.

As there is difficulty in obtaining more pontoons from England, I write to enquire whether a few of these can be supplied from India.

2. Experience in this country has established the fact that the Indian pattern pontoon is not so servicable and handy as the English one, and has justified the complaint made in my predecessor's No. 760-II-25-Q., dated 15th May 1916.

It would however be easy to obviate two of the principal defects of the Indian pattern, *viz.*, by providing the English standard pattern of cam lever for coupling the half pontoons, and by making saddles of the English bi-partite design.

3. I would enquire whether pontoons with these improvements could be made, and if so in what time fifty could be supplied.

(Sd.) J. C. RIMINGTON, *Major-General,*

Engineer-in-Chief, G. H. Q.

28th June 1917.

APPENDIX 49.

No. E.-284 68.

Engineer-in-Chief's Office.

General Headquarters.

29th June 1917.

Copy of a Memorandum No. 5-F., dated 27th June 1917, from Superintending Engineer, Hindiyah Irrigation Works, to Engineer-in-Chief, G. H. Q.

I have the honour to enquire whether it is possible to take any steps to reduce the flow of water through the breach in the Euphrates bund above Felujah, now that the river is nearing its summer level?

At the present moment I believe that about 12,000 cusecs are flowing through the breach, and, in consequence, all crops irrigated by the Euphrates below Felujah are suffering from want of water. Small canals like the Latifiyah and the Mahmudiyah are dry or nearly so, while at the Barrage I am forced to rotate the supply between the Hindiyah branch and the Hillah Canal. In the case of the Hillah this means that the canal receives full supplies for 15 days in the month and from one-third to one-half full supply for the rest of the month. I estimate that the reduction in the area of the rice crop planted this year will be between 15,000 and 20,000 acres, which represents a direct loss of revenue of Rs. 1,50,000 to Rs. 2,00,000 for this canal alone, besides reducing the quantity of grain available for purchase for the Army. If nothing is done to reduce the flow through the breach shortly, I am doubtful whether I shall be able to continue giving the Hillah Canal full supply even by rotation, as the river is falling and the maximum amount of heading up at the Barrage allowed for by Sir W. Willcocks is 4 metres.

In view of the serious damage to the regulator pavement reported by me yesterday, I consider that I shall probably increase the extent of the damage if I allow this 4 metre overfall, but at the same time I do not think that the extent of the damage will get out of hand or be more than I can repair during the repair season of September and October, provided the materials I have asked for are available, so I intend working up to the designed overfall if I find it necessary to do so, to give the Hillah Canal full supply during its term of rotation.

I am influenced in my decision to risk the chance of heavier expenditure on repairs, by the fact that the people in the Hillah district, besides suffering badly last year at the hands of the Turks, are again suffering this year on account of scarcity of water, and I consider it imperative that we should do all in our power to preserve such crops as they have been able to irrigate with reduced amount of water available.

At the same time I would point out that if immediate steps are taken to close or reduce the flow of water through the breach, they would if successful, ensure a proper supply of water for the Hillah Canal and remove the necessity of taking any risks of damaging the Barrage.

May
Wednesday 26 - Working parties resumed to fill in about dawn - casualties during the night. Three men wounded - Sent stretcher party across Ghou canal - as parties were returning from work carried shell splinters in rear of company but no damage was done.

Very hot day - Bright sunshine - Battalion on rest during the day -

Sat May 26 Apparently it appeared by the Field Marshall Commanding in Chief the issue in the field dated E.T.A. 22nd May 1915 message being sent containing the following:-

"Officers are granted the temporary rank of Captain whilst Commanding a Company: -

Lieut R.B.T. Baker & 2nd Lt Nottelim & Lt Whiteman & B. Sam Reg.
dates 15th May 1915 - of 309 men 15
A Special conference Rank Allows 15
carry out special work towards about 4pm Remainder of Battalion at rest -

Working party continues to fill about midnight - no casualties -

Lieut (?) Jack goes behaving 5th - Miniature asst. goes the Battalion for duty.

May
Wednesday 26 continues
fills reserves to replenish the expense of ammunition at that night -

Anno myth -

Thursday 27th - Fine day relieved Moonby this morning by parties of Canada's Battalion marched from fields at DICKEBUSCH by a few minutes near OUDERDOM and VLAMERTINGHE to about HUTS on HUTS & HUTS OF SISSER. After which it was from S.R. fields. Bridges through ??? Kitchen. Battalion arrived at first cantonment start of hyrain and at our next our business to settle down to 4 miles arrival to furnish parties which number H.S. quite near H.S.

Between Patrick Marcus & Commandant between 7.30pm and 5:30pm marching on some sort of our route back of YPRES are continuing communicating trench in square 11 and 11

Place at BELGIUM -

Friday 28 - Battalion returned to business about 1.30am and remained on rest during the day -
Very day but rather cold - Read Isabella's Service-

I am arranging for a sufficiency monthly of superstructure.

(Sd.) J. C. RIMINGTON, *Major-General*,

Engineer-in-Chief, G. H. Q.

21st June 1917.

Telegram No. 398-A., dated 11th June 1917.

From—Communications, Basrah,

To—General Headquarters.

" Reference your E.-407, and your E.-420. No materials now available in Basrah to make more than one or two pontoons of any service pattern and only prompt source of supply in India, who could presumably only send materials to make Indian pattern pontoons. Works Army suggests that Indian pattern if connected by same type cam lever as is used in British pattern, which would be easy to arrange, would be equally suitable and could be made up in India far better than here. Presume you refer to pontoons which can be used for same purposes as portable service pontoons and not to boats like those in Kotah or mahaila bridges or other types solid construction."

APPENDIX 37.

No. E.-217-187.

Engineer-in-Chief's Office.

General Headquarters.

21st June 1917.

D. Q. M. G.

Reference your No. Q.-1284-1, dated 20th instant.

1. The approximate cost of the piping may be £20 a ton, but the very extraordinary conditions existing make it impossible to say with any degree of accuracy.

2. There is about 20 miles of 4" pipe in reserve at Basrah.

3. The nesting of the pipes means that pipes of different sizes pack inside one another, thus the five miles of 6", 7" and 8" would be nested together, the remaining five miles of 6" would have to come separately.

The pipes are 9' to 12' long. Each nest would therefore consist of an 8", a 7" and a 6" pipe and would be 9' to 12' long.

4. I find I under-estimated the weight; the total weight would be about 260 tons dead weight, but as the pipes are light and bulky they would probably take up 500 shipping tons of 40 c. ft.

(Sd.) J. C. RIMINGTON, *Major-General*,

Engineer-in-Chief, G. H. Q.

APPENDIX 44.

C. G. S.

I put up a draft for approval :—

Chief of the General Staff,

Army Headquarters, India.

There are in this country 500 service pontoons of which 300 are of the English and 200 of the Indian pattern.

From these four bridges will probably be required across the Tigris, which, when the river rises, will account for about 2,000 yards of bridge, and in addition it is likely that a certain number of smaller bridges will be wanted for crossing smaller streams and canals.

May
Friday 26th continues.
10 to 2 am B Battalion made a bombing
raid in our front and
Tuesday is quite our YPRES- MENIN road
when Bn. head qrs. accompanied
troops down the line at [?]
south of the new road
11 am 17?
Laganville. 3 new reinforcement
Officers night.
Working parties returned trenches about
5 am am[?]

Saturday 27th - fine bright day - strong
wintry [?]
Battalion all night sweeping the day
A fine day itself B Battalion a short
distance from Battalion Bivouac affords
shelter to some observers the horse
situation was an —
A and B companies were detailed to
carry on work not being done at
our camp and left trenches about
6 pm
Remainder of Battalion on rest —
2.5 other ranks joined the Battalion
Quiet night.

Sunday 28th - Working parties arrived back
in bivouac about 2.30 am —

May.
Sunday 28th continues.
Bivouac during the
morning —
Some light rain —
Battalion at rest during the day —
Lieut Malcolm Grier
10 am. B company left bivouac
about 5 pm —
Bn. [?] no casualties but
some alarm of gas on the
[?] [?] Highlanders from
21st London Highlanders
Quiet night —
Fine [?]

Monday 31st. Work on which transport
[?] [?] another party
[?] to [?] a short distance
in rear - 6 [?] [?] a manoeuvre
Battalion at rest during the day —
Quiet. I am anxious [?] officers
commenced our courses at [?]
7 am
Our [?] mill [?] the remains of the No 2 9th
who are most anxious [?] the [?] [?]
[?] [?] [?]
[?] [?] [?] [?] [?] [?]
[?] [?] the day -

APPENDIX 35.

No. E.-297-5.

Engineer-in-Chief's Office.

General Headquarters.

21st June 1917.

D. Q. M. G.

In reply to your No. Q.-1169-3, dated 21st instant.

1. *Your paragraph 1.*—The Merryweather Valiant pump is a steam driven pump burning coal, but as it is really a fire engine it can raise steam very quickly.

We had nine of these pumps with the Force last year and they were very efficient and most popular.

A pump only burns 1 cwt. of coal in 10 hours, and in that time could pump 60,000 gallons.

2. *Your paragraph 2.*—The pump requires no foundations and can be used on its carriage or anywhere.

3. *Your paragraph 3.*—The weight of the pump is 6½ cwt. or 728 lbs. so it can be carried in an A. T. cart (load 800 lbs.).

I would propose that one extra cart be allotted to each Sapper troop and company to carry these.

4. *Your paragraph 4.*—Sufficient L. and F. pumps are available to provide for troops on the move, but as a L. and F. pump only gives about 12 gallons a minute and weighs 84 lbs. complete, it would require 8 or 9 such pumps to produce the equivalent water delivery of 1 Merryweather "Valiant" pump, and these would have to be worked by tired men.

The essence of my proposal is to relieve the men of unnecessary work after a hard day, whilst providing a quickly obtained and efficient water supply.

5. *Your paragraph 5.*—I cannot give the price, and in fact any statement of such would probably be quite inaccurate as all prices have changed during the war. In peace time they would probably cost about £180—200 apiece.

(Sd.) J. C. RIMINGTON, *Major-General,*

Engineer-in-Chief, G. H. Q.

APPENDIX 36.

C. G. S.

In a note, dated 7th June 1917, you said that the Army Commander was not prepared to order more pontoons from England, and as we had asked the Base if they could make up any, you would like to know the result of local manufacture and how long it would take them to make up one pontoon.

The attached copy of a telegram from the I. G. C. shows that we cannot expect any to be made up in Basrah.

The state of the case in regard to pontoon equipment is as follows :—

We have in the country about 500 pontoons and a number of trestles; some of the pontoons will always be under repair, but the trestles can be allowed for in their stead.

Thus we have about 2,500 yards of bridge, of which 40 pontoons, or 200 yards of bridge, will be at Nasiriyah, the remainder 2,300 yards will be concentrated above Baghdad.

The Army Commander has said he will require four main bridges at the front, which may be taken at 2,000 yards of bridge, leaving 300 yards spare.

This makes no allowance for minor bridges over canals, etc.

The reserve of pontoons should be sufficient *provided* the bridging trains do not get heavily under fire or the demands for bridges are not increased.

Mon.
Monday 31st continued.

The undermentioned officers from the Regiment
this day:-
1 Captain T. Arnold Vernard Marsden
3 2nd Lieut Ralph Elliott
      Henry Broadhurst
      Roland Alexander Henning

"A" all South Generals Regiment
A + D Companies were kept as company
attack as mortars having an
incursion to dea the enemy at
WITTEPOORT FARM at Square 1113. Leaving
bivouac about 6 p.m.

On this date the Battalion numbered
as follows:-
Major Lt. T. Wilson & Sam R. Lemming Hay
Captains St Venant
Lieuts A. Bains & Arme Morris Office
1 Lt. Q. Young + Sant & Carlie + Adj't.
6 2nd Lt. A. Reid ......
    St. Venac
    ......
Sergeants A. Sparl, Clark, R. Lemn. Gwin
           A.O. Shiel, R. Smart
           R.S. Sr Ball
6 & Whitehead Stewart R.
about J. Snow Geo't S. Smart

Monday 31st continued

2nd Lieut. W.S. Sillars
        R. Snape
        C.M. Drew
        J.S. Malting
        G.T. Hopple
        ......
        ......
       & Sergt Hook
        R. Wilson Known Sayn
       about 900 other ranks.
       the strength of the Battalion

       established Strength
       1 Colonel to Sergt Major
       1 Sergeant + Drum Major
       1 Mayer S't Donkey
       ......

about 70 other ranks on strength of the
Battalion in addition to the numbers
mentioned above but not actually serving
with it, are employed on various outside

No. D.-7.

B. M., R.E., G. H. Q.

Reference your E.-455 of 15th, *re* fitting E. P. pontoon wagon for launch.

In the absence of a wagon of this type or of any detailed plans of one, it is only possible for me to indicate generally what is required.

1. It must be arranged to enable the launch to be run off, or on, behind, running on rollers. The wagon is run down backwards into a pit, dug to correspond with height of platform.

A prepared way, carried on the wagon, is then put across and the launch run off on rollers, and continued thus into the water. To assist in pulling it down or up a tackle should be provided on each side.

2. The wagon should be fitted down the centre with rollers at 3 ft. intervals or so for the keel to run on.

3. The platform can be of some simple construction, collapsible if necessary for convenience of carriage. It should be long enough and strong enough to carry the launch over a 12 ft. gap, or more if possible. Three loose rollers should be provided to run the launch over this platform and later along the track (made of spare bridging timber) to the water.

4. While taking on and off, the launch is kept upright on its keel on the rollers by men on each side hanging on to lines coming from the gunwales.

5. When in correct position, launch must be fixed by three sets of chocks, three on each side, two ends and centre. These chocks have to be *shaped for the particular launch to be carried,* and where in contact with the boat must be well padded to prevent injury to boat when jolting across country. They must be movable to enable the launch to run off or on, but it must be possible to fix them *firmly* bearing *tightly* up against the launch. Some sliding or hinged arrangement might work, or combination of the two, worked by screw arrangement.

6. Arrangements for securely lashing the launch down are also necessary, but need no special mention.

(Sd.) F. V. B. WITTS, *Captain, R.E.*,

O. C., No. 2 Bridging Train.

16th June 1917.

APPENDIX 33.

D. A. G.

The advantages of closing the Sakhlawiyah breach are :—

1. Prevents any possibility of damage by floods from the Euphrates to the western portion of Baghdad, also to the Advanced Base.

2. Prevents the road to Museyib and Hillah, and the Decauville Railway to Mufraz being interrupted by floods.

3. Provides more water down the river for the cultivation of the fertile districts south of Museyib.

4. Removes an interruption of road communication along the left bank of the Euphrates (important both from the civil and military point of view).

5. The shrinking of the Lake will leave a large area of splendid grazing.

I am afraid I cannot apportion the monetary value of these advantages between the military and civil.

(Sd.) J. C. RIMINGTON, *Major-General,*

Engineer-in-Chief, G. H. Q.

21st June 1917.

May -
Monday 31st continued -
Such as Brigade Pioneers, Miners with R.E.
Companies, Sanitary duties, Lines of
Communication etc -

R. Cotton. Major
Commanding 2nd S. San. S -

APPENDIX 21.

No. E.-217-133.

Engineer-in-Chief's Office.

General Headquarters.

19th June 1917.

D. Q. M. G.

Lieutenant Norrie, R.E., has suggested to me that we should get some of the piping used in the mines in the Malay States. This consists of rivetted steel sheet pipes with stove pipe joints. The advantages of it are :—

(*i*) that it is very light ;

(*ii*) it is easily transported as the pipes " nest " inside each other ;

(*iii*) it is quickly laid and as quickly removed ;

(*iv*) it is strong and will stand quite a big head.

2. The Army Commander at the conference yesterday morning expressed a desire that we should have a reserve of piping, and I am sure this type would be the best for the reasons given above.

3. I would recommend that we ask India to get 20 miles of it, *viz.*, 10 miles of 6 inch, and 5 miles each of 7 inch and 8 inch.

I do not know the weight, but probably the whole consignment would not weigh more than 200 tons, including specials.

4. If approved, I will draft a wire explaining what is wanted.

(Signed) J. C. RIMINGTON, *Major-General,*

Engineer-in-Chief, G. H. Q.

APPENDIX 22.

No. E.-293-17.

Engineer-in-Chief's Office.

General Headquarters.

19th June 1917.

D. of S. and T., G. H. Q.

MEMORANDUM.

I understand you have undertaken the preparation of 2 wagons for transport of launches by Bridging Trains.

2. I recently asked O. C No. 2 Bridging Train for suggestions as to conversion of an *E. P. pontoon wagon* for carrying a launch.

3. As he has had much recent experience of requirements in the field, I forward a copy of his report in the hope that it may be of use to you. Occasions may arise when the tactical importance of being able to bring a launch up under cover, and put it in the water rapidly, may be very great, and I shall be glad if you can arrange for all possible facilities to be provided in the wagons now under preparation.

(Signed) J. C. RIMINGTON, *Major-General,*

Engineer-in-Chief, G. H. Q.

7th Inf.Bde.
3rd Div.

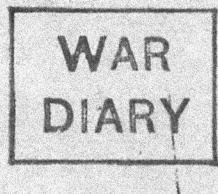

2nd BATTN. THE SOUTH LANCASHIRE REGIMENT.

J U N E

1 9 1 5

2nd Batt'lion South Lancashire Regiment -
War Diary - 1st to 30th June 1915 -

Tuesday 1st. Working parties returned to bivouac about 3 am. One man wounded -
Battalion at rest during the day -
Very hot day -
Usual activity amongst artillery during the early morning - much quieter during the day -
Local situation fairly quiet -
2nd Lieut. William August Wassner, 3rd S. Lan. Regt reported his arrival and joined for duty -
B, C and D Companies forming working parties left bivouac about 8 pm -

Wednesday 2nd. Casualties during the night.
1 Sergeant killed - 8 other ranks wounded -
Parties returned to bivouac about 3 am
The work on which companies had been engaged was as follows -
B Company constructing defensive post north of YPRES - MENIN road in Square I.15.a.
C Company constructed 250 yards of support trench in Square I.11.a.b.
D Company constructed a communication trench in same area -

June.   57
Wednesday (continued)
    Battalion did not [suffer?] any [casualties?]
    [Br...]
    Heavy shelling by enemy most of the
    day - a large number of shells [fell?]
    in vicinity of battalion [Headquarters?] but
    no damage was done.
    [During?] the afternoon orders were received
    [that?] [we?] were [required?] to [prepare?]
    [Brigade?] for Battalion to be prepared to
    [move?] at short notice -
    Trenches in vicinity of HOOGE [shelled?]
    heavily by enemy all day -
    Battalion "Standing by" till about 5 pm
    when A & B Companies left bivouac
    for work in area East of YPRES.
Thursday 3rd. Companies arrived back in
    bivouac about 3 am -
    A and B Companies had been detailed to
    construct a communicating trench from
    Western edge of wood in I.18.c to a house
    in I.19.b [where?] it was [proposed?] to
    establish a defensive post. On arrival at
    the [point?] mentioned, [after?] a
    reconnaissance was made [before?] commencing
    work when it was discovered that the
    house was occupied by the enemy -
    The proposed work was abandoned and

~~May~~ June
Thursday 1 - continued.

The two companies returned to bivouac.
A Company one man wounded slightly
remaining on duty.
B Company one man wounded.
C Company was engaged in constructing
a communication trench from G.H.Q. line
just south of railway in the vicinity
of ÉCOLE de BIENFAISANCE.
Casualties in this company were one man
killed and two wounded.
Fine bright day.
A portion of the day was devoted to company
training and musketry drill. Beyond this
battalion at rest during remainder of the
day.
Lieut. Colonel F.A. Dudgeon due to return
from leave, but a communication received
this morning from Lieut. Dudgeon and
troops to the effect that this officer
was unfit for duty and orders had been
issued for him to be examined by
a medical board in England.
Considerable shelling by enemy during the
afternoon along VLAMERTINGHE - YPRES road
and in vicinity of battalion bivouac.
No damage done to the battalion.
A. C. and D. Companies left bivouac for

May. June.   59
Thursday 3rd continued –
    work about 6 p.m.
    About this hour our artillery in the
    vicinity became very active –
Friday 4th. Some activity took place about
    1 a.m. amongst units of 9th Brigade. Otherwise
    the event [illeg] was nil.
    'C' Company continued work on trench
    commenced last night and returned to
    bivouac about 3 a.m.
    'A' and 'B' companies were engaged in
    improving the position in vicinity of same
    referred to last night, and returned to
    bivouac shortly after 3 a.m.
    Total casualties – two men wounded –
    Rather dull morning – inclined to rain –
    Bright and warm by afternoon –
    All companies carried out musketry
    training during a portion of the day.
    Otherwise Battalion at rest.
    Following message received about 4 p.m. –
    " O.C. E. S. Lan. R.
        B.M. w/o – 4th.
    3rd Div wires that your Battalion will
    come under command of 9th Bde from
    receipt of this order and that 2 of
    your companies are placed at the
    disposal of C.R.E. for work tonight.

May-June.

Friday 4 Continued.

"The Brigadier wishes me to thank you very
"much for the good work you have
"done while attached to this Brigade.
"   Brigade Major 8th Brigade"

"B" Company detailed for work and left
bivouac about 7.30 pm.
Remainder of Battalion at rest during night.

Saturday 5th. "B" Company returned to bivouac
about 3 am. No casualties.
This Company was engaged in repairing
trenches on South side of road in
vicinity of village of HOOGE. These trenches
had been badly damaged during last
two days by enemy's shell fire.
Fine bright day. Very warm.
All Companies at training during the
morning. 1200 Smoke helmets issued to the Battn.
Local situation throughout the day, quiet.
During the afternoon several heavy
shells passed over the Battalion bivouac
and pitched in the vicinity of
VLAMERTINGHE.
"A" and "D" Companies detailed for work
and left bivouac about 7.30 pm.
Very fine evening. Aeroplanes very active.

Sunday 6th. Companies returned to bivouac
about 3 am. Casualties - two men wounded.
Battalion machine guns took up position in Brigade Sector.

~~May~~ June
Sunday 6th continued.
D Company had been engaged in carrying
on the work on which B Company was
engaged last night.
A Company constructed a new fire trench
in the sector.
Ringers had a day's practice.
All companies carried out inspections
and training during a portion of the
day.
180 Smoke helmets received.
2nd Lieut. Francis Alfred Bernard Wassner
3rd B. Sam. R. and 29 other ranks joined
the Battalion.
By this date the Sector in which the
Battalion was employed had been taken
over by 7th Infantry Brigade.
During the evening B and C Companies
moved forward to vicinity of J.13 where
they were to remain for three days
instead of returning to Battalion bivouac
after each night's work. By this
arrangement men will be able to do
more work and the long march from
bivouac to the Brigade Sector and return
will be avoided.
Considerable activity in the Sector during
the evening and most of the night.

June.

Monday 4th. Very hot day.
No change in disposition of Battalion.
'A' and 'D' Companies at training.
Considerable activity amongst our own and enemy artillery during the afternoon and evening.
Quite a number of large shells were pitched by enemy in vicinity of Battalion bivouac, apparently searching for our guns which had recently caused them some annoyance.
As far as is known no damage was done in our area.
'B' and 'C' Companies employed during the night in constructing and improving trenches. Casualties during the night:-
Captain N. G. F. Salter and one man killed. Two other men wounded.

Tuesday 5th. Disposition of Battalion unchanged.
Dull day. Thunderstorm during the afternoon.
Local situation quiet during the day and night.
'B' and 'C' Companies continued work already commenced.
Remainder of Battalion at training.
Battalion machine guns still in position.
Casualties - 5 men wounded.

June.

Wednesday 2 - Battalion dispositions unchanged.
Very warm day - Very hazy.
2nd Lieut. W. Rokos reported sick and sent to Field Ambulance.
Captain Frank Adams Rafey, b. Lauth reported his arrival and assumed command of "B" company.
Following messages were received during the day.

"I. O. b. 2. D. Sam R.
B.M. w- 9.
The undermentioned N.C.O's have been awarded the D.C.M. and should be informed of such please.
6432 C.S.M. Sgt. J. Fearnehough
6922 Sgt. A. Cleveland
8892 Sgt. B. Yorke
B.M. 7. Inf. Bde.
9.10.30 am."

"I. O. b. 2 D. Sam R.
B.M. v- 9.
The Brigadier wishes to congratulate the men of your Battalion who have won the Distinguished Conduct Medal.
7th Inf. Bde. 12.15 pm"

2nd Lieut. K. S. Gilmour reported sick at position occupied by "B" and "D" companies and sent to Field Ambulance.

June,
Wednesday 2nd Continued—

During the day an experiment with asphyxiating (chlorine) gas was carried out under the supervision of the A.D.M.S., in a section of the G.H.Q. line of trenches where this cuts the POPERINGHE — VLAMERTINGHE Road

A large cylinder containing the gas was placed on top of the trench in such a position that the gas poured into the trench and was carried along by the breeze.

Parties of Officers, N.C.O's and men from Units of the Division attended the demonstration and actually moved about the trench amongst the gas, each wearing the official gas helmet.

The Battalion was represented by Major Bolton and several other officers, N.C.O's and men — each of whom moved about the trench amongst the gas, which they were able to do quite freely by using the gas helmets issued to them.

Major Bolton personally carried out exhaustive trials and specially asked for the amount of gas to be increased. This was done until it was so dense that he could not see objects at arms length. He was able to pass through safely wearing the "gas helmet"

June
Wednesday 7th Continued.
issued.

The test demonstrated the full value of
the helmet and proves to those present
that the soldier has nothing to fear
when attacked by gas, if he only adjusts
his helmet properly, according to the
instructions issued for its use.

A further issue of 300 helmets made
to the Battalion.

Local situation very quiet during the
day and night.

Very heavy rain during the night.

"B" and "D" Companies continued work on
improvements already commenced.

Casualties – 6 Other ranks wounded.

Thursday 8th – Wet morning. Disposition of
Battalion unchanged up to 2.30 pm.
About this time following orders were
received from Head Quarters 7th Infantry
Brigade –

Head Quarters of Battalion and two companies
"A" and "D" in bivouac to move as soon
as possible to billets on East side of YPRES,
relieving 1st Wiltshire Regiment who would
take over Battalion bivouac.

This move was completed by about 6 pm.

Information was also received to the

June,
Thursday 10th Continued–

effect that two companies – 'B' and 'C' – would
withdraw from position on HOOGE after
work tonight and rejoin the Battalion –
During the afternoon several of enemy's
shells pitched in vicinity of field
occupied by Battalion transport –
One horse severely wounded & had to be
destroyed –
Two men R.A. passing on road were
wounded – No casualties amongst transport
personnel –
Five men wounded during night of 9th – 10th.

Friday 11th

'B' and 'C' Companies withdrew from
position on which they had been engaged
since 6th and rejoined the Battalion at
YPRES, about 3 am
Casualties during the night – ten men
killed, four wounded –
Battalion at rest during the day –
Considerable activity in Sector occupied
by the Brigade, East of YPRES.
Reinforcement of 120 all ranks arrived at
POPERINGHE during the evening and
moved into bivouac in vicinity of G.17.b.
Whole Battalion moved out about 8pm
and proceeded to I.17.b. for work on
South side of YPRES – MENIN road –

June.   67
Saturday 12th – Companies return to billets
   at YPRES about 3 am.
   Warm day but rather dull.
   Battalion at rest during the day.
   Considerable activity amongst our artillery
   in vicinity of YPRES, commencing about
   2 am and continues practically all day.
   Several enemy shells pitched near billets
   occupied by Battalion – one near "A"
   Company's billet killed one man and
   wounded several others.
   Total casualties up to noon today being
   1 man killed and 7 wounded.
   Reinforcement moved from bivouac in
   vicinity of VLAMERTINGHE and join the
   Battalion in YPRES.
   Whole Battalion moved out about 6 pm
   to work in same area as last night.
   During the evening the village of
   VLAMERTINGHE was heavily shelled by
   enemy and the church there was set
   on fire and completely destroyed.
   By this date all units of the 7th Infantry
   Brigade, except "A" Coy "K", had been
   relieved and withdrawn to bivouac in
   vicinity of C in K.
Sunday 13th – Companies returned to billets at
   YPRES about 3 am. – Casualties during the

June.
Sunday 1st Continued.

night. One Sergeant killed, two other ranks wounded.

All Units of 7th Infantry Brigade (less this Battalion) paraded at 10 a.m. in the bivouac of the Brigade and ribbons of the Distinguished Conduct Medal were presented by General Inderwick, G.O.C. in C. 3rd Division, to several N.C.O's and men of various Units of the Brigade. Owing to the Special work on which the Battalion was engaged it was only possible for a small representative party to attend the parade.

Amongst the recipients of the ribbon were
　　Coy. Sergt. Scarisbrough.
　　　　Corpl. Harcourt.
　　　　　　Yorke.

In each case the presenting officer explained the circumstances for which the award of the medal was made and afterwards addressed the troops.

Battalion at rest during the day.

400 gas helmets issued.

Considerable activity, especially amongst artillery, during the day, in vicinity of YPRES.

June.   69
Sunday 13th Continued -
   Battalion moved out about 8.30pm to
   continue work on [trenches?] engaged last
   night -
Monday 14th - Battalion returned to billets
   about 3am -
   Casualties during the night - two men
   killed - three men wounded.
   Heavy firing by our Artillery commenced
   about 3am -
   Several heavy shells from enemy guns
   pitched in vicinity of our guns on
   West side of YPRES -
   Battalion at rest during the day.
   Dull and rather cold day - [two?] [battalion?]
   Companies left billets about 8 pm [erased?]
   and proceeded to area back of
   YPRES, and commenced construction of
   "Assembly trenches" in vicinity of road
   running North in 11d. D Company
   [working?] [east?] of the road - A. B and C
   Companies West of the road -
   The first named Company being nearest
   the enemy's trenches was much exposed
   to rifle fire - the other three were
   exposed to considerable shell fire
   for about two hours -
Tuesday 15th - Companies returned to billets

June
Tuesday 1st Continued.
about 3am. On this occasion the
casualties were heavier than usual
and are detailed below.

	Killed	Wounded	Missing	Suffering from Shock
A Coy	2	15	1	2
B "	2	5		
C "		4		
D "	1	3		
Total	5	32	1	2 = 40

Of the wounded 9 were able to
carry on their duties.
Lieut. Shotting accidentally sprained his
ankle but remained with the Battalion.
Bright warm day.
Battalion at rest during the day.
Considerable activity among aeroplanes
of both sides but none were
engaged.
2nd Lieut. Grady & Hyman Jebens,
L. Lancashire R.ft. reported his
arrival.
A and D Companies left billets about 8pm
and proceeded to same vicinity as last
night for the purpose of completing
"Assembly trenches" which had been left
incomplete by another unit detailed for

June.
Tuesday 15 continued –
the work.
These two companies had to work very hard as the trenches were required for immediate occupation by Units who were moving East of YPRES to take part in operations near HOOGE.

B and C Companies remained in reserve at YPRES.

During the evening the whole of the Units of 3rd Division moved from their bivouacs, marching in an Easterly direction through YPRES, in preparation for an attack on enemy's line in vicinity of HOOGE.

Beyond this movement there was very little activity in the Sector.

Wednesday 16th. The work on which A and D Companies were occupied was completed soon after midnight, when they withdrew to reserve at YPRES.

Casualties – 4 other ranks wounded, 2 of whom died of wounds during the night.

The whole of the "Assembly trenches" which had been constructed during the past few nights were occupied by various units before 2 a.m.

Shortly after that hour the whole of our guns East and West of YPRES opened

June.

Wednesday 16 continued -

a heavy fire on enemy's line in vicinity of HOOGE, and about an hour later the infantry of 7th, 8th and 9th Brigades moved forward -

The enemy's trenches were successfully carried and a number of prisoners taken -

The Battalion, still in reserve at YPRES, was detailed to take over and dispose of all prisoners, in accordance with Special orders issued on the subject -

During the whole day fire from our guns and those of the enemy was very heavy - many of the enemy's shells pitched into YPRES, and these, together with falling buildings, placed the Battalion in very considerable danger -

Whole Battalion moved forward from YPRES about 9 pm to consolidate the ground won and still held by units of 4th Brigade -

As companies moved up to the position they were exposed to enemy's fire of shrapnel, high explosives, and gas shells, sustaining a number of casualties, and the move was very slow -

On arrival at the position there was a certain amount of confusion amongst

June.
Wednesday 16th continued –
the Units in occupation and it was
found impossible to carry out the work
intended.

Thursday 17th. As work could not be
carried out, B, C, and D companies withdrew
to YPRES, arriving about 3 am.
Casualties in these three companies were
as follows – Other ranks –

	Killed	Wounded	Suffering from gas	Missing
B. Coy.	–	3.	7	4
C "	4	18.	1	–
D "	3	4	–	–

2nd Lieut. G. Pitten-Thomas was also killed.
A Company, under command of Captain
Reuel, remained in occupation of a
fire trench, under the orders of 8th Infantry
Brigade.
During the morning a small party of
the enemy, apparently bomb throwers, made
an attempt to approach the trench
occupied by A Company, but they were
at once repulsed and practically all
killed.
B, C, and D companies at rest during
the day – Left billets about 9 pm
and proceeded to ground in rud to

74

June.
Thursday 17th Continued -
construct a communication trench -
"D" Company relieved "A" Company during
the evening - the latter withdrawing to
billets at YPRES.
Total casualties in "A" Company were -
2nd Lieut. Leigh-Mallory - wounded.
Other ranks - 6 killed, 34 wounded,
1 missing -
6 of those wounded were able to continue
at duty -

Friday 18th - B and C Companies completed
allotted work and returned to billets at
YPRES about 3 a.m.
A, B and C Companies at rest during the
day. D Company still in fire trench.
Very warm day.
Local situation rather quiet -
Major Jack Burke, 4th Lancashire
Fusiliers, joined the Battalion.
D Company was relieved during the evening
and withdrew to billets at YPRES.
Whole Battalion remained at rest.
Casualties in D Company - 5 other ranks wounded.
3 of these were able to continue on duty.
During the morning the area in which
"A" Company was billeted in YPRES was
shelled by enemy - Captains A.K. Rathkins,

75

June.
Friday 18th. ntinues

2nd Lieut. F.A.B. Wasenir and 5 other ranks wounded.

Saturday 19th. Bright and very warm day.
Local situation fairly quiet.
Battalion at rest during the day.
Orders received to move to area in vicinity of HOOGE.
Head Quarters, together with 'B' and 'C' Companies, left YPRES about 8.45 p.m. and moved to SANCTUARY Wood South of YPRES—MENIN Road and occupied fire trenches about J.15.c and J.19.a.
Casualties — none during relief.
'A' and 'D' Companies remained in billets at YPRES.
Fairly quiet night.

Sunday 20th. — Fine bright day. Warm.
Local situation quiet during the day.
Disposition of Battalion unchanged until evening.
'A' and 'D' Companies left YPRES about 9 p.m. and joined the Battalion in area referred to yesterday.
Casualties up to 12 noon today — other ranks.
B. Company 2. (including C.S.M Bagshier who was able to continue on duty). C. Company 1.
'A' and 'D' Companies reached the position

June -
Sunday 20th

without casualties -

Bullets from enemys trenches, (which were only a very short distance from ours) and snipers, continually dropping in the wood, caused a certain amount of annoyance although doing no damage.

During the night Major Becke and Lance Corporal Drinkwater reconnoitred the ground for about 200 yards to the front on north side of the wood and discovered a large working party of the enemy apparently improving trenches.

This Officer and N.C. Officer returned safely.
Fairly quiet night.

Monday 21st - Very hot day - No change in disposition of Battalion -

During the morning the party discovered last night could be seen at work as, although men were not actually seen, earth was being thrown up. Rapid fire was opened from our trenches and this apparently dispersed the workers, as no further movement was seen during daylight.

Casualties up to 12 noon - 3 men wounded.
2nd Lieut Roscoe rejoined the Battalion from hospital and resumed duty as

June.   77
Monday 21st Continued.
    Machine gun Officer.
    Local situation rather quiet.
    About 11 pm 2nd Lieut. Thompson, working
a trench mortar, pitched 10 bombs into
enemy trenches in quick succession, causing
a certain amount of damage.
    Hand rifle fire slackest whole day and
increased at night, but otherwise the
night passed off quietly.
Tuesday 22nd. Bright hot day.
    Disposition of Battalion unchanged.
    Local situation fairly quiet during the
day.
    Heavy bombardment commenced by our
artillery about 7.30pm and continued for
some time. This was apparently in
connection with some movement of units
of 42nd Infantry Brigade and part of 7th
Infantry Brigade.
    Casualties during the day:-
    2nd Lieut. Roscoe and 6 other ranks wounded.
one of the latter subsequently died of wounds.
    Fairly quiet night.
    Captain J. Martin, Royal Irish Rifles, transferred
to South Lancashire Regt. 20 June 1915.
~~Two Howitzer wagons and four horses~~
~~~~

June.
Wednesday 23rd –

Very warm day but rather dull and inclined to rain. No wind.

General disposition of the Battalion unchanged.

"A" and "D" Companies relieved "B" and "C" in fire trenches – later withdrawing to support in SANCTUARY WOOD.

During the morning a sniper in the enemy's lines, who had caused us some annoyance, was located at an opening in a building about 400 yards in front of our trenches. No. 9433 Pte. W. Peel "A" Company was detailed to watch for this sniper and about 9 am succeeded in hitting him as he was seen to fall through the opening, being subsequently removed by a party of enemy's stretcher bearers.

Local situation quiet.

Casualties during the day – three other ranks wounded.

The following letter received today gave great satisfaction to all ranks of the Battalion –

" The Officer Commanding   G/3610.
   2nd Battalion South Lancashire Regt.

The Major General Commanding the 3rd Division desires to convey to the

June.
Wednesday 5th Continued.   79

Officer Commanding 2nd Battalion South Lancashire Regiment his appreciation of the excellent work which this Battalion has done during the period that it has acted as Pioneer Unit of the Division. The experiment of employing a battalion as such has, through the zeal and energy of all ranks of the 2nd Battalion South Lancashire Regiment, proved most successful and it has been possible to execute a large amount of work of an important nature in a short period of time. The battalion, in whole or part, has nightly worked in close proximity to the enemy's front line, has often been under fire for several hours, and has suffered not a few casualties. Yet the tasks allotted have been unfailingly executed, and the Royal Engineer officers who have supervised have spoken highly of the quick manner in which the working parties have fallen to and carried out their work.

As, owing to losses lately incurred in the 7th Infantry Brigade, it is probable that the 2nd Battalion South Lancashire Regiment will now return to Trench

June.
Wednesday 3rd continued.
"duty, the Major General Commanding feels
"sure that the knowledge which it has
"acquired in executing field work with
"rapidity will be of great value to it
"during the remainder of the war –

"(Signed) A. J. Sillem Lieut. Colonel
" A. A. & Q. M. G. 3rd Division
"23 June 1915.

Lieut. Kenneth Butler R.A.M.C. reported
for duty with the Battalion in relief of
Lewis, whose graphic leave –
Fairly quiet night.
Two blanket wagons and four horses
handed over to O.C. A.S.C. Train.

Thursday 24th – Bright hot day.
The following is an extract from Despatch
dated 31. May 1915 by the Field Marshal,
Commanding-in-Chief, published in daily
papers of 23. June 1915. "mentions" –
– 2nd S. Lancashire Regiment –
Dudgeon, Lt.Col. (Temp Col.) F.A.
Bullen, 2nd Lieut (Temp Lt.) W.E.N.
No change in disposition of Battalion.
Local situation quiet.
Casualties during the day – 6 other ranks
wounded. Night fairly quiet.

June.
Friday 25th - Dull day with rain.

A list of honours published in daily papers of 24th June 1915, in connection with Despatch referred to yesterday, contains the following :-

Military Cross - Lieut. W. E. M. Boulton.

C.B. - Lieut. Colonel Frederick Annesley Dragoon Prince of Wales's Vols. (South Lancashire Regiment).

Distinguished Conduct Medal. for acts of Gallantry and Devotion to Duty.-

6922 Sergt. A. Clarkson.
6432 C.S.M. L/Sgt. J. Fairclough.
8892 Sergt. B. Yates.

2nd Lieut Frederick Albert Holden, South Lancashire Regiment joined the Battalion.

No change in general disposition of Battalion.

Local situation fairly quiet during the day.

About 10.30pm enemy opened a heavy rifle and machine gun fire on a working party engaged in the vicinity of MAPLE COPSE. The Transport of the Battalion en route to the Battalion position with supplies at this hour came under this fire, but fortunately sustained no damage beyond injury to one horse.

June.

82

Friday 25th continued.
Heavy rain during the evening caused tracks used by transport to become very heavy, making progress very difficult. Casualties during the day - Other ranks 2 killed, 6 wounded.

Saturday 26th - Bright and clear day - Very hot.

During the afternoon 'C' and 'D' Companies were relieved from fire trenches by 'B' and 'A' Companies and withdrew to supports. No casualties during relief. Local situation fairly quiet during the day, but at intervals YPRES and roads to East were heavily shelled.

During the afternoon, trench B6, occupied by 'A' Company was heavily enfiladed by enemy machine gun and rifle fire and much damaged. This was soon repaired by occupants who suffered no casualties. This was largely due to the promptness of the men taking immediate cover during the period of the hostile fire.

2nd Lieut. R. Lodge proceeded to the G.H.Q. machine gun school of instruction.
2nd Lieut. R.B. Gilmour rejoined from hospital.
During the night YPRES and roads leading

June.   83
Saturday 26. Contd...
The Battalion positions were again heavily
shelled by enemy, and transport
conveying supplies was much harassed,
but suffered no casualties.
It was yesterday noted that an
unusually large number of the enemy's
shells were this number failed to explode.
The following officers South Lancashire
Regiment who had been previously attached
to 2nd border Reg.mt reported their arrival
this day -
  2nd Lieut. Robert Gordon Spalding.
    "   "   Alan Carre Penton
    "   "   Alfred William Gates
    "   "   Kenneth Morrison Brown.
Casualties during the day -
R.S.M. Knightley Killed. 3 men wounded.
Fairly quiet night in Battalion Sector -
Sunday 27th - Rather dull day with rain -
         .... quiet. Nothing unusual
during the day - no change in both defences.
During the night some annoyance was
caused by an enemy sniper and it was
decided to make efforts to locate him.
Casualties during the day - 5 other ranks
wounded -
Rather quiet night -

June.   84
Monday 2ⁿᵈ - At dawn the sniper referred
to yesterday was located in a pit
some little distance in front of the
Battalion sector, by 2/9 R. S. Livesey
and shot by him. The enemy also
succeeded in hitting two other men
who came to the assistance of the
sniper. [illegible]
[illegible] from our own
trenches [illegible]
later under [illegible] cover [illegible] the
enemy.
[illegible] day, with some showers -
frequent heavy storms of rain.
Local situation unusually quiet during today
no change in general disposition of
the Battalion.
During the morning a working party
located in [illegible] area [illegible]
to the trenches, were exposed to heavy
rifle fire of enemy, one man being
killed.
Roads running east of YPRES to Battalion
position shelled frequently by enemy
during the evening and nights, harassing
transport taking supplies, very much -
About 11 pm our guns opened a heavy
fire on enemy trenches in vicinity of

June.   85
Monday 28th (continued).

HOOGE. This was replied to by enemy's
guns, a number of their shells pitching
on to the road leading to our position.
Battalion transport moving along this
road was in considerable danger but
there was only one casualty — one man
being wounded by shrapnel.
    Total casualties up to 12 noon today
were 1 man killed, 4 wounded.

Tuesday 29th — Dull and very showery day.
Disposition of Battalion unchanged.
During the day a working party of 'B'
Company successfully completed an advanced
observation and listening post in front
of B4 trench. This work was designed
by and completed under the supervision of
Captain J. A. Breul, and was found to
be of great value for "Observation" and
"Listening" purposes.
    Snipers' posts were also established by
Captains Bagley and Taylor. Selected men
were placed in these posts and caused
much annoyance to the enemy.
    2nd Lieut. Gillespie and Pte Gurney were
amongst those who took a turn of
duty in these posts.
    2nd Lieut. Gillespie succeeded in hitting one

June
Tuesday 29th continued.   86

of the enemy snipers and M. Gunney
amounting to over 20 others. The bodies of
these three men could be clearly seen
from our trenches.

Shelling spur day and night except that
during the sniper all ranges were
again shelled by enemy at frequent
intervals.

Between 6 pm & 12 midnight today were
3 men wounded.

Wednesday 30th. Keep three days.
Little fire indulged in unchanged during the
day.
Local situation fairly quiet. Usual
sniping.

During the evening the battalion took
over billets in G. 4 Division Sector
B & C.

"A" and "B" Companies were relieved from
fire trenches by about 9 pm and
withdrew to bivouac in vicinity of
HQrs. 1 man wounded during relief.
"C" and "D" Companies remained in the
position and were employed in constructing
a special communication trench.
3 men of above companies were wounded
during the night. Situation fairly quiet.

June.   87
Wednesday 30th Gallipoli

Notification received that Lieut Schuling
5th Wiltshire Regiment attached to the
Battalion had been promoted to Captain
with effect from 5th April 1915.
The following officers were on the
strength of the Battalion on this date —
Major H.F. Colton L. Lanc. formerly Batt.
     " Y. Buckle Army Ser Corps brevet Major
Capt'n J.K. Cook L. Lanc Quartermaster
Lieut A.B. Sloan R.A.M.C Medical officer
2nd "   C.C. Thompson L. Lan.R acting adjt
     "   S. Brast "   Transport officer
Captain F.A. Briers Gloster Reg comm'g "A" Coy
   "   F.A. Bayley L. Lanc.   "   B "
   "   C.A.J. Taylor   "   "   C "
        C.P. Whitaker Gloster Reg   "   D "
2nd Lieut H.B. Gilmour L. Lan R
    "   T. Bousfield-Escott "
    "   R. Gregg   "   (M.G. Section)
    "   J.W. Ashworth   "
    "   J.G.T. Strickland   "
    "   E.P. Stedanum   "
    "   A.S. Wilson Lan Fus
    "   G.L.A. Rees L. Lan R
    "   R. Gillespie   "
    "   H. Broadhurst   "
    "   C.A.H. Hogg   "

June,
Wednesday 30th Continued –
    2nd Lieut. W. A. Wassner, 2 Tank
    "   F. R. Jolins,   "
    "   F. A. [illegible],   "
    "   H. G. Spalding,   "
    "   R. F. [illegible],   "
    "   A. W. Gale,   "
    "   Wm. [illegible]   "
Captain J. C. Schustz, Medical Corps.

The total other ranks [illegible] on this
date were about 650. In addition to
this number about 50 men attached for
miscellaneous duties such as Pioneer and
R.E. Details duties, Army Communication
kemen, attached with Army Services
and Hygiene and Sanitation.

                    [signature] Patton, Major
Commanding, 2 L Tank.

7th Inf.Bde.
3rd Div.

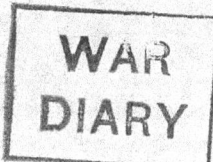

2nd BATTN. THE SOUTH LANCASHIRE REGIMENT.

J U L Y

1 9 1 5

(25 pages) 89

2nd Battalion South Lancashire Regt -
War diary.   1st to 31st July 1915 -

Thursday 1st -
A and D Companies completed allotted task and withdrew to bivouac with remainder of Battalion, about 3 a.m.
Rather dull day -
Local situation very quiet.
Battalion at rest in bivouac in H11d Sheet 28 Belgium -
A party of 100 men of B Company under 2nd Lieut: Beaulrient and others left bivouac about 6.30 p.m. and proceeded East of YPRES where they were employed in constructing special trenches for protecting telephone wires to various sectors of the front line.
Quiet night.

Friday 2nd - Working party returned to bivouac about 3 a.m.
Bright warm day.
Disposition of Battalion unchanged -
Companies at training during the day.
Local situation exceptionally quiet all day -
Very fine evening. Many aeroplanes about.

July -
Friday 2nd Continued -
Quiet ~ night. Battalion not disturbed.
Saturday 3rd. Bright hot day.
Battalion still in bivouac. A portion of the day allotted to company training. Local situation generally quiet but between 7 and 9 am enemy pitched a number of shells - "crumps" and shrapnel - in vicinity of bivouac, apparently searching for guns, but no damage done. Two parties of 1 officer and 50 men each furnished by the Battalion were employed most of the day in constructing trenches to give cover to telephone wires from positions East of YPRES to batteries in vicinity of that town. No casualties. Enemy shells again pitched during afternoon and evening in same area as this morning. -
During the evening the presence of obnoxious gases was experienced in the area occupied by the Battalion and caused some anxiety. -
Fairly quiet night -
Sunday 4th. About 5 am. Shelling by enemy again commenced and continued at intervals till about 8 am.
Shells pitched in same vicinity as

91

July.
Sunday 4th Britannia.
Yesterday - This caused some annoyance
but no damage done.
Very hot day.
2nd Lieut. Wilson admitted to Field
ambulance.
Between 10 am. and noon many very
heavy shells from enemy guns
pitched some little distance from
Battalion bivouac, but there were
no casualties although many large
splinters dropped amongst the men.
A couple of these shells hit a
dressing station about 400 yards away, almost
demolishing the building and causing
some casualties there.
It is interesting to note the following
events which took place actually
with heavy shells passing overhead.
The Battalion on Divine Service with
Holy Communion in the company lines.
Twenty yards away two men of the
Battalion were being tried by F.G.C.M.
for a serious offence.
And quite close a suspected spy
dressed as a French N.C.O., was
arrested by Divisional Police assisted by
2 men of the Battalion. The cause

92

July.
Sunday 4th _continued_ =
of the arrest was the suspicious behaviour of the soldier in endeavouring to obtain information regarding our guns.
Working parties similar to those yesterday were again engaged in constructing trenches for telephone cables. Owing to heavy shelling the men were obliged to leave their work several times and take cover but fortunately there were no casualties.

Captain Whittaker represented the Battalion at a demonstration by Chemical Experts in the correct method of donning gas helmets.
Very hot day. Battalion disposition unchanged.
Quiet night.

Monday 5th - Rather dull close day.
Local situation quiet.
No change in disposition of Battalion during the day. Usual parties employed burying cables.
About 8.30pm "A" Company moved to Ramparts on Eastern side of YPRES relieving one company of 4th B. Som R.
Remaining three companies remained in bivouac.
Reinforcement of 132 other ranks joined the Battalion.
Quiet night.

93

July
Tuesday 6th - Heavy firing from guns North of
YPRES commenced about 4 am and continued
for some time. It was understood this
was in connection with an attack by
our troops on the left of Sector held by
3rd Division.
Very hot day.
Disposition of Battalion unchanged.
Various parties engaged in constructing trenches
for cable East of YPRES.
Local situation generally quiet.
Quiet night.

Wednesday 7th - Very strong winds. Dusty and
inclined to rain.
No change in disposition of the Battalion
during the day. 1 Officer + 50 men employed burying cables.
The following movements took place during
the evening -
About 5.30 pm "B" Company under command of
Captain Bagley moved from Battalion bivouac
to ramparts of YPRES and occupied billets
there.
"A" Company, commanded by 2nd Lieut. Case until
arrival of Captain Taylor due from leave
tomorrow, left Battalion bivouac about 8.30 pm
and moved to trenches in G.H.Q. line with
instructions to occupy portion of line as
follows - Sect resting on track I16 b.3.3. Right

July.
Wednesday 3rd Continues -
resting on track 11 b d.1.3. and including
MOATED GRANGE 11 b c.6.6.
100 men, with 2 Officers furnished from
companies in ramparts of YPRES were employed
during the night in burying cables East of
YPRES, leaving billets at 8.45 p.m.
Wet afternoon and evening - cold winds -
Quiet night.
Captain Breul and 2nd Lieut Strickland due
to return off leave did not arrive.

Thursday 4th Dull boisterous day - S.W. wind.
Local situation fairly quiet.
Information received from War Office, through
Brigade Head Quarters, that 2nd Lieut. Strickland
due to return off leave yesterday, has been
granted sick leave until 20th July 1916.
No change in disposition of the Battalion
during the day.
Party of 1 Officer and 50 men employed in
burying telephone cables.
During the evening the following movements
took place:-
Battalion Head Quarters moved to ramparts
at YPRES.
Two platoons of "A" Company moved from
ramparts, and "D" Company from bivouac,
to SANCTUARY WOOD, under Command of Major Burke.

July-
Thursday 8th Continued-
Two machine guns with teams to fire trenches occupied by 8th K.I. Rifles, under the orders of O.C. that Battalion.
Battalion disposition now as under -
Head Quarters-
Half Detachment Signallers. ⎫
Two machine guns with teams ⎬ Ramparts
Two platoons A Company. ⎭ YPRES.
B Company.
C Company - Same position as last night.
D. Company. ⎫ SANCTUARY
Half Detachment Signallers. ⎬ WOOD.
A working party of C Company 100 men were employed during the night in burying telephone cables-

Friday 9th - C Company completed work about 1.30am and returned to position -
No Casualties-
Very dull day-
No change in disposition of Battalion during the day.
Guns East of YPRES very active several times during the day in bombarding enemy's trenches-
During the morning and afternoon enemy pitched considerable number of gas shells in vicinity of YPRES. Many of these fell near

July.
Friday 9th Continued —

Battalion Head Quarters and company billets, causing some discomfort to all ranks —
The gas hung about considerably, there being no wind, and it was necessary to wear respirators for some time —
The following moves took place during the evening —
"D" Company, relieved "C" in G.H.Q. Line held by them during past two nights —
"C" Company, with the exception of a working party of 2 officers and 100 men engaged on burying telephone cables, withdrew to billets at YPRES —
Disposition of "A" and "B" Companies unchanged. Parties of these companies were employed during last night in improvements in vicinity of SANCTUARY WOOD —
No. 4450 Pte. J. Baldwin, Adjutant's groom, who was conveying Officers mail to Companies in various positions, was wounded by Shrapnel in YPRES. This man had performed this duty for several months past, often under most difficult circumstances and at considerable risk, earning for himself an excellent reputation — His arrival daily with mails was eagerly looked forward to as the "event of the day" —

July-
Friday 9th Continued-
Other casualties up to 12 noon were-
"A" Company. 1 man wounded
"B"   "   Nil
"C"   "   5 men wounded-
"D"   "   Nil
Very quiet evening and night-
During the day information received that
Captain Breul who should have returned
from leave on 7th July, had been granted one
months sick leave in England-
2nd Lieut- Esdaile Frederick Burkitt Wyatt,
3rd S. Lan R, rejoined the Battalion-
During the afternoon an aeroplane flying
S.W. of YPRES was hit by enemy's shell and
brought down well inside our lines and not
far from Battalion Transport. The machine
was wrecked and pilot killed-

Saturday 10th
An escort consisting of
No. 6372 Regtl. Serjt. Major S. Birkett. S. S Lan R.
    9912 Pte. W. Franklin   S. Lan R
    5750 "   S. Campbell   "   -
arrived from England in charge of No. 8306
Pte. 4336 Pte. Thomas Redmond-
This man had been granted leave and had
failed to return being arrested by civil police
St. Helens-
The escort was attached to the Battalion

July
Saturday 17th continued –

Party of "B" Company working during the night
withdrew to billets at YPRES about 2 a.m.
No casualties.

Bright warm day.

Disposition of Battalion unchanged.

Great situation fairly quiet during the day;
about 2 p.m. and again about 7 p.m. our
guns East of YPRES bombarded enemy positions
in vicinity of HOOGE causing some damage to
his trenches there.

About 9 p.m. artillery fire of considerable
volume could be heard North of YPRES.
This continued for an hour or more and
was apparently in connection with operations
by troops on our left.

Whole Battalion engaged during the night
in improving Brigade Sector of fire trenches
generally, companies or various portions
each been allotted separate tasks.

During the evening the Commanding Officer,
Adjutant and Medical Officer visited the
several detachments of the Battalion, leaving
YPRES about 9 p.m. and returning about
12 midnight.

Casualties 12 noon yesterday to 12 noon today –
"A" Company. 1 man died of wounds.
"D" "   1 " wounded.

July. 1915.

Sunday 11th - Working parties completed tasks on which engaged and withdrew to original position about 2 am.
Casualties - one man wounded.
Dull boisterous day - Rather cold.
Battalion disposition unchanged.
Local situation fairly quiet. Enemy shells pitched into YPRES, in vicinity of our guns West of the town and along YPRES-VLAMERTINGHE-POPERINGHE Road. These cause some annoyance but practically no damage done.
Party in SANCTUARY WOOD - D Company and two platoons 'C' Company. And B Company in G.H.Q. line, employed during the evening and night in improving positions generally.
Fairly quiet night.

Monday 12th - Working parties returned to positions about 2 am.
Bright day - cold winds.
No change in Battalion disposition during the day. 2nd Lieut. Wedderburn reported sick and sent to F.A.
Local situation quiet until evening when artillery - both our own and enemy's - became very active. Large number of aeroplanes about all evening until dark.
Battalion relieved after dark by Suffolk Regiment, 8th Infantry Brigade, with orders to march to bivouac about three miles West of POPERINGHE.

July 1915.
Monday 12th Continued -
    Two platoons 'A' Company and 'B' Company
left YPRES about 9 p.m. together with Bn. Head Qrs -
'C' Company left position in G.H.Q. line about
11 p.m.
    Two platoons 'A' Company and 'D' Company
employed on Special work in SANCTUARY WOOD
during the night.

Tuesday 13th. Two platoons 'A' Company and 'C'
Company arrived at bivouac about 1.30 a.m. -
'B' Company arrived about 4 a.m.
    The march from YPRES to bivouac was about
11 miles and in view of the fact that men
had been engaged in special trench work
for over a week and had not done
marching for a considerable period, the
march to bivouac was performed in
excellent order, only about four men
falling out -
    As the party from SANCTUARY WOOD had been
working most of the night they were conveyed
from YPRES to bivouac in motor buses arriving
about 4 a.m. -
    Entire day - Battalion at rest -
    2nd Lieut. Lodge rejoined from Machine gun course -
Following extract is taken from London Gazette
dated 10 July 1915 -
Prince of Wales's Volunteers (South Lancashire

July 1915.

Tuesday 13th & continued -
Regiment) - Major H. T Cotter to be temporary
Lieut. Colonel - June 23. 1915.
2nd Lieut. Randolph D. Gilmore to be Lieut.
Dec. 26. 1914 -

Wednesday 14th - Fine bright day -
Battalion at company training till 1 pm
at rest remainder of day -
2nd Lieut. William Rose rejoined from
hospital, and assumed charge of machine guns -
2nd Lieut. Francis Leslie Roe I. S. San R.
joined the Battalion -
A... wet night -

Thursday 15th - Very heavy rain during the
night and early morning - Fine later.
Training continued during the day.
2nd Lieut. Wigath proceeded to join 9th
Infantry Brigade as Brigade Machine Gun
Officer -
Regimental Sergt Major H. Bartlett I. S. Leath
and two Privates I. Smith who arrived
on escort duty on 10th July 1915, returned
to England -

Friday 16th - Rather dull day and inclined
to rain -
Training continued -
Extract from London Gazette dated 14 July 1915.
"Prince of Wales's Volunteers (South Lancashire

July 1915.
Friday 16th. To inner –
"Regiment) – 3rd Battalion.
" See Army (corr. quotation) Talbot Street-Escott
" to be confirmed in his rank.
" See London to for Smith – May 25, 1915.
" Talbot L. Street.
" Edward P. Williamson.
" Spencer H. Goldsmith.
These three officers are borne on the
strength of 2nd Battalion.
Very wet afternoon and evening.
A "Bombing party" of 100 other ranks
formed and commenced special training
under 2nd Lieuts. Case and Gates.

Saturday 17th – Heavy rain all night and
during the morning –
Fine and brighter about 10 am –
Heavy rain commenced about 12 noon
and continued until about midnight.
Bivouac very uncomfortable –
2nd Lieut. H. Broadhurst reported sick and
sent to Field Ambulance –
training continued during the day –

Sunday 18th – Fine morning. Bright sunshine –
Battalion at rest – no parade except for
Divine Service.

Monday 19th – Fine day – No change in disposition
of Battalion. Training continued –

July 1915.
Tuesday 26 - Fine bright day. Disposition of Battalion unchanged.
Training continued.
Orders received for Battalion to be prepared to move to Trenches - Vierstraat to relieve 13th Infantry Brigade.
Following officers left Battalion bivouac during the morning with a view to visiting trenches to be taken over -
Commanding Officer.
Senior Major -
Adjutant -
4 Company Commanders.

Wednesday 21st - Very hot day - Order for actual move to trenches changed - Battalion to go into Divisional reserve.
Marched from bivouac about 4 pm to small wood at H.26.b, arriving about 6 pm and occupying huts there.
Transport moved at same time and was accommodated at farm H.31.b.4.4 Sheet 26. Belgium.
2nd Lieut. Strickland rejoined from Special Sick leave -

Thursday 26 ns - Warm day - Rather dull and inclined to rain -
Companies at training during the day -
Very wet afternoon and evening -

July 1915.
Friday 23rd - Raining heavily throughout the night and early morning.
Showery with cold winds all day.
Battalion disposition unchanged.
Company training continued as far as possible. 2nd Lt. Bennett-Goldney rejoined sick tent to F.A.
Transport moved from position occupied on 21st, to field at H.31.b.8.3, about 400 yards East.
This area was heavily shelled during the afternoon and evening, causing some discomfort - no casualties.
Orders received during the afternoon for Battalion to be ready to move to trenches tomorrow in relief of 1st Wilts Regt.
During the evening the position to be occupied was visited by the following officers -
Commanding Officer
Senior Major
Adjutant
4 Company Commanders.

Saturday 24th - Showery up to noon. Fine later. No change in disposition of Battalion during the day. Training continued.
Area occupied by transport shelled at frequent intervals during the day. No casualties.
Draft of 30 Other ranks arrived about

July 1915
Saturday 24th Continued.
9 pm and bivouacked with Transport for the night.
Battalion moved from billets taken up on 24th, about 8 pm to relieve 1st Wilts Regt, occupying position in vicinity of ST. ELOI.
A, C & D Companies, with half B Company occupied trenches at ST. ELOI.
Head Quarters of Battalion and half B Company in "dug outs" at VOORMEZEELE.
Relief completed by 11.30pm when relieved Units withdrew to huts vacated by the Battalion.
No casualties during relief. Quiet night.
No change in situation of Battalion Transport.

Sunday 25th. Dull morning with heavy thunder Storms. Fine afternoon and evening.
Aeroplanes very active during the evening.
A hostile aeroplane was brought down by our anti-aircraft guns about 6 pm and fell in front of Brigade sector occupied by 2nd Dorsets R.? on our left.
No change in disposition of the Battalion.
Casualties up to 12 noon today — Nil.
Local situation quiet — Quiet night.

July 1915.
Sunday 25th trenches
Reinforcement which arrived last night
was taken forward to the Battalion
with supplies, and posted to companies
as under:-

$$\left.\begin{array}{r} A - 3 \\ B - 7 \\ C - 10 \\ D - 11 \end{array}\right\} = 30$$

Monday 26th - Showery and warm.
No change in general disposition of the
Battalion.
Local situation fairly quiet during the
day.
During the evening trenches on our
right occupied by 2nd R.B. were heavily
shelled.
About 10pm enemy exploded a mine in
front of R.3 trench, occupied by "D" Company.
The actual explosion was short of the
trench and did no damage to the
trench or occupants.
About the same time enemy guns opened
heavy fire, but this was directed towards
trenches on our left occupied by 3rd
Worcesters.
It was apparent that the enemy had made
some error either in exploding his mine,

July 1915.
Monday 26th.

or the direction of his artillery fire.
Immediately after the explosion our
guns at once opened fire and this,
together with heavy rifle fire from
our trenches, prevented the possibility of
any forward movement on the part of
the enemy.
By midnight situation had quietened down
and remained fairly quiet during
remainder of the night.
Casualties during the day - Sergt.
Chambers (Signalling Sergeant) wounded.

Tuesday 27th. About 10am enemy artillery
became very active and shelled all
trenches at intervals throughout the day.
Our guns replied and apparently
caused some damage to enemy's
trenches.
Battalion casualties during the day
were - Other ranks - 3 killed - 14 wounded.
Six of latter were able to continue
at duty.
Bright day.
General disposition of Battalion unchanged.
A number of shells pitched in
vicinity of Battalion Transport bivouac
but no damage done.
Quiet night.

July 1916.
Wednesday 28th - Bright day - Strong South
Westerly wind.
New Brigadier - Lieutenant Cushing R.R.R.C. -
paid the Battalion a visit assuming
command of 5th Inf Bde, and inspected
the Batter in billets during the morning.
No change in general disposition of the
Battalion.
Billeting fairly quiet during the day.
Germans this morning trenches R.2 and 4,
occupied by 'A' Company under the
command of Captain Scholey, were
heavily shelled by enemy, causing
some damage and loss, the casualties
being - 2 men killed, 6 wounded and
2 suffering from shock.
About 8.30pm enemy exploded a mine
in vicinity of trench Q1 occupied
by 'b' Company. About 8 yards of
parapet damaged but no casualties -
Casualties up to 12 noon were 7 other
ranks wounded, 3 of these were able to
carry on their duties.
About 10 pm Major Becke moved in front
of our fire trenches with a small
reconnoitering party of 3 men - Ptes Drinkwater,
McLoughlin and Hogan, discovering a
working party of the enemy about 12

July 1915
Wednesday 28 Continued -
midnight - These workers were protected
by a covering party and Major Beckes
succeeded in getting to within ~~a~~
a short distance ~~a copse~~ of their flank by crawling
through long grass. After ascertaining
their actual position the officer and
men withdrew, reporting to our artillery
who opened fire and dispersed the
working and covering parties.
No further incident during the remainder
of the night which passed fairly
quiet although considerable activity was
noticeable about the N.E side of the
Salient at HOOGE.
2nd Lieut Jebens and 21 other ranks
joined Brigade reinforcements today -

Thursday 29th - Dull day - Very fine night -
Disposition of Battalion generally unchanged.
Battalion Sector visited during the
morning by G.O.C. in C. 3rd Division -
Major General Haldane -
Nothing unusual occurred throughout the
day. Local situation fairly quiet -
Casualties from 12 noon yesterday to
12 noon today were - Other ranks, two
killed, eight wounded -
Quiet night -

July 1915.
Friday 30th — During the early hours some
activity was noticed on the line N.E. of
our Sector in the vicinity of HOOGE and
about 3am it was reported that an
attack was in progress. The bursting
of shells and grenades could be seen
from our trenches and was a very
wonderful sight.
The bombardment continued for some time
and later it was reported that our
troops holding the line at HOOGE had
been driven from some of their trenches
but the news was not definite.
No change in disposition of the Battalion.
General quiet of Artillery during the
day. Otherwise local situation quiet.
About 8.30pm enemy exploded a mine
in front of trenches R1 and 3, but short
and no damage was done.
About the same time a shell from
enemy guns struck the parapet of the
trench occupied by B Company, close to
the spot where Captain Bagley was
standing. This officer was wounded
slightly but suffered severely from shock
and was removed to Field Ambulance.
No further incident occurred in our
Sector during the night but the activity

July 1915.
Friday 30th. Strain
near HOOGE again continued throughout
the night.
Casualties 12 noon yesterday to 12 noon
today were - other ranks. 2 killed - 5
wounded.

Saturday 31st. Bright hot day.
General disposition of Battalion unchanged -
Much activity in Sectors occupied by
other formations on left of 7th Infantry
Brigade in vicinity of HOOGE - Heavy
shelling most of the day and part
of the night.
Local situation fairly quiet -
Enemy shelled our trenches frequently
during the day but did very little
damage.
Several shells fell close near Battalion
Head Quarters "dug out" but did no
harm. These were apparently searching
for a "fixed" machine gun and
"rifle battery" which were laid on to
certain special points in enemy trenches
and causing him some annoyance -
Casualties from 12 noon yesterday to
12 noon today were - other ranks - 3
wounded - one of these men was able
to continue at duty -

July 1915
Saturday 31st — continued —

On this day the Battalion mustered as follows —

- Lieut Col. H. T. Cotton. D. Sant. Commanding
- Major J. Bucke L. San. F. Senior Major
- Captain A. T. Boast. D. Sant. Quartermaster
- 2nd Lieut C. E. Thompson ... Acting adjt.
- " J. S. Boast ... Transport officer
- " W. Roscoe ... Machine gun
- Lieut A. B. Cheves N. A. M. C. Medical Officer
- Captain J. H. Schnier Midd Rgt. Commdg 'A' Coy
- Lieut K. S. Gilmour D. Sant. 'B'
- 2nd Lieut F. A. Holden ... C
- Captain H. P. .... Forest R. D
- 2nd Lieut R. Sage D. Sant
- " H. W. Goldsmith ...
- " J. B. T. Strickland ...
- " R. Gillespie ...
- " C. A. H. Legg ...
- " W. A. Wassner ...
- " R. G. Spalding ...
- " A. J. Ventris ...
- " A. W. Gates ...
- " B. M. Browne ...
- " F. S. Roe ...

Total feeding strength on this date was — all ranks 935 —

July 1915.
Saturday 31st continued -

The following officers absent from the
Battalion for reasons stated are borne on
the strength still -
Captain R.A.O. Taylor. S. Lank. Sick in England -
    "   F.A. Breed. Gloster R.   "   "   "
2nd Lieut G.R.a. Case S. Lank   "   "   "
Captain F.A. Bagley   —.—   Hospital
2nd Lieut C.P. Widdowson —.—   "
  "   A.D. Wilson   —.—   "
  "   H. Broadhurst —.—   "
  "   T. Sweet-Escott —.—   "
  "   F.H. Jebens   —.—   Brigade miners.

P. Cotton
Lieut-Colonel
Commanding 2. S. Lancashire Regt

7th Inf.Bde.
3rd Div.

WAR DIARY

2nd BATTN. THE SOUTH LANCASHIRE REGIMENT.

A U G U S T

1 9 1 5

1st Battalion South Lancashire Regiment.
War Diary. 1st to 31st August 1915.

Sunday 1st. Very hot day.
Disposition of Battalion unchanged.
Frequent outbursts of shelling during the day by enemy's guns. This caused us some annoyance but little damage done. Otherwise local situation quiet.
Casualties up to 12 noon - 2 men wounded.
About 10pm enemy exploded a small mine in front of our trenches.
2nd Lieut. Thomas Varley S. Lan R. joined the Battalion.

Monday 2nd. Very boisterous day with frequent heavy showers. Strong southerly winds.
Orders received that Battalion would be relieved during the evening by 6th Dorset Regt. Later this was cancelled and Battalion ordered to remain in position.
Throughout the day our trenches were subjected to heavy hostile shell fire and for the first time the Battalion came under enemy's aerial torpedo bombardment. The latter made a most terrific explosion and gave our men some concern.
Our fire trenches were very badly damaged

August 1915.
Monday 2nd.

and casualties were from amongst the general situation was an unsatisfactory barometer of the men from other ranks. 3 killed, 10 wounded.

During the evening the other units in Lakior attacher of 6 Infantry Brigade were relieved by units of 5th Infantry Brigade. The 1st Devon Regt which had been relieved as was temporarily attached to 6th Infantry Brigade and are now in billets with 5th Infantry Brigade.
No change in disposition of battalion. Large men fully occupied during the night in repairing damage done during the day. Strong party from 4th Battalion also employed on this work.

Tuesday 3rd. Weather very unsettled. Very much rain. Strong winds.
No change in disposition of battalion. Enemy commenced shelling our trenches about 4 am and this continued practically all day. As an instance of this it is estimated that between 400 and 150 shells into practically one spot in our trench. The result of all this was that the repairs carried out during last night were again destroyed.

August 1915
Tuesday 3rd continued.

3/

The situation generally was very uncomfortable but in spite of the fact that our casualties were again heavy, all ranks were determined to hold the position at all costs and the men were quite prepared to repulse any advance on the part of the enemy who took good care not to expose themselves. It was decided to construct a new trench slightly in rear of the original one, our arrangements made to carry this out tonight. At the same time it was decided by the Commanding Officer not to abandon the original fire trench but to reduce the garrison, having just sufficient to hold it. The remainder being in the trench in rear ready to move forward at a moment's notice.

About 10 am enemy exploded another mine in front of our position but very little damage was done to us — in fact it was apparent that he had miscalculated and that his own trenches were damaged. As a proof of this, the explosion carried a German soldier's jacket which actually fell into our trench.

During Monday–Tuesday night, No. 9 Platoon – B Company – who were in reserve at Battalion

August 1915
Tuesday 3rd August

Head Quarters were moved forward to the trenches occupied by 10th Battalion West Yorkshire Regiment to ascertain that there was occurring a grip of the situation. After a few hours the Station withdrew to our Battalion Head Quarters.

By this time the Rector on our right and left were being held by troops of the New Army recently arrived from England. The following Officers were wounded during the day:—

Lieut [?]
2nd Lieut Jekins " "
   " Thompson – Able to continue on duty.
Other casualties up to 12 noon were:—
Other ranks – 3 killed – 20 wounded. Some of the latter severely, and although sent to Field ambulance they were not expected to survive.

Except situation during the night was [?] – the work of repairing fire trenches and constructing new trenches was carried on. In this work every available man, and about 400 men of 10th Battalion, were engaged.

Communication received to the effect that 2nd Lieut Barr, due off leave tomorrow, was on sick list in England.

August 1915.

Wednesday 4th - Very wet miserable day -
General disposition of Battalion unchanged -
During the morning local situation fairly
quiet. Trenches were shelled by enemy
but not so heavy as hitherto.
During the afternoon the shelling increased
and part of parapet of C. 1.
occupied by "A" Coy. was partly
damaged -
About 1 a.m. this morning one Company of 18th
West Yorkshire Regt. moved from SCOTTISH
WOOD to Battalion Head Quarters and
remained there in Reserve.
Casualties up to 12 noon were - other ranks -
16 wounded -
About 200 men of the Battalion were engaged
during the night in assisting in the
repairs to trenches etc -
Fairly quiet night -

Thursday 5th. Fine bright forenoon -
No change in general disposition of Battalion.
Local situation much quieter than usual.
Very little shelling -
Nothing of any special importance in
Battalion Sector -
Casualties to 12 noon - 9 other ranks
wounded - 2 of whom were able to continue
at duty -

August 1915.   6

Thursday 5th continued -
    Reinforcement of 50 other ranks arrived and
remained for the night in trench mint
bivouac.

Friday 6th - Rather miserable day - South Westerly
breezes with frequent very heavy showers.
General disposition of Battalion unchanged
during the day.
    Local situation very quiet. Occasional
shelling by enemy - Not very severe and
very little damage done.
    Casualties 1 other rank wounded & 1 other rank
evacuated.
    During the afternoon orders received that two
Companies - A and B - would be relieved by
two Companies of 7th East Yorkshire Regiment.
Relief completed by about 11.30p- when A and
B Companies returned to bivouac in Bazaar(?).
No casualties during relief. Quiet night.
Reinforcement posted to Companies as under -
        A. 25. B. 7. C. 6. D. 12 - 50
A and B Companies joined their Companies
in bivouac referred to above. Others remained
attached for the night.

Saturday 7th - Very squally day. Southerly winds.
A and B Companies at rest in bivouac.
No change in disposition of remainder of the
Battalion.

August 1915.   7

Saturday 7th. Nieuwe-
Local situation remarkably quiet considering
what it was like a few days ago.
Occasional shelling by enemy during the
day, but practically no damage done.
Usual rifle fire day and night.
Casualties up to 12 noon - 3 men wounded.
A number of Shells fired by our guns
from positions in rear fell almost in
our trenches without exploding. This caused
us some concern and the matter was at
once taken up with our Artillery, who
succeeded in making some improvement.
Fairly quiet night.
Parties from 4th Battalion engaged in
repairing and improving trenches.
Reinforcements for 'C' and 'D' Companies taken
forward with transport conveying rations.

Sunday 8th. Fine warm day but not bright.
Disposition of Battalion unchanged.
Local situation fairly quiet. Very little
shelling.
Casualties to 12 noon - 1 Sergt wounded.
Several officers and N.C.O's of 6th South
Staffordshire Regiment arrived at Battalion
Head Quarters and were attached to
Companies in position for instruction,
remaining all night.

August 1915.
Monday 9th
About 2.30 am our Artillery opened a very heavy fire on enemy's position in vicinity of HOOGE. Apparently all guns in our line from near DICKEBUSCH to North of YPRES took part in the bombardment which continued for several hours and must have done considerable damage to the enemy. Later it was reported that our troops, 6th division in vicinity of HOOGE had made a very successful attack.

The sector held by the Battalion was not affected by these operations.

No change in general disposition during the day - casualties to 12 noon - 1 man wounded. Local situation fairly quiet. Our guns shelled, at frequent intervals, the ground in front of our trenches, causing the enemy some annoyance.

During the evening 'B' and 'D' Companies were relieved by 'A' and 'C' Companies. The former, on relief, withdrew to bivouacs vacated by latter.

Relief completed by about 10 pm.
No casualties during relief.

Tuesday 10th - Very hot day.
No change in disposition of Battalion.
Local situation exceptionally quiet.

August 1915.   9/
Tuesday 10th 6
  No unusual incident in Battalion Sector.
  Casualties to 12 noon - 1 man wounded.
  2nd Lieut C.C. Thompson slightly wounded
  during Monday-Tuesday night but was able
  to remain on duty.
  Captain F.A Bagley rejoined from hospital.
  Draft of 78 other ranks arrived and
  remained for the night at Transport
  bivouac.
  Quiet night.
Wednesday 11th - Fine bright day.
  Local situation quiet.
  No change in disposition of Battalion during
  the day.
  During the evening the Head Quarters of
  the Battalion and "B" company were relieved
  and withdrew to bivouac at Kaia S.2.
  The Head Quarters of the Sector were taken
  over by 7th East Yorkshire Regiment and "B"
  company was relieved by a company of 8th
  South Staffordshire Regt.
  Relief completed by about 11.30pm. No casualties.
  "A" Company under Captain Belverly and
  Machine guns under 2nd Lieut Srage remained
  in the Sector.
  Draft which arrived yesterday were distributed equally
  amongst the 4 companies - 19 each. Those of

August 1915

Wednesday 11th. Stamer -
B. C. and D Companies joined their respective
companies in Battalion bivouac. Those of A
Company remained in transport bivouac -
Duller hill.

Thursday 12th. Fine day -
Battalion disposed as follows -
A Company under Captain Scholey, Machine
guns under 2nd Lieut Lodge, and scouts
bombers still in trenches. One man wounded.
Remainder of Battalion at rest in bivouac.
[illegible] for Division reported from
6th line and [illegible]
Local situation quiet.

Friday 13th. Dull day - Frequent heavy rain -
No change in dispositions of the Battalion
during the day -
About 10 am enemy pitched four shells into
Battalion bivouac -
Casualties - [illegible] killed - C.Q.M. Sergt.
Kingham wounded.
2nd Lieut Roe reported sick and sent to Field
Ambulance.
During the evening D Company under Captain
Whitaker moved to Br trench St ELOI Sector, in
relief of A Company, the latter withdrawing to
bivouac on relief about 11 pm.
No casualties.

August 1915

<u>Saturday 14th</u> - Fine bright day.
No change in disposition of the Battalion during the day.
Companies at training during the morning.
At rest during the afternoon.
Machine gunners of the Battalion relieved from position and withdrew to bivouac.
Local situation quiet.
DICKEBUSCH heavily shelled by enemy but none reaching Battalion bivouac.

<u>Sunday 15</u> - Heavy showers throughout the day.
Battalion remained at rest in bivouac during the day.
Signallers withdrew from positions during the afternoon to bivouac.
Orders received for Battalion to be prepared to move.
"D" Company still in trenches.
Casualties - 1 man killed. 2 men wounded.
Orders received for Lieut Colonel V. A. Turzon to be prepared to join the 152nd Infantry Brigade and take over command.
Battalion moved from bivouac at 9.30 pm and marching via OUDERDOM to about M4b. Sheet 28. occupying huts and bivouac there.
Notification received that "D" Company would be relieved during the night.
Local situation quiet -

August 1915.   12

Monday 16th - "A" Company arrived at new
    bivouac about 5am.
    Battalion paraded at 10.30am and
    addressed by Colonel Surgeon on handing
    over command. His remarks were much
    appreciated by all ranks.
    Colonel Surgeon left bivouac by motor
    car about 11am to join 152nd Inf Brigade.
    As he moved off the whole Battalion
    turned out and cheered him most heartily.
    Companies at training during the morning
    at rest during the afternoon.
    Major Barton assumed command of the
    Battalion. "A" Company drill island.
    Bivouac visited by B.G.C. 50th Inf Brigade.

Tuesday 17th - Bright morning broken by heavy
    thunder storm. Local situation quiet.
    Companies at training up to 1 pm
    No change in disposition of the Battalion.
    Sports during the afternoon and evening.
    Quiet night.

Wednesday 18th - Rather dull damp day.
    Disposition of Battalion unchanged.
    Companies at training during the morning.
    2nd Lieut Textier proceeded for duty with 172nd
    Tunnelling company in relief of 2nd Lieut
    Wassner.
    Sports continued. Quiet night.

August 1915   13

Thursday 19th - Rather cold Northerly winds.
   Dull day.
   Companies at training till 1 pm.
   At rest remainder of day.
   Disposition of Battalion unchanged.
   4 Officers and 130 Other ranks to engage
   on Special work in SCOTTISH Wood under the
   orders of C.R.E. 14th Division.
Friday 20th - Bright warm day.
   Disposition of Battalion unchanged.
   Companies at training till 1 pm.
   2nd Lieut Rice rejoined from hospital.
   Draft of 50 Other ranks arrived and
   was posted to Companies as under —
   A.12 B. 9 C.15 D 14.
   250 men under Captain Whittaker left
   bivouac at 5.30pm for the purpose of
   constructing cable trenches.
Saturday 21st - Working party returned to bivouac
   about 2.30 am, after completing about 1500
   yards of cable trench in an Easterly direction
   from KRUISSTRAAT.
   Very wet day.
   Company training in progress as far as
   possible up to 1 pm.
   2nd Lieut J. D. Boast sent to 10 C. C. Station for
   examination by "X Rays".
   Local Situation quiet. Sergt. Herbert accidentally
   wounded at grenade practice and sent to F. A.

August 1915.   14

Sunday 22nd — Bright morning with occasional
showers.
    Battalion attended Divine Service.
    During the evening aeroplanes were
unusually active. Their hostile planes
passed immediately over Battalion bivouac
flying exceptionally low. These were
fired at by anti-aircraft guns but they
were not hit. Two of the shells failed
to explode and fell into Battalion
bivouac causing some alarm but doing
no damage.
    Captain Mitchell & Matthews Blow, 1st
Lancashire Regiment joined the Battalion.
2nd Lieut J.S. Croot rejoined from 10
C.C. Station.
    Quiet night.

Monday 23rd — Fine day. Very warm.
Company training in squads.
    Orders received that 7th Infantry Brigade
would proceed tomorrow to position in
vicinity of HOOGE.
    Commanding Officer, adjutant and four
company commanders left Battalion bivouac
about 8.30am and visited the sector
to be taken over returning about 5pm.
During the afternoon men were
engaged in football matches and other

August 1915.   15.
Monday 23rd continued.
        games and in the evening some very
        interesting boxing contests were organized
        and thoroughly enjoyed by all.
        Battalion undisturbed during the night.
Tuesday 24th. Bright and very warm day.
        Battalion at rest during the day.
        2nd Army Order ...... took effect ..
        England on 1st August 1915, against the
        Battalion. Strength Officers 7 20 men approx.
        Companies moved from bivouac about
        6 p.m. and proceeded to position about
        1.15 p.m. relieving 3rd Battalion Rifle Brigade
        who withdrew on relief.
        Relief completed by about 11.30 p.m.
        No casualties. Transport moved to H31.b.6.3. that PM.
Wednesday 25th. Very bright and warm.
        General disposition of Battalion unchanged.
        Hdqt Quarters established on Southern edge
        of SANCTUARY WOOD.
        Battalion fairly quiet during the day.
        Continuous rifle fire from both our trenches
        and the enemy's throughout the night.
        A large number of men of the Battalion
        engaged most of the night in fixing wire
        obstacles in front of our fire trenches.
        This was badly needed as very little wire
        had been fixed since the last attack by

August 1915.
16

Wednesday 25th. Contd. —
British troops which took place in the vicinity recently.
Casualties up to 12 noon — 6 other ranks wounded.
Between 11 pm and midnight, aircraft, apparently an aeroplane, passed to and fro over SANCTUARY WOOD and vicinity, but it was not possible to say whether it was ours or hostile.
Supplies, and large quantity of miscellaneous R.E. Stores, taken up from transport bivouac.

Thursday 26th. Very hot bright day.
Aircraft, both ours and enemy's, very active. Unusually so.
General disposition of Battalion unchanged.
Casualties to 12 noon — 1 man killed — 2 wounded.
During the day the B.G.C. 7th Inf. Bde. visited the sector held by the Battalion and expressed great satisfaction at the amount of work done by the various Companies.
A large number of men were again engaged during most of the night in improving the situation generally, facing wire obstacles etc.
A large quantity of R.E. Stores were again taken up with Supplies.
About 11 pm 2nd Lieut. _____ with a small reconnoitring party, located a

August 1915.   17

Thursday 26th — continued.
working party of the enemy a short distance
in front of our fire trenches. They were
dispersed by the rifle fire of our men.
Several of the enemy were hit but
our party sustained no casualties.
Artillery was again active during the
night. Several aeroplanes could be heard
passing over.
During Wednesday night 'A' Company completed
a new fire trench about 150 yards in front
of trench held. The new trench was in the
vicinity of the HOOGE Chateau Stables and
being on the forward slope, gave a much
better command, and field of fire.

Friday 27th. Work of improvement
continued till daylight and communication
trench from new to old fire trench completed.
Workers were covered by a party of
"bomb throwers" under 2nd Lieut. Bourne.
This officer located a machine gun in
a trench from which the enemy had
been driven. Several of the enemy, apparently
machine gunners, were lying dead near the
gun. With the exception of ammunition belts,
the gun was complete with tripod and
was removed under Battalion arrangements.
Very hot day.

August 1915.
Friday 27th (cont)
General disposition of the Battalion unchanged during the day.
Casualties to 12 noon - 3 other ranks wounded.
During the evening - after dark - the Battalion was relieved by companies of the 3rd Worcester Regt.
A, B & D Companies with signallers and machine gunners, withdrew to the Ramparts at YPRES, arriving there in parties between 10pm and midnight.
"C" Company, under Captain Taylor, remained as a working party in the sector, a party of bombers under 2nd Lieut Brown remaining as a covering party.
Battalion Head Quarters also remained in connection with the work to be carried out by "C" Company.

Saturday 28th - About dawn "C" Company withdrew to "dug outs" at ZILLEBEKE POND and Head Quarters of Battalion to Ramparts at YPRES.
The work on which "C" Company had been engaged was rather exposed and the following casualties were sustained -
2 men killed - 2nd Lieut Gates and 11 other ranks wounded. The officer named and 3 of the others wounded were able to continue at duty.

August 1915.
Saturday 28th. continued.

19

Very warm day.
Battalion at rest during the day.
The area in which Battalion was
 resting was subjected to occasional
hostile shell fire but there were no
casualties.
During Friday-Saturday night aeroplane
could be heard passing over but could
not be seen.
During the tour of trench duty - Tuesday
to Friday - just completed, a very considerable
amount of hard work was carried out.
On taking over the Sector, trenches were
practically in progress only, in consequence
of the recent operations in the area.
All ranks worked very hard and
most cheerfully and the B.G.C.
expressed his satisfaction at the result.
The following is an extract from a
"Fourth Supplement Gazette" dated 25 August
1915:-
 "His Imperial Majesty the Emperor of
Russia has been graciously pleased to confer,
with the approval of his Majesty the King,
the undermentioned rewards for gallantry
and distinguished Service in the field;
Cross of the Order of St. George 3rd Class -

August 1915.   20/

Saturday 28th. afternoon.
    No. 6437 Co. Qm Sergt Joseph Scarmbrough
      2nd South Lancashire Regt.
    Medal of St. George 3rd Class.
    No. 6942 Lce. Corp. Arthur Lawrence Cleveland
      2nd South Lancashire Regt.
Sunday 29th. Very wet boisterous day.
    General disposition of Battalion unchanged.
    Companies at rest during the day.
    Local situation generally quiet.
    'A' and 'B' Companies detailed as special
    working parties leaving billets about 7.30pm.
Monday 30th. Working parties returned to billets
    about 3am. No casualties.
    Dull day. Very showery.
    Battalion at rest during the day.
    Orders received to be in readiness to
    move to position in SANCTUARY WOOD.
    Companies moved forward about 7.30pm
    relieving 3rd Worcester Regiment who withdrew
    on relief.
    Relief satisfactorily completed by about
    midnight without casualties. Companies
    being disposed as follows:-
    D Coy under Captain Whittaker in Fire trenches.
    B   "   "   "   Hayley   on YEOMANRY POST.
    C   "   "   "   Taylor   on ZOUAVE WOOD
    A   "   "   "   Schooling at BURLINGTON ARCADE.

August 1915
Monday 30th continued —
Just before companies moved off to take
up position our guns shelled enemy's
trenches [illegible]

Tuesday 31st — Warm bright day —
General inspection of battalion postponed —
About 8 am our guns opened heavy
fire on enemy's lines which continued
for about ½ hour. Enemy replied by
heavy shrapnel fire which was directed
mainly on & in vicinity of our ques-
tion [?] shells bursting over our
fire trenches caused some damage to
parapets but fortunately the casualties
in the battalion was only one man
wounded —
During the night all companies were
engaged in repairing damage done,
digging new communication trenches and
[illegible] trenches —
Today the equipping of all ranks with
new pattern "tube" smoke helmet was
completed.
1 Officer and 1 N.C.O per company proceeded
to HAZEBROUCK to witness a demonstration
in "bomb throwing" at the Head Quarters
2nd Army — also to receive instruction in

August 1915.
Tuesday 31st continued.

manipulating the "Newton-Pippin" bomb
and a new pattern incendiary bomb.
On this date the battalion mustered
as follows —

Lieut Col   H.C. Lowther S.Lanc R   commanding
Major   J. Reeke   Lan Fus   2nd in command major
Captain   D.T. Brest S.Lanc R   quartermaster
2nd Lieut   C.E. Thompson   acting adjt.
     "   J.D. Brest   transport officer
     "   J.T. Roscoe   machine gun
Lieut   R.C. Adams R.A.M.C.   medical officer
Captain   J.L. Scholey, Middx Rgt temmry. O.C. Coy
            F.A. Bagley S.Lanc R   "   "
            ....   "   "
Captain   C.P. Whitaker Dorset R. "   D   "
Lieut   A.W. Goldsmith S.Lanc R
2nd Lieut   ....
     "   A.F. Ventris   "
     "   K.M. Browne   "
     "   G.R.A. Case   "
     "   R.J. Spalding   "
     "   ....   "
     "   ....   "
     "   J.S.T. Strickland   "
     "   C.A.H. Hogg   "
     "   J.L. Roe   "
     "   W.A.L. Vanndall   "

August 1915
Tuesday 31st Cont...
   2nd Lieut. B. ... ...
   Captain A. M. ...
   2nd Lieut. ...

The fighting strength of the Battalion
on this date was ...
...

W. Cotton

7th Inf.Bde.
3rd Div.

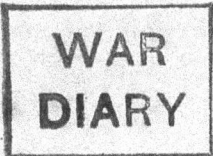

2nd BATTN. THE SOUTH LANCASHIRE REGIMENT.

S E P T E M B E R

1 9 1 5

2nd Battalion South Lancashire Regt.

War diary — 1st to 30th Sept. 1915

<u>Wednesday 1st</u>. Warm but very showery —
About 4 a.m. our guns again opened a heavy
fire on enemy's positions, and continued till
about 6 a.m.
This was replied to immediately, by hostile
artillery fire directed mainly at our position
and causing considerable damage to our
front lines —
A desultory fire from both our guns and
those of the enemy, was maintained
throughout the day — the hostile fire
was directed mainly at our "fire"
and "support" trenches —
Our casualties during the day were —
2nd Lieuts. Gater and Varley wounded — the
former was able to continue on duty —
Other ranks, 1 killed, 9 wounded —
Battalion dispositions unchanged —
Companies again engaged during the night
in repairing and improving the position
generally —
Position of Battalion Transport moved to Q.16.b.b.b.
Party returned from instruction in "bomb-
throwing" this evening —

September 1915.
Thursday 2nd - Very wet day - rain exceptionally heavy by evening - This caused the approaches to and surroundings of Battalion position, to become very heavy, making movement very difficult.
Artillery, both ours and enemy's, very active throughout whole day.
Trenches occupied by the Battalion were subjected to a very heavy fire from enemy guns in position about Hill 60. But considering the intensity of enemy fire, our casualties throughout the day were remarkably low.
2nd Lieut Messervé and 14 other ranks wounded.
During the night the work of repairing and improving the position was continued. G Company relieved F Company in fire trenches - no other change in disposition of the Battalion.

Friday 3rd Sept. - Wet boisterous day - heavy rain during whole day.
Heavy artillery duels throughout the day.
Enemy fire was of a very effective nature and caused considerable damage to the trenches occupied by the Battalion - guns in position near Hill 60 again used and fire very effective - Support and reserve trenches suffering equally with fire trenches

September 1915.   3

Friday 3rd Co Trines-
    The trenches generally were now most
    uncomfortable from the recent rains and
    men much fatigued-
    Casualties during the day again
    remarkably low - other ranks 2 killed and
    2 wounded-
    Battalion relieved during the night by
    3rd Worcester Regt-

Saturday 4th - Very wet night - Relief
    completed by about 1 a.m. no casualties
    during relief-
    Companies withdrew as relieved and
    marched to bivouac at Hsa.d.5.2 arriving
    there about 2 am -
    Raining heavy all day-
    Battalion now attached temporarily to
    8th Infantry Brigade and about 3pm
    marched to bivouac at H8.c.9.2 arriving
    there about 4pm-
    Temporary shelters were erected by the
    men and Battalion settled down for the
    night-
    Nothing unusual to record-

Sunday 5th - Very showery - Battalion at rest.
    Divine service held-
    2nd Lieuts. William Arthur Lloyd Poundall
    and Geoffrey Lease joined the Battalion-

September 1915.

Sunday 5th Co. mess.
Captain K.R.O. Taylor accidentally injured by a fall from his horse and sent to hospital at MONT DE CATS.

Monday 6th - Bright warm day.
Battalion disposition unchanged.
Training continued.
Local situation quiet.

Tuesday 7th - Bright hot day.
Local situation quiet.
Disposition of Battalion unchanged.
Company training continued till 1 pm. At rest remainder of day.

Wednesday 8th - Very hot day.
General disposition of Battalion unchanged.
Companies at training till 12 noon.
Battalion inspected at 2.30pm by Lieut. General Sir H.L.S. Plumer K.C.B.
Reinforcement of 19 other ranks joined the Battalion and posted to companies as under.
R.7. B.5. B.3. D.4.

Appx 2
A
One officer from each company proceeded to positions at SANCTUARY WOOD about 12 midnight for purpose of making a reconnaissance of trenches and to make observation reports of enemy's work in progress.

Thursday 9th - Officers returned from SANCTUARY WOOD about 6 am.

September 1915.   5.

__Thursday 9th__ - Bright warm day -
Training continued -
Disposition of Battalion unchanged -
Issue of 1 Blanket per man completed -
Aeroplanes, both our own and enemys, were
unusually active during the afternoon and
evening -
Considerable activity amongst our Artillery
East of Battalion bivouac, apparently on line
ST. ELOI - YPRES - during the evening and night -
Battalion not disturbed -
During the day Lt.Colonel H.J. Cotton visited
the positions and trenches held by Units of
7th Infantry Brigade in vicinity of HOOGE for
the purpose of making a reconnaissance of
same -

__Friday 10th__ - Bright day - Strong N.E. winds -
Company training continues -
Orders received for Battalion to be held
in readiness as "Corps Reserve" and be
prepared to move at short notice -
Aeroplane and Artillery activity continued
throughout whole day -
Many heavy shells from enemy guns
could be seen from Battalion bivouac
pitching into vicinity of VLAMERTINGHE
and DICKEBUSCH, apparently causing some
damage there -

September 1915.
Friday 10th Con'd.

Information received that Lieut. A.B. Shreves, Medical Officer to the Battalion had been promoted to rank of Captain with effect from 7th August 1915.

Battalion not disturbed during the night.

Saturday 11th. Bright day. Hostile aircraft. Companies at training.

Aeroplanes and artillery again very active. Several Officers of battalion visited trenches of Sector to be occupied.

Orders received to be ready to move tomorrow.

Machine guns under 2nd Lieut. Roscoe and a Section of bombers under 2nd Lieut. Bourne moved to positions during the evening.

Local situation quiet.

Sunday 12th. Very hot day.

Battalion attended divine service. At rest during remainder of day till evening.

8th Infantry Brigade, of which Battalion still formed part, moved during the evening, to position in vicinity of HOOGE, relieving 7th Infantry Brigade.

Battalion was allotted left portion of Brigade Sector and took over from 1st Wiltshire Regt. commencing about 10pm.

September 1915.
Sunday 12th (continued).

On this occasion 'A' Company under Captain
Schooling and 'B' Company under 2nd Lieut.
Lodge, who were to occupy the forward
trenches, were conveyed from bivouac to
Kruisstraat by motor buses, leaving about
5 pm.

Remainder of Battalion proceeded by march
route leaving bivouac about 6.30pm.

A party of 50 other ranks, under 2nd Lieut.
Strickland, remained behind under the
orders of B.G.C. 8th Inf. Brigade, for instruction
in "bombing". This party was attached, for
accommodation, to Details 2nd Royal Scots.

Transport of the Battalion moved from
G.15.c.9.5 to G.11.a.0.9, the latter being the
new bivouac area allotted to the Battalion.

Information received that 2nd Lieut. E.F.K.
Wyatt had been granted the temporary
rank of Captain while holding the
appointment of Brigade Machine Gun Officer,
9th Infantry Brigade", dated 15th July 1915.

Monday 13th. Relief completed by about 1 am
when relieved unit - 1st W.Y.R. Regt. withdrew
from position.

By this time the companies were disposed
as under -

'A' Company fire trenches.

September 1915.
Monday 13th - dinner -
    "B" Company Support trenches.
    "C"   "   less 1 Platoon in fire trenches
    "C"   "   1 Platoon in Support trenches.
    D Coy & HdQrs in Support trenches.
Bright warm day -
Fire trenches shelled by hostile guns causing some damage -
Casualties - 2 men wounded -
During the evening and early part of the night enemy guns were very active, shelling all roads and approaches to position. This caused some inconvenience to transport moving forward with supplies -

Tuesday 14th - Dull warm day -
No change in disposition of Battalion -
Our Artillery very active shelling enemys trenches nearly all day - This was replied to continually by hostile guns -
During the morning information was received that our guns were to shell the enemys trenches immediately in front of those held by "C" Company. As the distance between the trenches was only very short it was considered advisable for the garrison of our trench to withdraw a short distance while the shelling was in progress. The company withdrew to a communication trench but the

September 1915   9
Tuesday 14th Contd:-
movement must have been seen by the
enemy, presumably by means of powerful
periscopes which it was believed they
possessed, as hostile shrapnel fire was at
once directed on to the trench causing
the following casualties -
2nd Lieut Austin Killed.
2nd Lieut. Lodge and 5 other ranks
severely wounded, 2 slightly, able to continue on duty
The last named officer and 1 man died
of their wounds very shortly afterwards -
In addition to these casualties 4 other
men were wounded during the day -
The shelling by our guns, referred to
above, had some effect on the enemy
and beyond occasional artillery fire
directed at our guns, the remainder
of the day was fairly quiet -
2nd Lieut. Fee reported sick and sent to
No. 10 Casualty Clearing Station via Field
Ambulance -
Drier misty - Slight rain -
Companies in support at work during
greater part of the night in digging
"assembly" trenches in the vicinity of the
position held by the Battalion -
Captain Blair assumed command of 'C' Coy -

September 1915

Wednesday 15th - Warm day - inclined to be dull with occasional sunshine -
Disposition of the Battalion unchanged during the day. Aeroplanes very active all day -
Our artillery very active during the morning -
Very little hostile reply -
Local situation fairly quiet -
One man wounded during the day -
During the evening C and D Companies, under Captain Bagley and Schooling respectively, moved forward to fire trenches in relief of A and B Companies who withdrew to supports -
No casualties during relief -
Very dark night with some rain -
1 Sergeant and 15 men detailed for "mining" duties and joined Section assembling at RAMPARTS YPRES.

Thursday 16th - Warm dull day - inclined to rain -
Captain K.B. Brown, R.A.M.C. reported at transport lines and joined the Battalion with supplies in the evening for temporary duty as medical officer, in relief of Captain A.B. Chives, R.A.M.C., granted special leave to proceed to England -
No change in disposition of Battalion -
Our artillery very active throughout whole

September 1915.   11

Thursday 16th - Contd -
day. Feeble reply from hostile guns and
there appeared no doubt that our
fire was superior to enemy's.
Local situation rather quiet during the
day and night.
No casualties, except one man slightly wounded.

Friday 17th - Bright and warm,
General disposition of Battalion unchanged.
Considerable artillery fire at frequent intervals
throughout whole day from both our own
and hostile guns.
Enemy's fire particularly heavy during the
evening but this was directed mainly on
to the Sectors - SANCTUARY WOOD and HILL 60 -
on right of that held by Battalion.
Very little damage sustained by the
Battalion and - as far as could be seen -
our guns appeared to have superiority
of fire - Casualties, 1 man killed - 7 others wounded.
Machine guns of Battalion relieved by
H.A.'s, and withdrew to bivouac at G11a.9.8.
Information received to the effect that leave
suspended. Captain Shewen rejoined the
Battalion and assumed his duties as
medical officer, Captain Snowie returning
to 7th Field Ambulance.
Fairly quiet night -

September 1915.
Saturday 18th - Bright day, wind do.
Considerable activity amongst our Artillery
commenced very early - about 5 am - and
continued throughout the day, causing
considerable damage to enemy's positions.
Hostile artillery fire was feeble, and
did practically no damage. Casualties during
the day 3 men wounded.
Battalion relieved by K.O.S.B. during the
evening. Relief carried out in good
order and completed by about 11 pm.
Companies withdrew from positions as
relieved and marched to bivouac at
E.11.a.9.8.
No casualties during relief.

Sunday 19th - Companies and other sub-
units of Battalion arrived in bivouac
between 1 am and 3 am.
Although the march was a long one
and men very tired, all ranks were
very cheerful.
Bright day with rather cold winds.
Battalion at rest all day.
Considerable activity amongst aeroplanes.

Monday 20th - Bright day. Very cold winds after
a cold night.
Companies at training during part of the
day - at rest during remainder.
Shells from hostile Artillery could be

September 1915.   13
Monday 20th continued -
heard passing overhead on to POPERINGHE.
Other heavy shells could be seen
pitching into VLAMERTINGHE.
A party of 50 men, under 2nd Lieut Gates,
detailed as a Special working party,
left bivouac about 6pm by motor bus
and proceeded to village of Kruistraat,
thence by march route to ZILLEBEKE, where
they were employed in constructing a
special "Scotch trench". The work was
completed by about 11.30pm, when party
withdrew and returned to bivouac by
march and 'bus, arriving about 2 a.m.
21st. No casualties.

Tuesday 21st. Very cold night - Bright
day with cold winds -
Company training continued till 1pm.
Special recommendation forwarded today
for C.S.M. Shore to be promoted to a
Commission. This N.C. officer, on 14th
Sept, showed conspicuous conduct on the
occasion when 2nd Lieuts. Lodge and Ventris
were killed. Full particulars were given
in the special report rendered.
Party of 2 officers and 200 men, under
command of Captain Schooling, detailed
to carry out certain work East of YPRES,

September 1915.
Tuesday 21st cont.
 Left bivouac about 5 pm.
 Nothing occurred locally to disturb Battalion's rest.
 New pattern Officers mess cart issued.
 Very bright moonlight night. Rather cold.
Wednesday 22nd. Working party returned to bivouac, in detachments, between 2 am 3 am.
No casualties.
Bright warm day.
Companies bathed at POPERINGHE.
Training continued.
Local situation quiet. Battalion undisturbed.
Bright moonlight night.
Thursday 23rd. Dull muggy day.
Battalion at rest during the day.
Orders received to be prepared to move forward in connection with an intended attack on enemy's position in vicinity of HOOGE.
Commanding Officer and Senior Major reconnoitred the position to be occupied by the Battalion.
Companies moved from bivouac G11a.9.5 about 7.30 pm and marched to H3a, occupying bivouac in vicinity of Chateau, about 10 pm.
Rain commenced as companies moved off and continued until about midnight. This made things generally uncomfortable.

September 1915.   15.

__Friday 24th__ — Very dull showery day.
Battalion at rest until evening.
Considerable activity amongst artillery, both
ours and enemy's, throughout the whole day.
Many shells passed over Battalion bivouac.
Battalion left bivouac about 6.30pm and
marched to position in vicinity of HOOGE,
arriving about 9pm, and at once proceeded
to occupy various trenches allotted, from which
an attack on enemy's position was to be
launched.
Rain had been falling most of the day and
during the evening, but during the night it
was very heavy and this hampered movement
considerably.

__Saturday 25th__ — Bombardment by our guns commenced
at 3.50am, and continued till 4.20am at
which hour the attack on enemy's position by
our Infantry was launched.
The Units on our right and left were 1st Gordon
Highlanders and 2nd Royal Irish Rifles respectively.
A curious coincidence of regiments — English, Irish
and Scotch.
The report of the operations has been made the
subject of a separate communication — being too
long for diary purposes but the following brief
facts must be recorded here.
The two assaulting companies were "A" on

September 1915.
Saturday 25th continued.

right under Captain J.L. Schooling and
'B' on left under Captain F.A. Bayley with
Major J. Beeke in command.

These companies moved forward at once on
completion of the bombardment by our guns,
but it appears that the left company of the
1st London Highlanders had moved off too soon
and finding the barbed wire in their front
to be insufficiently cut, they moved too much
to the left in an endeavour to force a
passage through the wire. This they were
unable to do and consequently as the right of
our right company - A - moved forward, they
were met by some of the London Highlanders,
who had been unable to press forward, and
this led to some confusion.

Our company also found the enemy's wire
uncut and were forced to retire.

Another combined effort by rallied men of
ours and Highlanders, met with no better
success.

Our bombers on this flank did good work
but they were unable to make headway
against enemy machine guns, which in the
half light, were difficult to locate.

Our left company - B - was held up by a
low wire obstacle, a short distance in

September 1915.   17
Saturday 25th C. [contd].
front of enemy's parapet. This [obstacle] came as
a surprise - our men falling over it before
they could see it.
The ground generally was very difficult owing
to being broken up by shell holes and
debris of all kinds.
All the officers and Sergeants of "B" Company
were casualties. 2nd Lieut. Strickland assumed command.
This Company got close up to the enemy parapet
and a few men got through.
Their casualties were 114 all ranks, out of a
total of 170.
The bombers on the left also did good work,
getting quite close to enemy's trenches, but,
being unable to make headway, were forced
to withdraw.
There appears no doubt that the enemy was
well prepared for the assault, as their
rifle fire was opened before our assault
was actually commenced.
The [Battn.] casualties were - other ranks -
Killed 26   wounded 175   missing 45 - Total - 246
In addition the following casualties occurred
amongst officers -
Killed - 2nd Lieut. D. W. Greenwood and 2nd Lieut.
       G. R. A. Case.
Missing - 2nd Lieut. R. Gillespie -

September 1915
Saturday 25th Continued -

Wounded - Major J. Peeke - Captain E. A.
Bagley - and 2nd Lieut. R.E. Spalding and
2nd Lieut. G. Case -
Suffering from shock. 2nd Lieut. H. A. H. Kay -
Throughout the day companies held the
original positions and were subjected to
continuous heavy shell fire -
Rain fell heavily all day, and the situation
generally was most uncomfortable -
During the night the Battalion was relieved
by 1st Wiltshire Regiment.

Sunday 26th - Relief in progress most of the
night, companies withdrawing as relieved -
Heavy rain still continued.
All roads and approaches were heavily
shelled by hostile guns making withdrawal
difficult -
By 6.30 am the last party of the Battalion
reached bivouac at G.11.a.9.8. but owing to
the state of the ground it was found
necessary to accommodate men temporarily
in huts in course of construction about
G.17 and 18 - where they rested until afternoon -
By 2 pm the weather had much improved
and companies moved to original bivouac &
resting for remainder of the day -
Rather cold night -

September 1915.   19

__Monday 27th__ - Mild day with occasional showers.
During the morning the Battalion was
visited by Lieut General E.H.H. Allenby, K.C.B.,
Commanding 5th Corps, who addressed the
men. His remarks were roughly as follows -
"I have come around to see you today and
am pleased to find you looking so cheerful
and well, after your most trying ordeal the
day before yesterday. You stood a heavy
bombardment from dawn to dark.
I congratulate you upon your splendid
conduct in the attack. You were up
against the enemy's wire and heavy fire and
your losses were great. The attack to you
may seem a failure but it was not so.
You attacked and hung on like bull-dogs.
So much so that the enemy could not
detach a single man or gun to reinforce
his line further south. It is you we thank,
and so will the people at home, for your
good work. The position you attacked
kept the enemy engaged and allowed our
1st Corps, and the French, to advance and
occupy positions they had fought for, for
nearly twelve months.
I congratulate you all and wish you very
good luck."
Battalion at rest during the day.

September 1915.

Monday 27th (continued).
2nd Lieut George Richard Kerr joined the Battalion.
2nd Lieut. Roe rejoined from hospital.
Wet dark night.

Tuesday 28th. Dull and rather cold day.
Battalion at rest and refitting.
Local situation quiet.
Heavy rain commenced about 7 pm and continued all night.

Wednesday 29th. Still raining hard.
Bivouac most uncomfortable. Everyone very wet.
Battalion at rest, but detailed as "Battalion on Brigade duty."
Continuous heavy rain.
By night the bivouac was a quagmire.
Rain continued practically all night.

Thursday 30th. Still raining.
Battalion at rest in bivouac.
Rain ceased by about noon.
Fine for a few hours – rain again. Every one most uncomfortable.
Considerable artillery activity could be heard from an Easterly direction. Many aeroplanes about. Both hostile and our own.
Battalion ordered to be prepared to move at ¾ hour notice.

September 1915.
Thursday 30th Continued.

Very wet night.
Following Officers joined the Battalion during the day:-
2nd Lieut. Robert Heal Powell.   } 11th North
    "   Henry William Milnehouse   } Staff. Regt.
    "   Thomas Bevan   3. S. Wam Regt.

The following Officers were present with the Battalion on this date:-
Lieut. Colonel H.J. Cotton.   S. Wam R. Commg. Battn.
Captain   S.T. Boast   ...   Quartermaster.
2nd Lieut.   J.S. Boast   ...   Transport Officer.
    "   W.T. Roscoe   ...   Machine guns
    "   R.M. Bourn   ...   Bombing Officer
Captain   A.B. Chaves. R.A.M.C   Medical Officer.
    "   J.H. Schooling Middx Regt Commg. A Coy
                A.M. Blair   S. Wam. R   C
2nd Lieut.   J.C.T. Strickland   B
    "   A.W. Gates   D
    "   F.K. Holden
    "   F.L. Roe
    "   W.A.L. Crundall
    "   R.H. Powell.   N. Staff. R.
    "   H.W. Milnehouse   "
    "   T. Bevan   S. Wam. R
    "   G.R. Kerr   "

September 1915.
Thursday 30th Continued.
The undermentioned Officers were on leave in
England on this date.
Captain C. P. Whitaker. Dorset Regt
2nd Lieut. C. E. Thompson. S. San. R.

The following Warrant Officers were present
with the battalion -
Class I. R. Sgt. Major T. V. Roberts. no. 4918
  "   I. R. Q. m Sgt. S. Riddock   " 6766
  "   C. Sgt Major [struck out]   [struck out]
  "   "   "   "   A. M. S. Edwards   . 5003 K.
  "   "   "   "   E. Shone   . 4539 C.
  "   "   "   "   A. Aldridge   . 9558 D.

The Total "feeding strength" on this date
was 646.

                    W Cotton.
                          Lt Colonel
              Commdg. 2. S. San Regt

7th Inf.Bde.
3rd Div.

Battn. transferred
with Bde. to 25th
Div. 18.10.15.

Battn. transferred
to 75th Inf.Bde.
25th Div. 26.10.15.

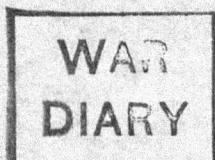

2nd BATTN. THE SOUTH LANCASHIRE REGIMENT.

O C T O B E R

1 9 1 5

- 2nd. Battalion South Lancashire Reg.t -
War diary. 1st to 31st Oct 1915.

Friday 1st Oct. - Dull, very showery, and cold.
Orders received for Battalion to be prepared to
move to trenches this evening.
Commanding Officer and Company Commanders
proceeded to reconnoitre the position to be
occupied.
Battalion left huts at or B11a.9.8 at 5 p.m.
marching via POPERINGHE - VLAMERTINGHE - YPRES
Road to H11a where a halt was made and
tea issued at about 9 p.m.
Battalion moved off about 8 p.m. to positions
about I.23.a.4.29.30 east of ZILLEBEKE, taking
over from 6th South.n Reg.t
Owing the bad state of the ground after the
continuous rain of the past few days the
relief was slow.
Very cold night.
Local situation generally quiet.

Saturday 2nd Oct. - Relief completed by about
1 a.m. when relieved unit withdrew from
position.
By this hour the Battalion was disposed as
under -
A. B. & D. Companies and machine guns in

October 1915.   24

Saturday 2nd Continued.

Fire trenches. "B" Company in reserve.
Casualties during relief. 1 man wounded.
Fine bright sharp day.
Captain A. B. Shiers R. A. M. C. Battalion
Medical Officer proceeding to England on
Special leave. private affairs.
Lieut. W. M. Snodgrass R. A. M. C. assumes duty
as Medical Officer to the Battalion.
No change in disposition of Battalion.
Local situation exceptionally quiet.
One Signaller accidentally wounded.
No other casualties during the day.
Very cold night.

Sunday 3rd. Fine bright day but cold.
No change in general disposition of the
Battalion.
Local Situation fairly quiet.
One man slightly wounded and able to
continue at duty.
Cold and very dark night.

Monday 4th. Very wet morning. Showery during
remainder of the day.
Enemy fired Shrapnel at intervals during
the day over trenches occupied by Battalion.
Otherwise situation fairly quiet.
During the evening "A" Company was
relieved by "B" in fire trenches. Former

October 1915.   25
Monday 4th Continued-
    withdrawing to Reserve.
    Casualties during the day:-
    One man killed.
    ?Lieut. Strickland wounded and sent to
    Field Ambulance.
    2nd Lieut. Morehouse slightly wounded and
    ~~sent to Field Ambulance~~ sent to C.C.S.
    Three other ranks wounded, one of whom
    was able to continue on duty.
    Very dark night.
    2nd Lieut. Holden sent to transport bivouac for
    short rest, having been slightly injured
    in the leg by a "Very" light.
    Considerable activity in progress all
    evening and while of the night in
    line north of YPRES. Much artillery,
    rifle and machine gun fire could be
    heard.
    2nd Lieut. William George Fletcher 11th North
    Staffordshire Regt. joined for duty and
    proceeded to Battalion in the evening.
Tuesday 5th. Dull wet day.
    The following is extracted from the London
    Gazette dated 1. Oct. 1915 :-
    Sec. Lieuts. to be Lieuts.
    J. Boast. 22. Jan. 1915.
    F. A. Holden. 27 Feb. 1915.

26

October 1915.
Tuesday 5th continued –

The undermentioned Officers joined at
Transport bivouac during the evening and
remained there for the night –

2nd Lieut. Ernest Frederick Brooks ⎫
   "   Mark Harold Giles   ⎬ S. San.
   "   Sydney Stevenson Jones   ⎪ Regt.
   "   Charles Grant Withers   ⎭

No change in general disposition of the
Battalion –
Casualties during the day – from 12 noon yesterday –
One man killed –
2nd Lieut. Strickland and two other ranks
wounded –
Local situation fairly quiet. Occasional
shelling by enemy guns –
Very dark cold night –

Wednesday 6th – Close and very muggy day –
No change in general disposition of the
Battalion except that the portion in
reserve was reduced to 2 platoons –
Local situation fairly quiet. Usual
occasional shelling –
Casualties – one man wounded –
2nd Lieut. Jack Gilmour O'Brien, S. San. Regt.
joined at Transport bivouac, and proceeded
during the evening, together with four other
officers, to join the Battalion, moving with

October 1915.   27

Wednesday 6th continued.

Supplies -

Transport moving up this evening was
exposed for some time to hostile shell
fire but fortunately there were no
casualties.

Very dark night.

1 Company 9th Suffolk Regt. and ½ a
Company 9th Norfolk Regt. attached to the
Battalion for instruction in Trench
work etc.

Thursday 7th. Bright day. Inclined to be warm.
2nd Lieut. Seers William Billinson D. San
Regt. reported at Transport bivouac and
proceeded to Battalion in the evening.

Draft of 55 other ranks arrived and
bivouaced with Transport.

400 special waterproof covers for rifles
received through Head Quarters 7th Infantry
Brigade.

No change in disposition of Battalion.
Quiet day except for occasional shelling
by hostile guns, and our own.

Casualties. 2 other ranks killed. 3 wounded.
all by shell fire.

Supplies for units attached, were taken
up with Battalion supplies during the

October 1915.
Thursday 7th Continued.
evening.
Very dark night.
Friday 8th. Dull cold day.
2nd Lieut. Vox arrives at Transport bivouac from trenches to await orders to proceed to machine gun School.
Following officers arrived and remained at Transport bivouac for the night.
2nd Lieut. Percy Easton Cornish.
 — . — Charles Richard Tattam. } S. San. R.
 — . — Oswald Thomas Walton.
No change in general disposition of the Battalion.
Detachments of 2nd Suffolk and 9th Norfolk Regiments relieved by parties of similar strengths from same Battalions.
Considerable activity amongst our own and hostile Artillery continuously during the day and at frequent intervals during the evening and night. Also considerable rifle fire.
Casualties during the day. 1 man killed. 2 others wounded.
During Thursday–Friday night D Company located a working party of the enemy in front of our fire trench. Rifle fire was opened on them and they

October 1915.   89

Friday 8th Continued.
were discussed.
Transport moving up this evening came
under considerable shell fire but there
were no casualties.

Saturday 9th - Very dull day - cold.
2nd Lieut Roe and Bough Parties left
Transport lines this morning for Head
Quarters 3rd Division RENINGHELST whence
they proceed to G.H.Q. for course of
instruction in machine guns.
Disposition of Battalion unchanged.
Considerable artillery activity on our side
most of the day and during the
night.
Three officers who arrived yesterday
proceeded to join the Battalion, moving
with supplies.
Casualties during the day - Nil -
Fairly quiet night.

Sunday 10th - Bright day - Cold wind.
No change in general disposition of Battalion.
Local situation normally quiet.
No casualties.
Considerable activity amongst artillery in sectors
North of that held by Battalion.
During the evening parties of 9th Suffolks
and 9th Norfolks withdrew from the

October 1915.   30.
Sunday 10th Continued.
positions with instructions to proceed to Transport
bivouac.
Between 9 and 10pm several of enemy shells
could be heard passing over Transport
bivouac travelling, apparently, in direction of
POPERINGHE.
Very fine clear, starlight night. Cold.
Draft which arrived on 7th moved forward
to join Battalion this evening. 40 of the
total number were posted to 'B' Company, the
remaining 8 were men discharged from
hospital and rejoined their original Companies -
A 3. B 2. D 3.
Monday 11th. One Company Suffolks arrived at
Transport bivouac about 1.30am. The other about
3.30am. They were made as comfortable as
possible and moved off at 11.45am.
Fine bright day but rather cold.
General disposition of Battalion unchanged.
Much activity in sector occupied by the
Battalion. Continuous bombing, rifle and
artillery fire throughout whole day and most
of the night.
Enemy appeared to be very restless - but our
fire apparently causing him some uneasiness.
Casualties during the day -
2nd Lieut. Gates slightly wounded. but able to

October 1915.   31

Monday 11th Continued.
  Continue at duty.
  Other ranks - one killed, 4 wounded.
  Exceptionally dark night and inclined to
  be wet.

Tuesday 12th - Very misty cold morning.
  Bright later and rather warm.
  Disposition of Battalion unchanged during the
  day.
  Artillery both our own and enemy very
  active but very few shells disturbed the
  Battalion, the majority passing right over
  our sector.
  No casualties during the day.
  After dusk hostile guns pitched a
  large number of shells on to roads and
  approaches to Vermelles.
  Battalion transport moving with supplies
  were exposed to this fire but the only
  casualty was one horse wounded.
  During the night the Battalion was
  relieved by 3rd Worc'ts Regt.
  Relief completed about 11 pm and Battalion
  withdrew.
  One man killed during relief.
  2nd Lieut Gates who was wounded yesterday
  and who remained at duty, was sent to
  Field Ambulance as his wounds were found

32.

October 1915
Tuesday 12th Continued.
to be more serious than they appeared.

Wednesday 13th. Battalion arrived at G11a.9.5.
about 2 am and went into bivouac there.
Still dark night.
Wet morning. Bright afternoon.
Battalion at rest.
Orders received to be prepared to move to
another formation.
A very heavy bombardment West of the
bivouac could be heard all the afternoon
and evening.
About 7 pm enemy shells commenced to
pass over bivouac, bursting in direction of
POPERINGHE. This continued for some hours.
Very dark night.

Thursday 14th. Dull day.
Battalion prepared to move.
Major General A.L. Hobbs, K.C.B. commanding 3rd
Division visited the bivouac about 12 noon,
The Battalion was formed up and the
G.O.C. addressed the men. His remarks
were roughly as follows:-
"I have come here today to wish you all
good bye, at least for a time, and to wish you
all the best of luck. I have been ordered
to send a Brigade from my Division to one
of the new Divisions and have selected the

October 1915.
Thursday 14th continued.

7th for this. You are a Battalion of this Brigade and are seasoned troops. I feel sure it is an excellent arrangement to mix such men as you, with your experience of French warfare, amongst the new troops who are arriving, and I know you will do your best to show them what to do and how to do it. I am sorry to lose you but am satisfied it is for the best. Before you leave I should like to take this opportunity to touch on the works done by the Battalion. Unfortunately there are very few of the original Battalion actually here now but most of you have seen a good deal. When I took over the 3rd Division in November last my predecessor impressed on me the good work done by the Battalion in the early days of the war and he was most anxious that I should see the Battalion as much as possible. For some time you were employed on Special Pioneer work, and as I explained on a former occasion, this work was always faithfully carried out. The Officer Commanding Royal Engineers and other officers of that Corps were strong

October 1915.
Thursday 14th Continued.

in their presence and it was fully
appreciated that when a task was set you
it was always completed up to time. For
some months prior to 25th September last, the
Battalion did not actually take part in
any special engagement but your work
in the trenches has always been well done.
I should like to say a few words regarding
the affair of 25th September, in which you
took part. As is well known now the
real object of the affair was to keep the
enemy occupied and prevent him from
detaching any of his troops or guns further
South where French and British troops were
attacking him. At the same time we hoped
to make some progress in the vicinity of
Hooge. The attack was a "containing" one
and it was quite understood that the task
allotted to the units of 7th Infantry Brigade
was a difficult one. Before the attack by
Infantry was actually commenced it was
thought the enemy's wire to your front
had been demolished, but, as you found out,
this was not so. Owing to the peculiarity
of the ground, observation for artillery fire
was difficult and although you succeeded
in reaching the enemy's wire you were

October 1915.   35
Thursday 14th Continued-
obliged to go back through no fault of
yours. Your work was gallantly carried
out under very trying circumstances and
your heavy losses are most regrettable.
Still the main object was attained and
the general result was very satisfactory.
You are now leaving the famous HOOGE
Salient and perhaps you are not sorry -
I know you will continue to do your work
in your new division as well as you
have done so here and I send you off
with the greatest confidence" -
After further remarks on various matters
the G.O.C. again wished the Battalion very
good luck.
The address was very much appreciated by
all ranks of the Battalion.
Battalion moved from bivouac at 2 pm
and marching via POPERINGHE, to about
L.21.d.5.4. Sheet 27 where they halted and
bivouaced for night.
Very misty and cold.

Friday 15th. Very dull damp day - cold.
Battalion bathed at POPERINGHE.
Otherwise at rest.
Orders received to be prepared to move
by march route tomorrow.
Battalion completed with waterproof rifle covers.

36.

October 1915
Friday 15th Continued.
Lt. Colonel H. T. Cotton proceeded on Special leave to England.
Captain C. P. Whitaker assumed temporary command of the Battalion.
Quiet night.
About 10pm a message was received to the effect that a reinforcement of 100 other ranks had arrived at POPERINGHE Station, where they remained at rest for the night.

Saturday 16th. Dull misty day.
Battalion at rest during the day under orders to move.
Left bivouac at 5.45pm and marching via ABEELE – GODEWAERSVELDE – FLETRE – and STRAZEELE to MERRIS where Battalion arrived about 10pm and occupied billets. The billets were very scattered but everyone had settled down by midnight.
Before leaving bivouac the reinforcement at POPERINGHE Station had joined the Battalion and was posted to companies as under –
A. 35.   B. 36.   C. 15.   D. 14.   = 100

Sunday 17th. Dull and rather cold.
Battalion at rest at MERRIS.
Nothing to record.

October 1915.   37

Sunday 17th continued.
   Captain A. B. Johnson R.A.M.C. rejoined
from leave and Lieut W. M. Snodgrass
R.A.M.C. returned to 143rd F.A.

Monday 18th - Bright day - Rather cold.
   Battalion still at MERRIS.
   Companies at training.
   Very cold night.

Tuesday 19th - Fine day - Cold winds.
   No change in disposition of the Battalion.
   Companies at training.
   Captain Blair reported sick and sent
to No. 12 C.C. Hospital HAZEBROUCK.
   Lieut J. B. Boast assumed command of
C. Company.
   2nd Lieut Bates rejoined from hospital
and assumed command of B Company.
   Cold night.

Wednesday 20th - Bright rather cold day.
   Disposition of Battalion unchanged.
   Training continued.
   Nothing to record.
   Battalion concert this evening.
   Cold night.

Thursday 21st - Bright day - cold.
   Disposition of Battalion unchanged.
   Inspected by Lieut. Gen. Sir C. Fergusson, Bt.
K.C.B, M.V.O, D.S.O. Commanding 2nd Corps.

October 1915.   36
Thursday 21st continued.
The Battalion was formed up in mass
by 10.30 a.m. -
After inspection Sir Charles addressed the
Battalion, his remarks being on the following
lines:-
" It gives me great pleasure today to renew
the acquaintance of the Second Battalion
South Lancashire Regiment - a Battalion
which served in my command in
Ireland a few years ago. At that time
I found it most efficient - well disciplined,
as you are now - always smart and well
turned out - a good shooting Battalion and
one with an excellent reputation.
Since May last you have been away
from the 2nd Corps and I take this
opportunity to welcome you back again -
In Ireland I knew the Battalion well
and I see a few familiar faces amongst
you - but I am afraid there are not
very many present who served with it then -
but it has the same good reputation and
I want to impress on you all the necessity
of living up to that reputation. You are
now on your way to your new
division after a very hard time in the
position you have just left - You will

October 1915
Thursday 21st Continues.

be a battalion of the only Regular Brigade in the Division and with the reputation you hold and the experience you have had of the present war, you will be expected to set the example to the newer units with which you will be associated. These units are very excellent ones — they have done good work and I am proud to have them under my command — but they will copy the example set by you, on the lines that "what Regulars do, we must do". It is this example I wish particularly to refer to now. It is well known that it is the well disciplined and well turned out men who make the best soldiers — all British soldiers can fight, some better than others — but the best are those with the best discipline — a fact which has been proved over and over again —

The trenches you will shortly take over are very good — much better than those you have recently occupied — and the general situation is much quieter — but you must not allow these facts to lessen your vigilance and activity — and remember, it is the duty of us all to kill the enemy — Don't think that because they

October 1915.
Thursday 21st continued.

are quiet you need not worry them. It is only by worrying and killing them that the war will come to an end. Any departure from this only gives the enemy opportunities to worry and damage us. Again, you may find the work of making new trenches and keeping others in repair very uninteresting, but in this you must remember to keep up the reputation you have already gained, of being good workmen. I have heard of the excellent work done by the Battalion in the 3rd Division. I want you to live up to this and I feel sure you will do your best to show a cheerful spirit to the new Battalions with whom you will come in contact. Any man can fight, but every man cannot fight and work. You have the reputation of being able to do both. What you are now is what I want the new troops to be and this will be gained by your good example. I shall see more of you when you are in the trenches and hope to find that you will always keep up the good reputation already earned by the Battalion."

After the inspection and address, companies

October 1915.   41
Thursday 21st Continued.
    marched back to billets and remained at
    rest during the remainder of the day.
    Information received through Head Quarters
    7th Infantry Brigade, that Company
    Sergeant Major C. Shone had been promoted
    to commissioned rank and ordered to join
    2nd Royal Lancaster Reg. in 26th Division.
    Very wet night.
Friday 22nd Oct. - cold little day.
    No change in disposition of Battalion.
    Companies at training part of the day.
    C.S.M. Shone on promotion to commissioned
    rank, left to join his new unit, much
    to the regret of all ranks of the
    Battalion.
    Remarkably clear night - very bright
    moonlight.
Saturday 23rd. Cold day - rather hazy.
    Lieut Colonel H.T. Cotton returned off
    leave and assumed command of the Battalion.
    Captain Whitaker rejoined his company.
    Disposition of Battalion unchanged.
    Battalion at rest. Paper chase organised in which
    Company which Battalion took part. 40 prizes given.
    Very cold night.
Sunday 24th - Dull cold day.
    Battalion disposition unchanged.
    Still at MERRIS.

October 1915.
Sunday 24th Continued.

At 10 am the Battalion paraded for inspection by Major General B.J.C. Doran C.B. Commanding 25th Division.

After the inspection the General addressed the Battalion, roughly as follows -

"I take this opportunity of visiting you, as tomorrow you move on the way to your area and I may not have such a favourable opportunity of speaking to you for some time. It is very cold and I don't want to detain you longer than necessary but I must tell you how pleased I am to know that the 2nd South Lancashire Regiment is joining my command, as I know what a good reputation you hold. I look on you as old friends as I often came into contact with the Battalion when I commanded the 8th Brigade - you being at that time in the 7th. You will shortly join the 75th Brigade and the other Battalions of that Brigade are looking forward to your joining them - You go to them with an excellent reputation and I want you to keep this up and help the newer Battalions by setting them the good example which you are well able to do - You will find the other Battalions of your

October 1915.
Sunday 24th Continued.

43

new Brigades, very good ones and I feel sure
it is a good thing to mix seasoned
troops, as you are, with the less experienced
ones. I shall see more of you later and
feel sure you will do well."

After the parade companies marched to billets
and remained at rest during remainder of
the day.

2nd Lieut. Cater reported sick and sent to hospital.
Wet evening. Fine later.

Orders received for Battalion to be prepared
to move to BAILLEUL tomorrow.

Rain commenced about 6pm. and continued
heavily all night.

Monday 25th. Still raining heavily.

Battalion marched from MERRIS at 9 am
arriving at BAILLEUL about 10.30 am and
occupied billets there.

Everyone very wet and uncomfortable.

Companies bathed at BAILLEUL.

Orders received for Battalion to be
prepared to move to PLOEGSTEERT and join
25th Infantry Brigade.

Billeting parties moved to new area at
1.15 pm.

Very heavy rain still continued.

Battalion at rest at BAILLEUL.

October 1915.
Monday 25th Continued -

2nd Lieut. Roe returned from machine gun course.
Captain Blair and 2nd Lieut. Roscoe proceeded to England on leave - first named officer from Hospital at HAZEBROUCK.
2nd Lieut. Roe assumes temporary charge of Battalion machine guns vice 2nd Lieut. Roscoe.
2nd Lieut. Giles proceeded to Bombing School at TERDEGAN for instruction.

Tuesday 26th - Fine day, but very cold.
Battalion left BAILLEUL at 6 am. arriving at PLOEGSTEERT about 9 am. and occupied billets there, relieving 17th Cheshire Regiment, being disposed as follows:-

Battn. Head Qrs. - Hospice PLOEGSTEERT	C.1.b.0.7.	Sheet 36
A Company - SOYER FARM.	06.b.5.5.	" 36
B " - DELINELLE FARM.	C.1.d.3.2.	" 36
C " - MAISON 1875 FARM.	C.2.a.5.5.	" 36
D " - ROUDEE FARM	U25.c.5.5.	" 28
Transport - In house near ROMARIN.	R.d.10.9.	" 36

Local situation quiet.
2nd Lieut. Garnish proceeded to Divisional Bombing School at NIEPPE for instruction.
Very wet night.

Wednesday 27th - Still raining hard. Very cold.
General disposition of Battalion unchanged.
2 officers and 100 other ranks from "A" and "B"

October 1915.   45

Wednesday 27th Continued -
  Companies employed in improving trenches.
  Lieuts. J.D. Boast and F.A. Holden and 70 other
  ranks proceeded by march route to BAILLEUL at
  9.30am to represent the Battalion in connection
  with the visit to that place of His Majesty the
  King.
  After taking part in a ceremonial parade the
  detachment returned to billets at PLOEGSTEERT.
  Very wet day.
  Local Situation quiet.
  Very quiet night.

Thursday 28th - Very wet day.
  General disposition of Battalion unchanged.
  2 Officers and 100 other ranks from 'C' and 'F'
  Companies employed in repairing and improving
  trenches.
  Orders received for Battalion to be prepared to
  move into trenches tomorrow.
  Local Situation quiet.
  Heavy rain continued all day and night.

Friday 29th - Very dull day. No rain but the
  roads and country generally in a very bad
  state after several days continuous rain.
  Battalion moved from billets to right Sector
  of line allotted to 75th Infantry Brigade, under
  the following arrangement. Starting point being
  MAISON 1875, where guides were to be found.

October 1915
Friday 29th continued —

	Company	Leave starting point	Trenches to take over
Firing line	C.	3 pm	101 to 104
	A.	3.15 pm	105 to 108
	D.	3.30 pm	109 to 112
Support	B	3.45 pm	LANCASHIRE FARM

Battalion Head quarters — Lawrence Farm.
Machine guns — In fire trenches.
Relief completed by about 5 pm.
Casualties during relief — nil.
The relieved Battalion — 8th Border Regiment — withdrew from the position and occupied the billets vacated by the Battalion.
Supplies were taken forward, after dusk, to MAISON 1875, where they were placed on trucks and conveyed to companies etc by means of a light tramway.
Situation very quiet —

Saturday 30th. Fairly bright day — Roads etc much improved.
No change in disposition of the Battalion.
Local situation quiet —
Casualties during the day — one man wounded.
Captain Frank Newstead Powell, 3rd S. San. Regt. joined the Battalion this morning —
A reinforcement of 40 other ranks arrived this evening and remained at transport bivouac for the night —

47

October 1915.
Saturday 30th continued.
  Quiet night.
  The following is extracted from the London
Gazette of 26th Oct. 1915.
  Prince of Wales's Vols. (South Lancashire Regt.)
Temp. Sec. Lieuts to be Temp. Lieuts -
  R.L. Thompson June 10, 1915.
  W. Roscoe   June 16, 1915.
Sunday 31st. — Very cold wet day.
  The following is extracted from a list of
awards made by the King, issued on 29th
Oct. 1915 —
        — Military Cross —
His Majesty the King has been graciously pleased
to confer the Military Cross on the undermentioned
officers, in recognition of their gallantry and
devotion to duty in the field —
Sec. Lieut. Alfred William Gates 3rd Battn. the
Prince of Wales's Volunteers (South Lancashire
Regt.) attchd. 2nd Battn. —
For conspicuous gallantry on the morning of Sept. 25,
1915, near Hooge. He advanced twice to the assault
with a party of bombers but was compelled to
retire owing to casualties. On the second occasion
he reached the enemy's wire entanglement, which
he personally endeavoured to cut under heavy
shell and rifle fire —
  Disposition of Battalion unchanged —

October 1915.
Sunday 31st Continued.

Local situation fairly quiet.
Casualties during the day - Nil.
About 2 pm enemy exploded a small mine
on right of trenches held by "B" Company -
practically no damage done to our trenches.
Those on our right, occupied by 8th North
Lancashire Regiment, were slightly damaged.
Continuous rains inclined to cause sides of
trenches to "cave in".
Reinforcement which arrived last night
moved forward to Battalion this evening
and were posted to companies as under -
A. 6 - B. 12 - C. 19 - D. 3 - = 40 -
2nd Lieut. Giles rejoined from Bombing Course.
Very wet night.

The following Officers were present with the
Battalion on this date -

Lieut Colonel	H.T. Cotton. S. Lan R	Commanding Battn.
Captain	S.T. Boast	Quartermaster.
Lieut	C.E. Thompson	Acting Adjutant.
2nd Lieut.	K. M. Bourne	I/c Bombers.
"	F. L. Roe	I/c Machine Guns
"	Lt. A. L. Poundall	I/c Snipers
Captain	A. B. Chevers R.A.M.C.	Medical Officer
"	J. H. Schooling Middx Regt	Commdg. "A" Coy
2nd Lieut	S. S. Jones. S. Lan R	"B"

October 1916.
Sunday 31st Continued -

Lieut J. D. Boot   S. Lan. R.   coming to camp
Captain L. P. Whitaker   Dorset R.   ..
    ..   F. M. Powell   S. Lan. R.
Lieut   F. A. Holden   ..
         K. K. Powell   N. Staff. R.
2nd ..   T. Bacon   S. Lan. R.
  .. .. G. R. Kew   ..
  .. .. G. F. Burtt   ..
  .. .. M. H. Giles   ..
  .. .. L. G. Withers   ..
  .. .. J. G. O'Brien   ..
  .. .. L. W. Collinson   ..
  .. .. P. G. Cornish   ..
  .. .. G. R. Tattam   ..
  .. .. O. T. Walton   ..
  .. .. W. G. Fletcher   N. Staff. R.

The following Officers on the strength of the
Battalion were absent for reasons stated -
    Captain A. M. Blair - on leave in England
    Lieut.   W. Roscoe.
    2nd ..   A. W. Gates. In hospital
The following warrant Officers were present -
Class I. No. 4918 Reg. Sgt. Major T. J. Roberts.
  .. I. . 6766   Q.M.Sgt.   J. Reddock
  .. II. . 9558 C.Sgt.Major A. Aldridge - D. Coy
Acting C.Sgt.Majors T. Ross 'A' Coy - A. M. G. Edwards 'B' Coy.
and E. Nicholson 'C' Coy. Total feeding strength - 759 -
                        H. J. Cotton Lt. Colonel.
         Commanding 2. S. Lancashire Reg -

3RD DIVISION
7TH INFY BDE

4TH BATTALION
STH LANCASHIRE REGT.
FEB - SEP 1915.

FROM UK

7th Inf.Bde.
3rd Div.

Battn. disembarked
Havre from England
13.2.15.

Battn. joined Bde.
24.2.15.

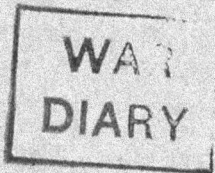

4th BATTN. THE SOUTH LANCASHIRE REGIMENT.

F E B R U A R Y

(10.2.15 — 28.2.15)

1 9 1 5

Army Form C. 2118.

WAR DIARY
or
INTELLIGENCE SUMMARY.   4th Bn. SOUTH LANCASHIRE REGT.
(Erase heading not required.)

Instructions regarding War Diaries and Intelligence
Summaries are contained in F.S. Regs., Part II.
and the Staff Manual respectively. Title pages
will be prepared in manuscript.

Hour, Date, Place		Summary of Events and Information	Remarks and references to Appendices
TUN BRIDGEWELLS	10th February	Instructions recd from G.O.C. S. LAN. BDE that 4. S. LAN. R would proceed abroad on 12th inst	
"	12th		
LA HAVRE	13th 5.30pm	4 S LAN R proceeded by train to SOUTHAMPTON & Embarked on SS QUEEN ALEXANDRA & SS TRAFFORD HALL	
"	" 7.30am	The Battn Sailed en route for HAVRE	
"	14th 4.30pm	The BATTN arrived at HAVRE	
BAILLEUL	15th 8pm	The Battn left HAVRE by special trains & proceeded to No 2 Rest Camp	
"	"	Ranks proceeding to ROUEN as 1st Reinforcement	10 officers + 420 O.R.
"	19th 10am	The Battn reached BAILLEUL	
LA CLYTTE	21st 10am	Half Battalion under Major G.R. Crosfield proceeded by march route to GRAPPERIES & LA CLYTTE	
"	"	Battalion Head Quarters arriving & Bn proceeded to LA CLYTTE	A 1/20 pm
"	23rd	Billets in huts	
LOCRE	25th	Received orders from 148 & 7 Inf Bde to proceed to LOCRE on 26th inst.	
"	26th 9.30am	The Battalion proceeded by march route to LOCRE	
"	" 6pm	"A" & "B" Companies marched to KEMMEL & occupied billets	
"	27th	" 4, 5 & 7 Coys G2 and S2 trenches	
"	28th	Casualties in trenches 2 other ranks	
		Casualties in trenches 1 other rank killed 3 other ranks wounded	

7th Inf.Bde.
3rd Div.

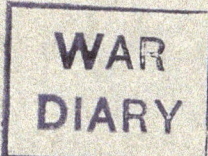

4th BATTN. THE SOUTH LANCASHIRE REGIMENT.

M A R C H

1 9 1 5

Army Form C. 2118.

WAR DIARY
or
INTELLIGENCE SUMMARY.
(Erase heading not required.)

4th South Lancs.

Instructions regarding War Diaries and Intelligence Summaries are contained in F. S. Regs., Part II. and the Staff Manual respectively. Title pages will be prepared in manuscript.

Hour, Date, Place		Summary of Events and Information	Remarks and references to Appendices
LOCRE. March 1st 1915		Casualties in week. 10 other ranks wounded	
"	3rd	" 1 other rank killed, 1 other rank wounded	
"	4th	" 2 other ranks wounded	
"	5th	11.30a	A & B Companies rejoined Headquarters at LUCRE.	
"		6 p.	A digging party 600 strong proceeded to a point about 2 miles N of WULFERGHEN for trench digging. Completing 500 yards of support trench. Casualties 3 other ranks wounded.	
"	7th		Reported from 7th F.A. AMBCE 2 men died of wounds.	
"	10th		Working party 600 R. & D. proceeded to a point in rear of ST Roland for purpose of digging supporting trenches, about 700 yards of trench was completed. 1 other rank killed, 2 died of wounds, 2 wounded. Prety relieved	
"		at 3.20 am 11th inst		
	N⁰. 5 usq.		Fatigue party proceeded to KEMMEL for purpose of carrying stores to fire trenches in E section. 1 other rank died of wounds.	
"	14th		Battn. orders ordered to KEMMEL to take on following orders of trenches. T 5, 6, G 1, 2, 3.	
"	15th		Battn. formed part of Army Reserve ready to move at 1 hrs notice.	
"	16th 6.30p		Battn. proceeded to KEMMEL to take over trenches of trenches as ordered	

Army Form C. 2118.

WAR DIARY
or
INTELLIGENCE SUMMARY.
(Erase heading not required.)

Instructions regarding War Diaries and Intelligence Summaries are contained in F.S. Regs., Part II. and the Staff Manual respectively. Title pages will be prepared in manuscript.

Hour, Date, Place	Summary of Events and Information	Remarks and references to Appendices
KEMMEL. 16th March 1915	Trenches G1,2,3 taken over from 2nd Bn THE BUFFS. Casualties nil.	
" 17th	Trenches F5, 6. Taken over from H.A.C. Casualties nil. Batt. Headquarters THE DOCTORS HOUSE KEMMEL	W
	Trenches F5, F6, G1,2, Exchanged over to 2nd Bn S LAN R.	
" 18th	Trenches F2,3,4, & F5, F6, G1, G2, Taken over from WILTS RGT. Casualties during 17th 2 O.R. killed. 8. O.R. wounded. Enemy shelled trenches F4. 5 in morning in afternoon no damage.	W
" 19th	Held trenches F2,3,4, & F5, F6, G1, G2 day & night. Weather fine. Casualties nil.	W
	Trenches quiet during the day. At night wire landed over on our front. F3 handed over to NORTHUMBERLAND FUS. F3, 4 & F5, F6, S2 handed over to 2ND CHESHIRE REGT. The Battalion then bivuacd Ravensyde to LA CLYTTE. Casualties OR. 1. wounded.	W
LA CLYTTE. 20th	The Battalion moved to LOCRE.	W
LOCRE. 23rd	The Battalion moved to WESTOUTRE.	W
WESTOUTRE 24th 10 PM	The Battalion marched to DICKEBUSCH. 15 officers visited trenches N5,6,10,01-5. Casualties CAPT H G ROBERTS. wounded	W

Army Form C. 2118.

WAR DIARY
or
INTELLIGENCE SUMMARY.

(Erase heading not required.)

Instructions regarding War Diaries and Intelligence Summaries are contained in F.S. Regs., Part II. and the Staff Manual respectively. Title pages will be prepared in manuscript.

Hour, Date, Place	Summary of Events and Information	Remarks and references to Appendices
DICKEBUSCH 26th March 1918 6 a.m.	The Bgd.m moved out and occupied trenches N5 a, b, c, d. c, O, P, Q, R, d, S was in Coull 36 MSG2 in rear Barracks at exit roads N6 a. Battalion in progress from 1000 hrs. 307 men in trenches worth 3rd left Trench. Headquarters Bent. Cos. per instr. Can copy. Casualties wounded 5th World R.O.	
27	The Bn. Remained in the Support Position. Casualties. O.R. Brown, was told round moved at 3.45 a.m. Died of wounds 6.30 p.m. wounded O.R Smith G 4 Pte Y (Probationer Lt P. K. Samuels)	
28	Trenches. Wounded O.R Smith G 4 Pte four (Reported Wounded & Miss on Mch 20 (Lieut R.W.A. Harden) Casualties Wounded O.R 4	
29	Trenches. Support Mr. 169 3 N.C.O. and Runnery Killed O.R. 2 wounded on 1.30 am 3 N.C.O.	
30th	The Bn. Remained in the Sgr. Sec. Casualties. Wounded O.R. 2	
31	Trenches. Occupied Gd. 3 6.5 Soft B trenches N.35. Wds and was withdrawn to B has slept Casualties. Wounded O.R. 2. Pat 1 man 2nd infantry	

7th Inf.Bde.
3rd Div.

WAR DIARY

4th BATTN. THE SOUTH LANCASHIRE REGIMENT.

A P R I L

1 9 1 5

Army Form C. 2118.

WAR DIARY
or
INTELLIGENCE SUMMARY.
(Erase heading not required.)

4. S. LAN. R.

Instructions regarding War Diaries and Intelligence Summaries are contained in F.S. Regs., Part II. and the Staff Manual respectively. Title pages will be prepared in manuscript.

Hour, Date, Place	Summary of Events and Information	Remarks and references to Appendices
DICKEBUSCH April 1st 1915	The Batt. held the following trenches Nos 5, 6, 10, 10A, O1, O2, O3, 2, F, & Redoubt S6. Batt. H.Q. BRASSERIE at cross Rds at cross Roads N½ of MILLEKRIUSE – KEMMEL & YPRES – KEMMEL Road	
8 am	Weather fine and warm. Quiet day.	
10.30 p.m.	Relief from 2nd Bn. S Lan R arrived to take over the trenches. The relief was completed at 2 am. The Batt. returned to DICKEBUSCH and occupied billets on DICKEBUSCH – LA CLYTTE Road.	H.J.
" 2nd	Weather fine. Quiet.	
7.30 p.m.	Digging party 300 men marched to BRASSERIE for working & communication trenches between BRASSERIE – DEAD DOG FARM – Casualties Nil	H.J.
" 3rd	Weather fine. Quiet. Digging party 200 men proceeded to vicinity Bois Confluent to complete erection of communication trench leading into that wood. Casualties nil.	H.J.
" 4th	Weather fine. Day quiet. Casualties nil.	H.J.
" 5th	Weather fine & colder, enemy shelled vicinity of Billets occupied by D. Company. Casualties nil.	H.J.
" 6th	Working party 300 continued trench DICKEBUSCH – KEMMEL Road in vicinity of farm BRAMERS – Bus Confluent	H.J.
" 7th	Weather showery weather cold – Enemy sent 4 or 6" shells in vicinity of farm billets occupied by C. Company. Casualties nil. 1 shell entered village in which Officers & Company Billets in Casualties 1 man killed, 1 wounded. The Batt. moved out & occupied the following trench No 6, No 10 on 10a, 01, 02, O3 O4 P. HQs returned to BRASSERIE Casualties 3 other ranks wounded.	H.J.

Army Form C. 2118.

WAR DIARY
or
INTELLIGENCE SUMMARY.
(Erase heading not required.)

4 S LAN R

Hour, Date, Place	Summary of Events and Information	Remarks and references to Appendices
TRENCHES DICKEBUSCH. APRIL 8th 1915	Weather fine & warm. Day quiet & normal (A. HOLDEN. Very slightly wounded in foot.), 1 other ranks killed	HWV
" " 9th	Weather fine & warm. Day quiet & normal Casualties 1 other ranks wounded	HWV
" " 10th	Bright fine weather. Day quiet & normal. Enemy shelling vicinity of BRIELEN in evening. Casualties 1 other ranks 1 killed 1 wounded	HWV
" " 11th	Weather fine & warm. Day quiet & normal Casualties. Other ranks 2 wounded	HWV
" " 12th	Bright fine weather. Day quiet. Zeppelin reported crossing our lines at 8.20 pm Casualties. Other ranks. 1 killed 1 wounded	HWV
" " 13th	[Battn. relieved at night] clear night. The Battn. has returned at 9 p.m. by a C./LAN.R. & moved to Billet at vicinity of BRIELEN	HWV
DICKEBUSCH " 14th	Weather fine & warm. Casualties. Other ranks 2	HWV
" " 15th & 16th	Heavy rifle & artillery fire coming from vicinity of ST ELOI. Enemy shelled road S. of DICKEBUSCH throughout day & night. Men in dug-outs partly behind Winches. Casualties Other ranks 2 wounded	HWV
" " 17th	Weather fine. day quiet. no casualties.	HWV
" " 18th & 19th	" " Very heavy rifle fire in N during day & night (flares). Casualties nil	HWV
" " 19th/20th	Enemy shelled vicinity of Bn HQrs. and afternoon & evening. One killed-struck by shell. Casualties from little fire Other ranks. wounded 2	HWV
7.30 pm	The Battn. moved out to the Winches & took over trenches from 2. S/LAN R. N6, N10, D1, 2, 3 & N5 A.S.P. No further Casualties.	HWV

Forms/C. 2118/10

Army Form C. 2118.

WAR DIARY
or
INTELLIGENCE SUMMARY.
(Erase heading not required.)

4 S L a n R

Instructions regarding War Diaries and Intelligence Summaries are contained in F.S. Regs., Part II. and the Staff Manual respectively. Title pages will be prepared in manuscript.

Hour, Date, Place	Summary of Events and Information	Remarks and references to Appendices
Trenches DICKEBUSCH April 20th 1915	Weather fine, cold. Day normal. Heavy rifle fire from trenches opposite to our casualties. Other ranks wounded 1.	W/
" " 21st	Weather colder, fine. Bayonets. Enemy fired 2 shells, wounding 1/Batt'n HQrs wounding our man. Casualties Other ranks killed 1. wounded 2.	W/
" " 22nd	Weather fine, warm. Bayonets. Casualty Lt A HATTON wounded in thigh.	W/
" " 23rd	Weather warm & cool. Bayonets - casualties nil	W/
" " 24th	Weather fine, warm. Very heavy rifle fire from N.W. Enemy shelled one of the trenches occupied by the Batt'n, destroying it. It was rebuilt during night. Casualties Other ranks wounded 3.	W/
" " 25th	Weather fine & warm. Bayonet. At 8.30 p.m the Batt'n was relieved by 2 S.L.an R and returned to DICKEBUSCH	W/
DICKEBUSCH " 26th	Day quiet. Some few enemy fire. Enemy fired about 10 heavy shells over our village wounding 2. Digging party of 300 men in trenches of VORMEZELE. Casualties wounded other ranks 3. (1 died of wounds)	W/
" " 27th	Day fine & warm. Enemy fired a few light shrapnel over the village at 1.30 p.m. The German aero fire about 20 rounds of shrapnel ammunition passing still no damage. Magazine blowing about 5.30 p.m damaging a few buildings. Casualties from shelling other ranks 1 killed & wounded. (1 other since died.) Digging party 300 men near ELZENWALLE.	W/
" " 28th	Day fine & warm. Digging parties 250 men in rear of 2 S Lan R trenches. Casualties other ranks wounded 6.	W/

Forms/C. 2118/10

Army Form C. 2118.

WAR DIARY
or
INTELLIGENCE SUMMARY.
(Erase heading not required.)

4 S LAN R

Hour, Date, Place	Summary of Events and Information	Remarks and references to Appendices
DICKEBOSCH April 29th	Day fine & warm. Quiet comparatively. Few trees hit. no village or church at night	
" 30th	weather fine & warm. day quiet. working party & 2D two pm filling in trenches at VIERSTRAAT at 9 pm. Casualties	
	(see month N.S.W.1/4 L	

7th Inf. Bde.
3rd Div.

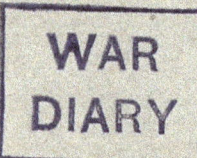

4th BATTN. THE SOUTH LANCASHIRE REGIMENT.

M A Y

1915

Army Form C. 2118.

WAR DIARY
or
INTELLIGENCE SUMMARY.
(Erase heading not required.)

4. S. Law R.

Instructions regarding War Diaries and Intelligence Summaries are contained in F.S. Regs., Part II. and the Staff Manual respectively. Title pages will be prepared in manuscript.

Hour, Date, Place	Summary of Events and Information	Remarks and references to Appendices
ETZENWALLE May 14th 1915	Weather hot. day quiet. Casualties Other ranks. wounded 1	Nil
" 15th	Weather fine, day quiet. Trench P1 was handed over to 1/5 A.A.C. and No 6 to WORCESTER REGT.	Nil
DICKEBUSCH " 16	Bn. N.S. proceed half East relieved 1/2 DCRF BATTN. No 4/6/ Bn remained in trenches No 2 and 01-5.	Nil
" 17th	Nearly / village shelled at 1 Am & 10 W. pm, billets damaged. Casualties other ranks killed 2. wounded 3.	Nil
" 18th	Weather hot. day quiet. Enemy shelled nearby / village at 11 p.m damaging billets & injuring 3 inhabitants. P.H. Casualties other ranks killed 1, wounded 1.	Nil
" 19th	Weather wet. day quiet. Casualties nil.	Nil
" 20th	" " Casualties other rank wounded 2.	Nil
" 21st	Weather fine. day quiet. Casualties other ranks. killed 1, wounded 6.	Nil
" 22nd	Weather fine. Even day quiet. Casualties other ranks. 1 killed 1 wounded.	Nil
" 23rd	" " "	Nil
" 24th	Weather fine rather warm, day quiet. Casualties nil.	Nil
" 25th	" " " " Other ranks wounded 1.	Nil
" 26th	" " Army pro clams press no in battle No 3rd Bean coming from another N.E of YPRES. Casualties nil.	Nil
" 27th	day fair. Casualties other ranks wounded 1. nil. nil	Nil

Army Form C. 2118.

WAR DIARY
or
INTELLIGENCE SUMMARY.
(Erase heading not required.)

4 S[outh] Lan[cashire] R[egiment]

Instructions regarding War Diaries and Intelligence Summaries are contained in F. S. Regs., Part II. and the Staff Manual respectively. Title pages will be prepared in manuscript.

Hour, Date, Place	Summary of Events and Information	Remarks and references to Appendices
DICKEBUSCH 28th Mar 1915	Weather fine & clear, day quiet. Casualties Nil	
" 29th "	Weather fine & warm, day quiet. Casualties Rifle route killed 1, wound 1	
" 30th "	" " " " " Oth ranks wound 2	
" 31 "	" " " " " killed 1	
	(26th - 31st 2 Cpl Butterworth 2 Coy killed)	Cas 144 - 3 [off], K.2, W.20

(9 29 6) W 4141—463 100,000 9/14 H W V Forms/C. 2118/10

7th Inf.Bde.
3rd Div.

```
┌──────┐
│ WAR  │
│DIARY │
└──────┘
```

4th BATTN. THE SOUTH LANCASHIRE REGIMENT.

J U N E

1 9 1 5

Army Form C. 2118.

WAR DIARY
or
INTELLIGENCE SUMMARY.
(Erase heading not required.)

4th Bn North Lancashire Regt.

Hour, Date, Place	Summary of Events and Information	Remarks and references to Appendices
DICKEBUSCH. June 18t & 2nd 1915	Two Companies in Huts in DICKEBUSCH, 2 Companies in Bivouac near VORMEZEELE	
3rd	The Bn moved at 5pm to (Bivouac near) KLAMERTINGHE. Ordered in to relieve	
	2nd LIFE GUARDS and 3 HUSSARS in	
4th at HOOGE	Surry Regt. & Buffs. Casualties nil	
	The Bn marched to YPRES to SANCTUARY WOOD relieving 2nd LIFE GUARDS and 3 HUSSARS in	
	trenches on south edge of HOOGE	
5th	Casualties Other ranks killed in movement up 4 A.?	
	B in trenches in SANCTUARY WOOD - Shelter Wood	
6th	Casualties Other ranks. Killed 1 Wounded 4	
7th	Shelter Wood. Casualties Other ranks killed 2. Wounded 2	
8th	Officer killed 1 (Lieut HOLDEN)	
	Other ranks killed 1 Wounded 2.	
9th	Casualties Other ranks, killed 1 wounded 1	
10th	Heavy rain during day	
11th	The Bn was relieved at 1pm by 5th & 6th NORTHUMBERLAND FUS, 4th Bn relieved 6	
	Bivouac 2.6 I PRIEST FARM. Sht 28 Sq G 17 D Casualties other ranks wounded 1	
BUSSEBOOM 12th–14th	The Bn proceeded at 7pm to Junction of YPRES-POPERINGHE Railway Wood East	
15th	Sht 28 Sq I 11 34.	
16th	The Batts took part in the operations to take HOOGE The Bn as part of 9 7th BDE ordered	
	in supporting troops to 9th (?) BDE who were attacking enemys trenches nr HOOGE	
	& Railway line. The attack commenced at 3.50am by artillery but at 5.20am advanced	
	1st & 9th BDE advanced to attack, the 7th BDE moving up to take up new advanced	
	trenches successfully held by 7 BDE. Very heavy the enemy's guns opened on our	
	supporting trenches. The assault by Royal Scotts Batt'n succeeds, waited for a time	
	under [illegible] heavy fire [illegible] but in the evening the 6th Corp ready to advance	
	trenches occupied later on in evening & wash party of the Bn was brought up to	
	support a second attack to the North of YPRES-Zonn Rd. These it was thought safe to	
	Practically no casualties were caused by shell fire. The Bn was relieved at about midnight	
	& developed to Bivouac Sq G 17 D	

Forms/C. 2118/10

WAR DIARY or INTELLIGENCE SUMMARY

Army Form C. 2118.

4. S. LAN. R.

Hour, Date, Place	Summary of Events and Information	Remarks and references to Appendices
N of HOOGE. June 16 (Cont)	Casualties. Officers - Killed 1 (Lieut S. L. Frost) Wounded 9 CAPTS ABLNYTON, SGTN THIRLOUGH, A SKINNER, & C H ROBERTSON, LIEUTS DICKSON, 2nd/LIEUTS QUINT, TRUTH, HERCHORN, ANSTIE.	
Busseboom " 17 - 20th	Other ranks killed 29 wounded 208 missing 11. Bn. remained in Bivouac refitting & refilling. Casualties Nil	
" 21st	Bn. marched at 7 PM to YPRES and was accommodated in ramparts. Casualties Nil	
YPRES " 22nd	Bn in Ramparts. Bombs arrived and 3 bombers of pr Bn to HOOGE to assist.	
" 23rd	Bn in Ramparts & Lewis Sergeant Casualties O.R. wounded 1. Casualties. Other ranks wounded 3	
" 24th	The Remainder of Bn moved to & relieved 7th R Scouts) in HOOGE defences with supporting troops in ZOUAVE WOOD. Casualties Nil	
HOOGE " 25th	Trenches at HOOGE. Quiet day not shelled much. Casualties O.R. wounded 1	
" 26th	HOOGE DEFENCES. Enemy's artillery very active. Shelling front line & ZOUAVE WD. supports in YPRES. Casualties O.R. wounded 3	
" 27th	HOOGE DEFENCES. Enemy fired minnewerpers & bombs. Killed 3 - Buried day. Our artillery retaliation Casualties O.R. Killed 3 wounded 1	
" 28th	Our R. Regt to WILTS Regt took our trenches and the Bn marched back to Bivouac about 1 mile N of YPRES (Route to MAP D 20115). Casualties Nil	
" 29-30th	Bn in Bivouac N of YPRES Route to Q YPRES. Weather fine & warm. Church Parade. Casualties Nil.	

Forms/C. 2118/10

7th Inf.Bde.
3rd Div.

WAR DIARY

4th BATTN. THE SOUTH LANCASHIRE REGIMENT.

J U L Y

1 9 1 5

Army Form C. 2118.

WAR DIARY
or
INTELLIGENCE SUMMARY.
(Erase heading not required.)

Instructions regarding War Diaries and Intelligence Summaries are contained in F. S. Regs., Part II. and the Staff Manual respectively. Title pages will be prepared in manuscript.

4th Bn. E. Lancashire Regt.

Hour, Date, Place	Summary of Events and Information	Remarks and references to Appendices
N.TH YPRES. 13 July 1915	[illegible handwritten entries]	
YPRES		
" 2ⁿᵈ "		
" 3ʳᵈ "		
" 4ᵗʰ "		
Ed. BOESINGHE		
" 5ᵗʰ "		
SANCTUARY WOOD 6.7	1 Coy provided 2 sentries & 4 Hoggs. Casualties nil	
" 8ᵗʰ "		
" 9ᵗʰ "		
" 10ᵗʰ "		
" 11ᵗʰ "		
" 12ᵗʰ "		
E.N RANGEMARK 13ᵗʰ		
" 14ᵗʰ "		
" 15ᵗʰ "		
" 16ᵗʰ "		
" 17ᵗʰ "		
" 18ᵗʰ "	Construction of trenches at Suffolk Farm	
" 19ᵗʰ "	A & B Coy rigging C & D Church Parade	
" 20ᵗʰ "	Battalion	

WAR DIARY
or
INTELLIGENCE SUMMARY.
(Erase heading not required.)

Army Form C. 2118.

4th South Lancs Regt

Hour, Date, Place		Summary of Events and Information	Remarks and references to Appendices
E. of BUSSEBOOM	21st	Bn in rest- Bay guard- Digging at supporting point H15E	AAA
"	22nd	Battalion furnished Promulgation Party & Firing Party for execution of 12295Pte F.Hughes 3rd Mounted Regt- 2 days desertion.	AAA
"	23	Digging at supporting point H15 & H16E	AAA
"	"	" " " "	AAA
"	"	Appointed "Pioneer" Battalion for 3rd Div under C.R.E 3rd Div for Discipline & administration.	AAA
"	24	Digging at supporting point H15 & H16E	AAA
"	25	" " " "	AAA
"	26	" " " "	AAA
"	27	" " " "	AAA
"	28	" " " "	AAA
"	29	A + C Coys proceed to H29b. B + D digging at supporting point. Total of 20 hours on from 6pm Coys at 6pm man pace	AAA
"	30	B + D Digging at supporting point. A+C digging by night. At Advanced trenches.	AAA
"	31	Casualties from 13th to 31st "NUL"	AAA

7th Inf.Bde.
3rd Div.

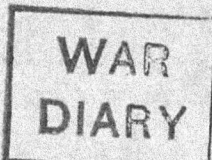

4th BATTN. THE SOUTH LANCASHIRE REGIMENT.

A U G U S T

1 9 1 5

Army Form C. 2118.

WAR DIARY
or
INTELLIGENCE SUMMARY.
(Erase heading not required.)

4th South Lancs Regt

Hour, Date, Place	Summary of Events and Information	Remarks and references to Appendices
E of BUSSEBOOM 1-8.15	Weather fine & warm. A & C in BIVOUAC at H.29. B & D digging at supporting point H.15.E. No casualties.	
" 2.8.15	" Battalion allotted New Billets in H.29 & 6.2 & 9. 5'6. Old Billet H.11. cleared by 9.20 A.M.	
N of DICKEBUSCHE "	" A & C in BIVOUAC H.29.6. D Coy at work on Communication trench. D Coy ordered to R.3. Fire trench with 2nd South Lancs Regt to Rebuild parapet destroyed by enemy shellfire. Casualty 1 O.R. Killed. Day quiet.	O.R.1
N of DICKEBUSCHE 3/8/15	Weather showery. A & C in BIVOUAC H.29.6. Day rest. work on R.3. trench during night & digging New trench in rear of fire trench. D Coy digging H.16.B. Supporting point. B Coy constructing shelter trenches in Billet H.29.6. Casualties 3 other Ranks wounded. Day quiet.	O.R.3
" 4/8/15	Weather dull & showery. A & C rest in BIVOUAC. Work continues on R.3. D Coy digging at Supporting point H.16.B. B Coy working at shelter trench & trenching Billet. D Coy carrying stores to VOORMEZEELE. Casualties 2 other Ranks wounded. Machine gun detachment attached to H.A.C. Day quiet.	O.R.2
" 5/8/15	Weather fine & Warm. A & C rest in BIVOUAC by day. Repairing fire trench. R.3. D Coy digging at Supporting point H.15.E. D Coy working at Shelter trenches in Billets & cleaning Camp. No Casualties.	nil

WAR DIARY
or
INTELLIGENCE SUMMARY.
(Erase heading not required.)

Army Form C. 2118.

Hour, Date, Place	Summary of Events and Information	Remarks and references to Appendices
N of DICKEBUSCHE 6/5/15	Weather dull. Morning. A & C in Bivouac H29b. Rest by day, work on repair of R3 & P1. Fire trenches, construction of R.Y. & communication trenches by night. Day work on supporting point H.15.c. B " in British at work on shelter trenches & clearing bumps. Night, at H.15c. relieved by A night at 6-3pm. No casualties by B & D Coy. shelled by shrapnel.	A/D
" " 7/5/15	Weather dull. A & C resting in Bivouac relieved by B & D Coy. 3 pm A & C to British in H.29b. B work on supporting point at H.15.c. Day in British digging & clearing bombs. B & D Coy at work on communication trench R.Y. 1 Battalion, 450 men carrying stores to VOORMEZEELE day gave no casualties.	A/D
" " 8/5/15	Weather fine Warm. B & D resting by day work on L of communication. Trench by night. A Coy to H.15.E. supporting point. C work on Shelter trenches and Brainy Camp. E work on Shelter trenches and Brainy Camp. Heavy Bombardment 1½ of YPRES, and at HOOGE. Casualties 6 Other Ranks wounded 10/1.	
" " 9/5/15	Weather fine & warm. B & D rest by day, work on communication trench R.Y. B 40 supporting point - H.15.C. A work on Shelter british & Brainy Camp. Heavy Artillery during day. No casualties. 1 Battalion a 450 men carrying stores.	A/D

WAR DIARY or INTELLIGENCE SUMMARY.

(Erase heading not required.)

Army Form C. 2118.

Instructions regarding War Diaries and Intelligence Summaries are contained in F.S. Regs., Part II. and the Staff Manual respectively. Title pages will be prepared in manuscript.

Hour, Date, Place	Summary of Events and Information	Remarks and references to Appendices
N. of DICKEBUSCHE 10/6/15	Weather fine. B. & D. rest by day. H.29. D. work on R.Y. communication trench by night. A. Coy to H.15.E. Supporting Point. C. Coy completing shelter trenches & gunide camp. 1 Officer & 30 H.Q. M.G. men arrived from Base. No Casualties. Company party 1 Officer 50 men.	Apl.
" 11/6/15	Weather fine. B. & D. rest by day. Work on R.Y. communication trench by night. A. Coy to H.15.E. Support on Supporting Point. A. Coy completing shelter trenches & clearing camp. Muster Parade 4 P.M. Army Act-read. No Casualties. Apl.	
" 12/6/15	Weather fine. B. & D. Coy rest by day. Work on R.Y. communication trench by night. A. Coy to H.15.E. Support on Supporting Point. C. Coy completing shelter trenches & clearing camp. 2 Battalions & 100 men carrying stores to VOORMEZEELE. 1 N.C.O. & 6 men collecting material. ELZINWALLE. No Casualties. Apl.	
" 13/6/15	Weather fine. D.+ B. Coy's rest by day, work on R.Y. communication trench by night. C. Coy to H.15.E. Supporting Point. A. Coy completing shelter trenches & clearing camp, carrying of material. H.24.B. shelled during morning. 1 N.C.O. & 6 men collecting material. Casualties nil.	Apl.

(9 29 6) W 4141—463 100,000 9/14 H W V Forms/C. 2118/10

WAR DIARY
or
INTELLIGENCE SUMMARY.

(Erase heading not required.)

Army Form C. 2118.

Hour, Date, Place		Summary of Events and Information	Remarks and references to Appendices
DICKEBUSCHE	14/6/15	Weather fine. B. & D. Coys relieved by A & C at H.29.6. A Coy at H.15.C on supporting Point. C. Coy garrisoning Camps A & C. Coy supply on R.Y. communication trench by night. Carrying party 2 officers 100 men supplied cartridges to VOORMEZEELE 1 N.C.O. & 8 men carrying stores and collecting material. Day party 1 Offr.	
"	15/6/15	Weather fine. B & D work on supporting point H.15.C. A & C returned from H.29.B. to H.29.D. 1 N.C.O. & 8 men collecting material for R.E. from ELZENWALLE. Heavy shelling in vicinity of Billets viz. DICKEBUSCHE. Grenadier hill & H.	
"	16/6/15	Weather showery. A & D work on supporting point H.15.C. B Coy in Camp Draining etc. 2 N.C.O. & 12 men collecting material at Ypres. 2 men killed, 5 injured by collapse of work. Day party, other casualties, 1 Offr.	
"	17/6/15	Weather showery. A & B work on supporting point H.15.C. VEERMOZEELE. C Coy in Camp. Cleanly inspected. Drawing from stores. 1 N.C.O. & 8 men collecting stores for R.E. VEERMOZEELE. Day quiet no Casualties.	1 Offr

Army Form C. 2118.

WAR DIARY
or
INTELLIGENCE SUMMARY.
(Erase heading not required.)

Instructions regarding War Diaries and Intelligence Summaries are contained in F.S. Regs., Part II. and the Staff Manual respectively. Title pages will be prepared in manuscript.

Hour, Date, Place		Summary of Events and Information	Remarks and references to Appendices
N. of DICKEBUSCHE	16/6/15 Weather fine	A.B. & C.Coy work on supporting point H.15.C. D.Coy work in camp, 1 H.C.O. & 8 men collecting material for R.E. at ELZINWALLE. Day quiet. 6 casualties.	A.P.M.
"	19/6/15 Weather fine	B.C. & D. Coys work on supporting point H.15.C. A. Coy work in camp, cleaning drains etc. 1 H.C.O. & 6 men collecting material at ELZINWALLE. Day quiet. 6 casualties.	A.P.M.
"	20/6/15 Weather fine	A.C. & D. Coys work on supporting point H.15.C. B. Coy work in camp. Draining etc. 1 H.C.O. & 8 men collecting material at ELZINWALLE. Day quiet. 6 casualties.	A.P.M.
"	21/6/15 Weather showery	A.B. & D. Coys work on supporting point H.15.C. C. Coy work in camp. Draining etc. 1 H.C.O. & 8 men collecting material at ABEELE. 1 Officer & 50 H.C.O. & men to ABEELE funeral in evening. Day quiet. 6 casualties.	A.P.M.
"	22/6/15 Weather showery	A.B. & C. work on supporting point H.15.C. D. Coy work in camp cleaning drains etc. 1 H.C.O. & 8 men collecting material at ELZINWALLE. 1 Officer & 55 H.C.O. & men. Hurdle making at H.15.D. 1 Officer & H.C.O. & 40 men in charge of supporting points. Day quiet. Casualties nil.	A.P.M.

WAR DIARY
or
INTELLIGENCE SUMMARY.

Army Form C. 2118.

Hour, Date, Place	Summary of Events and Information	Remarks and references to Appendices
N. of DICKEBUSCHE 23/6/15	Weather fine. Physical Drill all Ranks 6.30AM to 7.15AM. B,C & D work on supporting point H.15.C. A Coy work in Camp Cleaning drains etc. 1 R.E.O. & 8 men collecting material. 1 Officer & 55 R.E.O. & men furnish making in L.13.D. 1 officer & R.E.O. men in charge supporting points H.9. H.7. H.9. H.L. H & C. Day quiet. Casualties Nil.	Apl.
" " 24/6/15	Weather fine. Physical Drill all Ranks 6.30 AM to 7.15AM. 1 Officer 15 men to YPRES collecting material 2.30 AM. 1 N.C.O. & 40 men to R.E Park collecting material. A C.P.D Work on H.15.C Supporting Point. B Coy work in Camp cleaning drains etc. 1 R.C.O & 6 men collecting material. 1 Officer 55 R.E.O.& men furnish making L.13.D. 1 Officer 47 R.E.O. Men on supporting points. 9 Officers arrived from Base. Machine Gun Officer & detachment with 4 Guns sent to Y.P.O.W. for entire Duty. Day quiet. Casualties Nil.	Apl.
" " 25/6/15	Weather fine. Physical Drill all Ranks 6.30am to 7.15 A.m. A.B.& D to supporting point H.15.C. C.Coy in Camp Cleaning Drains etc. 1 R.C.O. & 8 men collecting material by R.E. 1 Officer & 55 men at L.13.D. Furnish training. 1 officer 47 R.E.O. in charge supporting points Machine Gun detachment on its 4th Day in Trenches. 1 Officer joined from Base. Day quiet. Casualties Nil.	Apl.

Army Form C. 2118.

WAR DIARY
or
INTELLIGENCE SUMMARY.
(Erase heading not required.)

Hour, Date, Place	Summary of Events and Information	Remarks and references to Appendices
N of DICKEBUSCHE 26/8/15 Weather fine	Physical Drill 6.30 to 6.4.15 a.m. A, B & C Coy to H.15.c. Supporting point for digging. D Coy work in camp clearing up. Remnants of R.E.O.& men collecting material for R.E. 1 officer 44 h. Coy 9 men in charge of supporting points, 1 officer & 55 h. Coy 7 men at # L.13.D. 1 officer 26 h. Coy 9 men attached to Y. Brigade Trench Entg. Hostile Aircraft over billets during day, nearly of hostile shells. Casualties 1 other ranks wounded.	[W]
" 27/8/15 Weather fine	Physical Drill 6.30 a.m. to 4.15 a.m. B, C & D Coys to H.15.c. Supporting point for digging. A Coy made in camp cleaning kit & draining 1 officer & 44 h. Coy men in charge of various supporting points, 1 officer & 53 h. Coy men at L.13.D. 1 officer 7 & men collected material for R.E. 1 officer 30 h. Coy men cleaning drain at ZILLEBEKE Y. 28/8/15 1 a.m 29/8/15 1 officer 26 h. Coy 9 men with & men attached to Y. Brigade Trench Entg. One officer of A & B Coy to Sanctuary Wood to inspect site of work to be carried out any guide to Casualties nil.	[W]
" 26/8/15 Weather fine	Physical Drill 6.30 a.m. to 4.15 a.m. C & D Coys to H.15.c. for digging. B Coy work in camp cleaning kit, draining A Coy by day under — orders to proceed to Sanctuary Wood to work on shelter left billets at 6.30 pm and worked on Communication trench during night. 1 officer 44 h. Coy 9 men in charge of supporting points, 1 officer 9 53 h Coy men at # L.13.D. 1 officer & 90 h. Coy & men attached to Y. Brigade Trench Entg, 1 officer 26 h. Coy 9 men work in R.E. Park. Any quiet. Casualties nil.	[W]

WAR DIARY
or
INTELLIGENCE SUMMARY

Army Form C. 2118.

(Erase heading not required.)

Hour, Date, Place	Summary of Events and Information	Remarks and references to Appendices
DICKEBUSCHE 29/8/15	Weather fine. Physical Drill from 6.0 to 6.30 A.M. B Coy 6.30 A.M. to YPRES. B & D Coys to H.15.c for Bridging. C Coy road in Camp Clearing pit site. A Coy at SANCTUARYWOOD rest by day, work on communication trenches by night. 1 Officer & 4 sect. of A. Coy Men in charge Tarriers supporting points. 1 Officer 53 h C.O.4 Men R.E. 2.13D tunnel miners supporting points. 1 Officer 30 h C.O. a Men work by night at ZILLEBEKE. 1 N.C.O. 7 12 Men work at "B" Bye Site. 1 Officer 26 h C.O. 9 Men work at "Burns" attached to Y Brigade for trench duty. Day quiet. Casualties Nil.	
" 30/8/15	Weather showery. C + D Coys 6.15 for Bridging. B Coy work in Camp clearing Pits Sites. A Coy rest by day at work for communication trench by night. 1 Officer + 4 sect. Men on a large working supporting point. 1 Officer 6 N.C.O. Men + 2.13D tunnel miners one Officer 30 h C.O. 9 Men working at ZILLEBEKE by night. 1 Officer 26 h C.O. 9 Men work at "Burns" attached to Y Brigade. 1 N.C.O. 12 Men work at R.E. Park. Day quiet. Casualties NIL.	
" 31/8/15	Weather fine. Physical Drill for Coys in Camp 6.30 to 7 A.M. C Coy to H.15.e for Bridging. D Coy in Camp Clearing pit + 2 parties to YPRES at 2.30 A.M. & 10 A.M. with 2 masons & 3 Lumley builders material for Hutments etc. A Coy rest by day. At work on communication trench by night. D Coy under orders to proceed to SANCTUARY WOOD for work on bivouacs with M.A.C. 1 Officer 4 N.C.O. Officers 9 Men at various supporting points, 1 Officer 53 h C.O. 4 Men at L.13D Hurdle making. 1 Officer 30 h C.O. 9 Men at night at ZILLEBEKE by night. 1 Officer 26 h C.O. 9 Men + 4 miners attached y/A Brigade trench duty. 1 N.C.O. 15 Men R.E. Park. 1 Officer 26 h C.O. 9 Men (BOMBERS) attached to 6 Brigade. Day quiet. Casualties Nil.	

7th Inf.Bde.
3rd Div.

Became Pioneers
12.10.15.

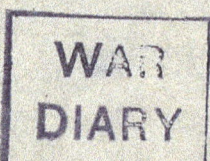

4th BATTN. THE SOUTH LANCASHIRE REGIMENT.

S E P T E M B E R

1 9 1 5

WAR DIARY
or
INTELLIGENCE SUMMARY.

(Erase heading not required.)

Army Form C. 2118.

Hour, Date, Place	Summary of Events and Information	Remarks and references to Appendices
N of DICKEBUSCHE 1/9/15	Weather fine. Rifle & Bayonet Exercise 6.30 AM to 7.15 AM. B. Coy to H/45 C. for digging. 6 Company in camp cleaning up. Bn. training etc. 1 Officer, 34 h. eoy & men on various supporting points. 1 Officer, 53 h. Coy men at L.13.D. Hurdle making. 1 Officer, 26 h. eoy men attached to 4 th Coy for trench duty. 1 Officer, 66 h. eoy men attached to 4 Coy for 6" infy Bde for "Bombing" 1 h. Officer & 15 men to R.E. Park. 1 Officer & 30 h. eoy men worked at ZILLEBEKE by night. A & B coy rest by day in SANCTUARY WOOD and MAPLE COPSE repairing & making trenches by night. Coy quiet. Casualties nil.	
" 2/9/15	Weather showery. Rifle & Bayonet Exercises 6.30 AM to 7.15 AM. C Coy to H.15.C for Digging. D Coy in camp cleaning kit. A & D rest by day in SANCTUARYWOOD and MAPLE COPSE repairing & making trenches by night. 1 Officer, 34 h. eoy men on various supporting points. 1 Officer, 53 h. Coy men. 1 h. Officer 26 h. Eoy men with 4 kings. Hurdle making at L.13.D. 1 Officer, 26 h. Eoy men attached to 4 Brigade for trench duty. 2 Officers 66 h. Coy men attached to 6" Bn. Hon. B" infy Bde for Bombing. 1 officer 30 h. eoy men work at ZILLEBEKE by night. 2 Lt & 9/20 men to K.16.D. R.E. fatigue. 3 h. W P9. 35 men fatigue at R.E. Park. Heavy Bombardment NW of YPRES Casualties nil.	
" 3/9/15	Weather fine. D. Coy Digging at H. 13 E. C by on Camp Brainings. 1 & 70 Coy Rest by Day repairing & making trenches by night. 1 Officer, 34 h. eoy men at various supporting points. 1 Officer 53 h. Coy men at L.13.D. 1 Officer 26 h. Coy men Hurdle making at L.13.D. 1 Officer 26 h. Coy & 1 h. eoy men with 4 m.G. attached 4/6 Brigade Trench duty.	

Army Form C. 2118.

WAR DIARY
or
INTELLIGENCE SUMMARY.
(Erase heading not required.)

Instructions regarding War Diaries and Intelligence Summaries are contained in F.S. Regs., Part II. and the Staff Manual respectively. Title pages will be prepared in manuscript.

Hour, Date, Place	Summary of Events and Information	Remarks and references to Appendices
N of DICKEBUSCH E. 4/9/15	2 Officers 66 h. coy men attached to 9th Bn ors 8th Brigade for Drilling. 1 Officer 36 h. 60 + 4 men work at ZILLEBEKE by night. 2 h. coy men at H16 & RE fatigue, 3 h. coy men to RE Park fatigue. Day quiet. Casualties 1 other Ranks wounded. Weather wet. D. Coy Road making & Draining Camp. 6 Coy reserve billets. A & B Coy met by Day working on Telephone trench by night. 1 Officer & 36 h. coy men on weapons supporting points at L.13.D. 2 Officers 1 Officer 5.3 h. coy 9 men trench mating at L.13.D. 2 Officers 68 h. coy 9 men detailed to 4th Brigade & 8th Brigade. Bombing 1 Officer 26 h. coy 4 men work at B. & attached to Brigade 1 Officer 36 h. coy 4 men work at ZILLEBEKE by night. 1 h. 20 men at H.16 & 7 E. fatigue. 1. coy+13 men at H.16 a constructing Bomb stores. 1 h. coy 20 men at 7E Park fatigue 1 h. coy 15 men at R.E. dark cooling timber. A Coy relieved by D Coy in SANCTUARY WOOD returned at 3 A.M. 5.9.15 Day quiet. Casualties 2 other ranks. 1 Officer Major Ll. Quidor on leave. Reported for duty.	App. App.
" " 5/9/15	Weather wet. A Company relieved by D. Company from Headquarters. B. Company in MAPLE COPSE. Working on Telephone trench at night. C. Company furnish fatigues Headquarters. 2 Officers Lt. Evans Bristol and Marks arrived and reported for duty. Casualties - nil. Detachments as usual.	App.

Forms/C. 2118/10

Army Form C. 2118.

WAR DIARY
or
INTELLIGENCE SUMMARY.

(*Erase heading not required.*)

Instructions regarding War Diaries and Intelligence Summaries are contained in F.S. Regs., Part II. and the Staff Manual respectively. Title pages will be prepared in manuscript.

Hour, Date, Place	Summary of Events and Information	Remarks and references to Appendices
N. of DICKEBUSCH. 6/9/15	Weather wet. A Company at Headquarters furnished all fatigues. B Coy relieved D Coy Headquarters & by march to MAPLE COPSE. 6 P.M. / D. Coy at SANCTUARY WOOD. worked in relays by night. Wired detachments. Dugouts. Casualties nil.	7M1.
" 7/9/15	Weather fine. A & B. Coys at Headquarters furnished all fatigues. C Coy in MAPLE COPSE and D in SANCTUARY WOOD working by night. detachments as before. Casualties - 1 other rank wounded.	4M1.
" 8/9/15	Weather fine. A & B Coys Headquarters furnished all fatigues. no casualties worked Camps. C & D Coys working by night in trenches. detachments as usual. Casualties - nil.	8M1.

Forms/C. 2118/10

WAR DIARY or INTELLIGENCE SUMMARY.

Army Form C. 2118.

Hour, Date, Place	Summary of Events and Information	Remarks and references to Appendices
No 9 DICKEBUSCH. 9/8/15	Weather fine. A & B Coys furnished all fatigues. C & D Coys working night in trenches. Detachments as normal. Bayonet considered.	fms
10/8/15	Weather fine. A & B Coys furnished all fatigues. C & D Coys worked by night in trenches. Detachments a usual. Casualties 1 O.R. wounded.	fms
11/8/15	Weather fine. A & B furnished fatigues. Bayonet drill cont. ogt. 2 P.M. 16". Rifle inspection Bayonet drill. A & B Coys & C Coy Bomb at 6.30 P.M. 16" relieve D Coy in SANCTUARY WOOD. A & C worked no. 9 the Km. Ry Sidings. Casualties 1 O.R. wounded.	fms
12/8/15	Weather fine. A + C Coys in trenches by night in SANCTUARY WOOD. C Company afterwards returning to Headquarters. B Company intensive during morning relieved C at night at MAPLE COPSE. D Company workers Camp in afternoon. Remainder of M.G. detachment Ramrod to Head Quarters. Worked detachments Bayonet. CASUALTIES. O.R. wounded 4. 1 R. died of wounds.	fms

WAR DIARY
or
INTELLIGENCE SUMMARY.
(Erase heading not required.)

Hour, Date, Place	Summary of Events and Information	Remarks and references to Appendices
N. of DICKEBUSCH.	**13/9/15** Weather fine - A & B Coy SANCTUARY WOOD. B Coy in MAPLE COPSE. Worked 2 parties by night. C. Company worked in camp. D. Coy H.I.6.d. Near R.E. Park in enlarging road. Detachments worked. Day Sunc. CASUALTIES - Nil	9pm
	14/9/15 Weather fine - A & B worked in trenches SANCTUARY WOOD. C Company H.16.d. Worked on Communication trench. D Coy in Huts 3 huts in YPRES & remainder worked in Camp. Detachments as usual. Day Sunc. CASUALTIES-Nil	9pm
	15/9/15 Weather Showery - A & B Companies worked in trenches SANCTUARY WOOD. C Company to H.16.d. enlarging road. D Company worked in Camp. Detachments as usual. Day Sunc. CASUALTIES. nil	9pm

WAR DIARY
or
INTELLIGENCE SUMMARY.
(Erase heading not required.)

Hour, Date, Place	Summary of Events and Information	Remarks and references to Appendices
N of DICKEBUSCH.	**16/6/15** Weather fine. — A & B Coys. worked in SANCTUARY WOOD. C Coy worked in repairing various SUPPORT POINTS. D Coy H.16.d. on corduroy roads. Detachments on wires. Day spent. CASUALTIES. 1 O.R. wounded.	
	17/6/15 Weather fine. — A & B Coys worked in Anchor & night in SANCTUARY WOOD. C & D Coys worked on supporting points. D & E Coy H.16.d. on duty roads. D.2.y H.16.d. Corduroy roads. Wires attachments. Day spent. CASUALTIES - Nil.	
	18/6/15 Weather fine. — A Coy returned to H.Q. relieved by D Coy. 'B' Coy worked on trenches by night. 'C' Coy worked on support points. D Coy to H.16.d. Corduroy roads in the hour & relieved A Coy at night. Wired detachments. Day spent. CASUALTIES 1 O.R. wounded.	

WAR DIARY
or
INTELLIGENCE SUMMARY.
(Erase heading not required.)

Instructions regarding War Diaries and Intelligence Summaries are contained in F.S. Regs., Part II. and the Staff Manual respectively. Title pages will be prepared in manuscript.

Hour, Date, Place	Summary of Events and Information	Remarks and references to Appendices
N⁰ 7 DICKEBUSCH.	Weather wet - A Coy to H.16.d. continuing road in the afternoon. B Coy returned to H.Q. being relieved by C. Coy from 'C' to H.16d in the morning afterwards relieved 'B' Coy at night. D Coy worked on trenches in SANCTUARY WOOD. Usual detachments from Sumr. CASUALTIES - Nil.	fm
20/5/15	A Coy to H.16.d continuing road. B Coy worked in Camp furnishing fwk'g 41 O.R. under 2nd Lieut. CHEERS to make BOMB STORES in CONDUIT STREET. C & D Coy worked in trenches in SANCTUARY WOOD by night. D Coy furnished 40 O.R. for making Bomb Stores in SANCTUARY WOOD under 2nd Lieut BARNISH. Usual detachments + 1 Offr. + 26 O.R. & Warden SALIENT C.T. 9. 1 O.R. wounded. CASUALTIES. 1 O.R. wounded.	fm

Forms/C. 2118/10

WAR DIARY or INTELLIGENCE SUMMARY.

(Erase heading not required.)

Instructions regarding War Diaries and Intelligence Summaries are contained in F.S. Regs., Part II. and the Staff Manual respectively. Title pages will be prepared in manuscript.

Hour, Date, Place		Summary of Events and Information	Remarks and references to Appendices
DICKEBUSCH.	21/9/15 Weather Summary	A Coy handed over fatigue to YPRES. remainder working in Camp. 'B' Coy to H.16 d. for ordinary work. C+D Companies worked in trenches SANCTUARY WOOD. Detachments as usual. CASUALTIES Nil	9pm
	22/9/15 Weather fine	A Coy to H.16 d. ordinary work. B Coy worked in Camp. C+D worked in trenches SANCTUARY WOOD. CASUALTIES 1 O.R. wounded.	9pm
	23/9/15 Weather wet	A Coy H.16 d. ordinary work. B Coy worked in Camp. C+D Coy worked in trenches in SANCTUARY WOOD. Usual detachments. CASUALTIES 1 O.R. wounded.	9pm

Army Form C. 2118.

WAR DIARY
or
INTELLIGENCE SUMMARY.
(Erase heading not required.)

Hour, Date, Place	Summary of Events and Information	Remarks and references to Appendices
No 9 DICKEBUSCH.	24/9/15 Weather showery. A Coy to H.16.d. Enduring walls. B & C worked in trenches. G.T.D. Coys worked in trenches SANCTUARY WOOD. At night the whole Battalion moved to RAMPARTS at YPRES. under the orders of C.R.E. 3rd Division during operations. Commencing morning of 25th inst. Usual awork. CASUALTIES. 1 O.R. Wounded.	9pm
25/9/15	Weather wet. Battalion in RAMPARTS. Bombardment commenced at 3.50 AM. Enemy shelled the RAMPARTS. no casualties. Bombers in action with the Gordon Highlanders. Machine Gunners attacked to 7th Bde in support. The Battalion moved up to SANCTUARY WOOD at 7PM and worked on front line trenches	7pm

WAR DIARY or INTELLIGENCE SUMMARY.

(Erase heading not required.)

Hour, Date, Place	Summary of Events and Information	Remarks and references to Appendices
N9 DICKEBUSCH.	25/9/15 and in communication trenches, afterwards returning to RAMPARTS. CASUALTIES. Killed. 1 Officer. 3.O.R. Wounded 1 Officer 19.O.R. Missing 16 O.R	am
	26/9/15 Weather fine. Battalion in RAMPARTS during the day. Attached A & B Coy worked on UNION STREE. C.T. C & D Coys worked on C.T. in SANCTUARY WOOD. Battalion returned to Camp at dawn. CASUALTIES. Killed 2.O.R. WOUNDED 5 O.R. MISSING 1 O.R. Heavy bombardment on both sides about 11 P.M. Started strong our attack of bombers, causing the above casualties.	am

WAR DIARY
or
INTELLIGENCE SUMMARY.

(Erase heading not required.)

Hour, Date, Place	Summary of Events and Information	Remarks and references to Appendices
N.4 DICKEBUSCH.		
27/9/15	Weather showery. Battalion rested in camp by day. A&B Coys would F ZILLEBEKE POND DUGOUTS at night. Usual detachments. Casualties—nil.	fmm
28/9/15	Weather showery. A&B Coys at ZILLEBEKE. Worked on trench at night. C Coy "rested" in camp. D Coy worked on scavenger road at H.16.d & KRUISSTRAAT. Picket to YPRES? collecting material. trench supplies. Casualties–nil.	fmm
29/9/15	Weather wet.	
	A&B Coys at ZILLEBEKE worked on trenches by night. C Coy in camp. D Coy at H.16.d & KRUISSTRAAT in building huts. Usual detachments. Casualties. 10 R. accidentally wounded.	fmm
30/9/15	Wet.	
	A&B Coys ZILLEBEKE worked on trenches at night. C Coy in training at H.16.d & KRUISSTRAAT D Coy worked in camp. CASUALTIES. 1 O.R. killed 1 O.R. wounded	fmm

3RD DIVISION
DIVL. TROOPS.

7 BDE

4TH BATTALION
STH LANCS REGT.
OCT-DEC 1915

To 55 DIVISION (PIONEERS)
Jan '16

1087

Pioneers.
3rd Div.

From 7th Inf.Bde.
3rd Div. 12.10.15.

WAR DIARY

4th BATTN. THE SOUTH LANCASHIRE REGIMENT.

OCTOBER

1915

WAR DIARY
or
INTELLIGENCE SUMMARY.

(Erase heading not required.)

Army Form C. 2118.

Instructions regarding War Diaries and Intelligence Summaries are contained in F.S. Regs., Part II. and the Staff Manual respectively. Title pages will be prepared in manuscript.

Hour, Date, Place	Summary of Events and Information	Remarks and references to Appendices
N.q. DICKEBUSCH. 1/10/15 Weather wet.	A & B Coys ZILLEBEKE worked in trenches by night. C Coy. worked in Camp. D Coy. worked in Coltivry road KRUISSTRAAT. Lieut. ANTROBUS killed. Attachments CASUALTIES. 1 Offr. ANTROBUS killed.	2 Lieut ANTROBUS was left B Company in command when shot by a sniper at about 15 yards range. The enemy front trenches faced the [ ] of SANCTUARY WOOD. JM
2/10/15 wet	A & B Coys ZILLEBEKE worked in trenches by night. C Company continuing road KRUISSTRAAT. D Company worked in Camp. 1 med Attachment. CASUALTIES. 1 O.R. wounded.	JM
3/10/15 fine	A & B Coys at ZILLEBEKE worked in trenches at night. B Company returned to camp on completion of job there. C Company relieved B Company at ZILLEBEKE at night. D Company bivouacked in YPRES - billeted in RUE D'ELVERDINGHE in cellars - & work on REGENT STREET. Usual detachments. CASUALTIES. 1 O.R. wounded.	Major Garry to hospital. JM
4/10/15 wet	A & C Coys at ZILLEBEKE worked in trenches by night. B Coy worked in KRUISSTRAAT continuing road from [ ]. D Coy at YPRES worked on REGENT ST at night and provided coming part to SANCTUARY WOOD. Usual detachments. CASUALTIES. 1 O.R. wounded.	JM
5/10/15 wet	A & C Coys at ZILLEBEKE worked in trenches by night. B Coy worked at KRUISSTRAAT on road by day. D Coy worked on REGENT ST by night. 3 baths YPRES. Usual material. Attachments. CASUALTIES. 1 O.R. wounded.	JM

WAR DIARY
or
INTELLIGENCE SUMMARY.
(Erase heading not required.)

Army Form C. 2118.

Hour, Date, Place		Summary of Events and Information	Remarks and references to Appendices
N of DICKEBUSCH.	6/10/15 Fine.	A & C Coys ZILLEBEKE worked in trenches at night. B Coy inducing road KRUISSTRAAT. D Coy at YPRES provided carrying party also working Regent St. Usual detachments. CASUALTIES nil.	
	7/10/15 Fine.	A & C Coys ZILLEBEKE worked in trenches at night. B Coy inducing road KRUISSTRAAT. D Coy at YPRES worked in REGENT ST. Draft 7 O.R. arrived from Base. Usual detachments. CASUALTIES 1 O.R. killed.	
	8/10/15 Fine.	A & C Coys ZILLEBEKE worked in trenches at night. B Coy continuing road KRUISSTRAAT. D Coy at YPRES worked in REGENT ST. Usual detachments. CASUALTIES nil.	
	9/10/15 Fine.	A & C Coys ZILLEBEKE worked in trenches at night. A Coy returned to camp in afternoon, whilst on return B Coy worked on corduroy road KRUISSTRAAT, were non-relieving A Coy at ZILLEBEKE at night. D Coy at YPRES worked in REGENT ST. also provided fatigue parties & carrying party for new tramway. Bombers returned to Headquarters from B & D coys detachments. CASUALTIES nil.	Appx

WAR DIARY or **INTELLIGENCE SUMMARY.**

(Erase heading not required.)

Army Form C. 2118.

Instructions regarding War Diaries and Intelligence Summaries are contained in F.S. Regs., Part II. and the Staff Manual respectively. Title pages will be prepared in manuscript.

Hour, Date, Place		Summary of Events and Information	Remarks and references to Appendices
N. of DICKEBUSCH	10/10/15 Fine.	B & C Coys at ZILLEBEKE worked in trenches at night. A Coy in Camp. D Coy at YPRES worked in REGENT ST. Bombers to Corduroy rds, transport road, KRUISSTRAAT. Horse detachments. CASUALTIES - nil.	JMW
	11/10/15 Fine.	B & C. Coys at ZILLEBEKE worked in trenches at night. A Coy + Bombers to Corduroy rd, KRUISSTRAAT. D Coy at YPRES. worked in REGENT ST. Horse detachments. CASUALTIES - nil.	JMW
	12/10/15 Fine.	B + C Coys at ZILLEBEKE worked in trenches at night. A Coy and Bombers on Corduroy road KRUISSTRAAT. D Coy at YPRES. worked in REGENT ST. Horse detachments. CASUALTIES - nil.	JMW
	13/10/15 Fine.	B + C Coys at ZILLEBEKE worked in trenches at night. A Coy and Bombers on Corduroy road KRUISSTRAAT. D Coy at YPRES. worked in REGENT ST. Horse detachments. CASUALTIES - nil	JMW
	14/10/15 Fine	B + C Coys at ZILLEBEKE worked in trenches at night. A Coy + Bombers on Corduroy road KRUISSTRAAT. D Coy at YPRES worked in REGENT ST. Horse detachments. CASUALTIES - nil	JMW

WAR DIARY or INTELLIGENCE SUMMARY.

Army Form C. 2118.

(Erase heading not required.)

Instructions regarding War Diaries and Intelligence Summaries are contained in F.S. Regs., Part II and the Staff Manual respectively. Title pages will be prepared in manuscript.

Hour, Date, Place	Summary of Events and Information	Remarks and references to Appendices
N°7 DICKEBUSCH. Tue. 15/10/15.	B & C Coys ZILLEBEKE worked in trenches at night. C Coy returned to Camp in completed daylight work. A Coy to continue road KRUISSTRAAT until noon - returned. C Company to ZILLEBEKE at night. Bombers to continue road KRUISSTRAAT from noon. Draft 70 OR arrived from base. Unwire detachments. CASUALTIES - nil.	(M)
Fri. 16/10/15.	A & B Coys at ZILLEBEKE worked in trenches by day. C Company in camp. Bombers at KRUISSTRAAT. D Coy at YPRES worked on REGENT ST. returning to Headquarters after dark. Detachment at usual. CASUALTIES - nil.	(M)
Sat. 17/10/15.	A & B Coys at ZILLEBEKE worked in trenches by day. Coys 1 platoon entry-ch of H16d. filling sandbags. Thursday. Support from Remainder + bombers to continue road KRUISSTRAAT. D Coy continued REGENT ST at night. Usual detachments. CASUALTIES. 1 OR wounded	(M)
Sun. 18/10/15.	A & B Coys at ZILLEBEKE worked in trenches by day. E Coy + bombers worked on continuing road KRUISSTRAAT. D Coy continued REGENT ST by night. Usual detachments. CASUALTIES. 2 OR wounded	(M)

Army Form C. 2118.

WAR DIARY
or
INTELLIGENCE SUMMARY.
(Erase heading not required.)

Instructions regarding War Diaries and Intelligence
Summaries are contained in F.S. Regs., Part II.
and the Staff Manual respectively. Title pages
will be prepared in manuscript.

Hour, Date, Place		Summary of Events and Information	Remarks and references to Appendices
No 4 DICKEBUSCH.	19/10/15 Weather fine.	A + B. Boys worked at ZILLEBEKE by day. C.Boy with Bombers continued work on conducting road (new Kempen road) KRUISSTRAAT D Boy worked on C.T's near MENIN RD. LIDDLE Road detachments. CASUALTIES. 1 O.R. wounded.	am.
	20/10/15 Weather fine.	A + B Boys worked at ZILLEBEKE by day on new C.T. which was named WARRINGTON AVENUE. C. Boy and Bombers continued road making at KRUISSTRAAT D. Boy worked on C.T's near MENIN RD. By night issued detachments. CASUALTIES nil 3/Lieut LINDEN discharged hospital returned to duty.	am.
	21/10/15 Weather fine.	A + B Boys worked at ZILLEBEKE by day on new C.T. HARRINGTON AVENUE C.Boy + Bombers at KRUISSTRAAT on conducting road. + Boy worked on C.T's near MENIN RD by night, A + B Boys and all detachments except hurdle makers at ABEELE and SUPPORT POINT WARDENS returned to Headquarters at night. CASUALTIES - nil. Billeting party proceeded to BERTHEN + commenced by midnight 2000 to BERTHEN	am.

(73989) W4141—463. 400,000. 9/14. H.&J.Ltd. Forms/C. 2118/10.

WAR DIARY
or
INTELLIGENCE SUMMARY.
(Erase heading not required.)

Army Form C. 2118.

Place	Hour, Date	Summary of Events and Information	Remarks and references to Appendices
DICKEBUSH	22/10/15	Battalion cleared up the camp by day. Transport convoy took to BERTHEN. Battalion marched off at 5.30 P.M. arriving at BERTHEN at 9.15 P.M. The night was clear and moonlight. the Battalion marching well. CASUALTIES nil.	P.M.
BERTHEN	23/10/15 24/10/15	2/Lt SHEPPERSON W.R.O.A joined. 2/Lieut WALMSLEY joined at BERTHEN	
	25/10/15	Battalion in the same Billets & Quarters. Route marches & Games of Football for teams from Reg'ts & Commands under C.O.	P.M.
	26/10/15	1 Officer 20 OR. proceeded to STEENVOORDE to represent the Battalion at an Inspection of I.V Corps at REMINGHELST by H.M. The King.	P.M.
	27/10/15	5 Officers & 15 men on the list of representatives of the Battalion & K Coy. included at 5 Coy 16 Lancashire Regt. by His Majesty KING GEORGE	P.M.
	28/10/15	2/Lieut R L BRISCOE joined for duty. Weather having been to heavy Walker.	P.M.

Pioneers.
3rd Div.

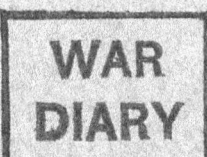

4th BATTN. THE SOUTH LANCASHIRE REGIMENT.

NOVEMBER

1915

WAR DIARY
or
INTELLIGENCE SUMMARY.

(Erase heading not required.)

Army Form C. 2118.

Hour, Date, Place	Summary of Events and Information	Remarks and references to Appendices
BERTHEN 29/10/15 to 2/11/15	Weather broken. Numbers, Supplies instructed, Battalion route marching, sub-calibre drill &c. Routine — not with 2n French Division & No 2n French Foreign Legion.	
3/11/15	Weather fine. Lieut. B.T. DICKSON joined for duty. Instruction as normal. HIS MAJESTY THE KING visited Corps.	
4/11/15	Weather fine. Debacle &c. normal. Practice, Ranging instruction continued. M.G. John (machine) M.G. replacement in routine & support.	
5/11/15	Weather wet. Battalion proceeded to OUDEZEELE at 7.45PM & billeted there arriving at abt 11.30 PM. W.G. Commander officer proceeded on leave to ENGLAND. Major CROSFIELD thereupon temporarily assumed command of Battalion. Casualties & names of officers to join & H.Q. in DIARY.	

Army Form C. 2118.

WAR DIARY
or
INTELLIGENCE SUMMARY.
(Erase heading not required.)

Hour, Date, Place		Summary of Events and Information	Remarks and references to Appendices
OUDEZEELE. J 14.a.5.1.	6/11/15 Weather fine.	The Battalion route marched in the morning by Companies.	AN
	7/11/15 Weather wet.	The Battalion route marched by Companies in the morning.	AN
	8/11/15 wet.	9 Officers 50 O.R. attended anti-gas demonstration at STEENVOORDE. Battalion under Company arrangements. Three day Course in Bombing for Officers commenced under Bombing Officer. 2/Lieut HOWES and 2 O.R. proceeded to GRENADE SCHOOL. ABEELE for Bombing Course.	AN
	9/11/15 Weather fine.	Battalion under Company arrangements in morning. A 173 Bde paperchase in the afternoon. C & B both marched.	AN
	10/11/15 Weather fine	Battalion under Company arrangements in morning. In the afternoon C & D Coys ran a paperchase. A & B route marched.	AN
	11/11/15 Weather fine.	Battalion route march via VERT VALLON (CASSEL) HARDIFORT - CORNHUYSE. Battalion under Company arrangements in the afternoon - Preliminary heats for short run off.	AN

Army Form C. 2118.

WAR DIARY
or
INTELLIGENCE SUMMARY.
(Erase heading not required.)

Instructions regarding War Diaries and Intelligence
Summaries are contained in F.S. Regs., Part II.
and the Staff Manual respectively. Title pages
will be prepared in manuscript.

Hour, Date, Place	Summary of Events and Information	Remarks and references to Appendices
OUDEZEELE.		
12/11/15. Wed.	Battalion under company arrangements during the morning for company feats of sports, bathing etc. Sports held in the afternoon, the weather having improved. No sports were of great success. Events for companies. Tug of war (on horses), bareback wrestling, tug of war on foot, Rugby race etc.	JML
13/11/15. Fri.	Battalion parade in morning for battalion drill. Afternoon holiday. Football matches played. Russian mechagh? range J.31.C for Mnus.	JML
14/11/15. Sun.	Church parade in a.m. afternoon 2/Lieut HOWES + 2.O.R returned from GRENADE SCHOOL. ABEELE.	JML
15/11/15. Wed.	'B' Company (1 platoon) completed range afternoon firing 20 rounds/p.r man. Machine Gun Section also fired. 2/Lieut BARNISH + 50. O.R commenced manufacture of Gabions. 2/Lieut BATCHELOR + 2.O.R to GRENADE SCHOOL. ABEELE.	JML

WAR DIARY
or
INTELLIGENCE SUMMARY.
(Erase heading not required.)

Army Form C. 2118.

Hour, Date, Place		Summary of Events and Information	Remarks and references to Appendices
OUDEZEELE.	16/11/15 Weather fine.	Attack practice in the morning under company arrangements. Afternoon A & C Coys ran before supper. B & D under company arrangements. B Coy fired 20 rounds per man on range. Battalion less C Coy rifle marched via HERZEELE, REXPOEDE, WEST CAPPEL, WYLDER & WORMHOUT.	am
	17/11/15 Fine.	C Coy on range fired 20 rounds per man. Coy practised the attack, & under Company arrangements. D Coy on range. Commanding Officer returned and resumed command.	am
	18/11/15 Wet.		am
	19/11/15 Fine.	Battalion less A Coy route marched via CRUYHUYSE, HARDEFORT, WORMHOUDT & HERZEN PUT. A Coy on range.	am
	20/11/15 Wet.	Battalion inspected & clothing etc. In afternoon practice machine gun instruction. Mining Camp. Range filled in & closed. Yphre sp. inire.	am
	21/11/15 Fine & cold.	Battalion moved to POPERINGHE at 8.45 AM, arriving about 1.30 PM. March about 14 miles. Battalion billeted as CONVENT SCHOOL RUE de BOESCHEPE.	am
POPERINGHE.	22/11/15 Wet.	Battalion at POPERINGHE awaiting orders. Supplying Road Wardens & Road MAIN BLEY 33 OR marched 8 AM. A & B Coys + H.Q. moved to VOORNEZEELE at 3 (5 Am taking over trenches from 12 SHERWOOD FORESTERS (11 INS Bde 4 th Div) C & D Coys under Captain RIDGWAY remained at POPERINGHE	am

Army Form C. 2118.

WAR DIARY
or
INTELLIGENCE SUMMARY.
(Erase heading not required.)

Instructions regarding War Diaries and Intelligence Summaries are contained in F.S. Regs., Part II. and the Staff Manual respectively. Title pages will be prepared in manuscript.

Hour, Date, Place		Summary of Events and Information	Remarks and references to Appendices
VOORMEZEELE.	23/11/15. Foggy.	Wet. Battalion strongly Manning defence of SCHOOL CASTLE & CONVENT. Revetting & improving C.T's. Saw front line built up in CASTLE and main CONVENT. A Coy Hqrs 1 platoon in SCHOOL, 1 platoon A Coy in CASTLE. B Coy in CONVENT. 2 platoons in Command of CONVENT wounding 2 men. 1 M.G. 12 WEST YORKS in SCHOOL defences. 1 M.G. " CASTLE " Casualties 2 O.R. wounded. Emeralds met marched.	AM
	24/11/15. First clear	Detachment at POPERINGHE met marched. A & B Coys each less 1 platoon continued improving defences. 1 platoon K.T.BRASSERIE worked on BOIS CONFLUENT C.T. 1 platoon in CONVENT LANE. Pioneers fixing duckwalks in ELZENWALLE C.T. Headquarters returned to RENNINGHELST at 5 P.M. Lieut. Major CROSFIELD in Command 2 Platoons worked on CONVENT LANE from 5 AM & 10 PM. Detachment moved to RENNINGHELST from POPERINGHEAD 1 P.M. arriving 3-15 P.M. Casualties nil.	AM
RENNINGHELST.	25/11/15. Fine & clear	1 Platoon of A worked on BOIS CONFLUENT. C.T. 1 Platoon of A worked at night on ELZENWALLE C.T. Remainder of A worked on CONVENT LANE. B Coy. on 1 Platoon worked on CONVENT LANE by day. 1 platoon B worked at CONVENT. D Coy moved to CANAL BANK. Casualties nil	AM

WAR DIARY
or
INTELLIGENCE SUMMARY.
(Erase heading not required.)

Army Form C. 2118.

Hour, Date, Place	Summary of Events and Information	Remarks and references to Appendices
RENINGHELST.		
26/11/15. Changeable - Some snow.	"A" Y/B at VOORMEZEELE worked from 8/30am till 3.30 PM. on CONVENT LANE. One platoon on ELZENWALLE. C.T. one platoon in dugouts and parts at CONVENT. D Coy Gieleng dugouts at CANAL BANK - worked on new C.T. at CANAL. Coy in Camp Specialist making and laying duckwalks. CASUALTIES - nil.	A.M.
27/11/15 Thursday	Worked carried on at VOORMEZEELE as 26th. CASTLE filled with H.E. Shrapnel. D Coy at OMAR working on new C.T - Supplied carrying party by R.E. Also worked in dugouts. H.Q. draining camp, making & laying duckboards etc. CASUALTIES - nil.	A.M.
28/11/15. Severe frost - bright sunshine.	VOORMEZEELE Shelled with H.E. Shrapnel. A Coy on CONVENT LANE. C.T. B Coy one platoon SCOTTISH WOOD to work on Cd. Arcy way to join up with BOIS CONFLUENT light railway. 2 platoons on BOIS CONFLUENT. C.T. 1 Platoon improving CONVENT + making dugouts at SCHOOL. B Coy relieved by C Coy. H.Q. Church Powell. Details informing Camp. 82 O.R. reported attached to battalion - Comes from various regiments. D Coy at CANAL revetting new C.T. + carrying stores for R.E. C.S.M. DAVIES R/for DICKEBUSCH. CASUALTIES. I.O.R.	p.m.

Army Form C. 2118.

WAR DIARY
or
INTELLIGENCE SUMMARY.
(Erase heading not required.)

Instructions regarding War Diaries and Intelligence Summaries are contained in F.S. Regs., Part II. and the Staff Manual respectively. Title pages will be prepared in manuscript.

Hour, Date, Place		Summary of Events and Information	Remarks and references to Appendices
RENINGHELST	29/11/15 Wed.	C Coy carried on with light railway, 1201 S CONFLUENT. C.T. & CONVENT. A Coy worked on CONVENT LANE. Some shelling @ VOORMEZEELE. D Coy at CANAL continued hutting C.T. & provided parties for R.E. B Coy at H.Q. working in Camp. 7 men & C.S.M. DAVIES at DICKEBUSCH Cemetery. 1/2 M.G. Section & 2 guns to VOORMEZEELE. Capt E. FAIRCLOUGH joined for duty from ENGLAND. CASUALTIES - nil.	
	30/11/15 Bullet=rain.	A & C Coy working on usual - making duckwalks, anchors, fascines. Commenced use of baths. D Coy working as usual. H.Q Coy commenced corduroy road at R.E. PARK. CASUALTIES - nil	

Pioneers.
3rd Div.

Battn. transferred to 55th Div. as Pioneers 9.1.16.

WAR DIARY

4th BATTN. THE SOUTH LANCASHIRE REGIMENT.

DECEMBER

1915

WAR DIARY or INTELLIGENCE SUMMARY

Army Form C. 2118.

December 1915

Hour, Date, Place	Summary of Events and Information	Remarks and references to Appendices
RENINGHELST. 1/12/15. Wet.	Work at VOORMEZEELE and KINGSWAY (CANAL BANK) as usual. Considerable shelling of SCOTTISH WOOD & ETZENWALLE C.T. Work stopped in ETZENWALLE in consequence. B. Coy in Camp - work as usual. Casualties NIL.	pm
2/12/15. Fine.	Work as usual. 'B' relieved 'A' at VOORMEZEELE. Casualties 2/Lieut A.J. MONKS & 3/Lieut BATCHELOR rejoined	pm
3/12/15. Slight rain.	Work as usual. Bishopping of ETZENWALLE C.T. completed. Casualties NIL.	pm
4/12/15. Rained all day.	CONVENT LANE collapsed in districts of 15 yards. Work as usual. 'A' Coy in Camp. Casualties NIL.	pm
5/12/15. Frost mild.	Work as usual. CONVENT LANE cleared. Casualties NIL.	pm
6/12/15.	Continuing extension of CONVENT LANE to R.W. 'A' relieved 'D' Coy at KINGSWAY (CANAL). Casualties 0 Killed.	pm
7/12/15. Frost Cold.	Usual work at KINGSWAY and VOORMEZEELE - heavy shelling on VOORMEZEELE. Company in Camp as usual. R.E. Parks & Scouril. Casualties NIL.	pm
8/12/15.	Work as usual at KINGSWAY and VOORMEZEELE on Communication trenches and H.Q. supplementary RUSH HOUSE. Work on own and R.E. Park & Scouril. Casualties NIL.	pm
13/12/15.		pm
14/12/15.	Work as usual. 10/R + 53 CR, to Gode to handle meching (GODEWAERSVELDE)	pm

Army Form C. 2118.

WAR DIARY
or
INTELLIGENCE SUMMARY.
(Erase heading not required.)

Instructions regarding War Diaries and Intelligence Summaries are contained in F.S. Regs., Part II. and the Staff Manual respectively. Title pages will be prepared in manuscript.

Hour, Date, Place		Summary of Events and Information	Remarks and references to Appendices
RENNINGHELST.	17/12/15 18/12/15	Took as usual as VOORMEZEELE, KINGSWAY and in camp. M.G. emplacement finished at O.S. HOUSE no casualties NIL. 17/12/15	JM
	19/12/15	At 4 A.M. on VOORMEZEELE heavy rifle fire heard for 10 minutes. 8 am R. and connected up telephones. Shell cleared 4.30 A.M. On 5 A.M. rifle fire broke out again in the direction YPRES. Together with very heavy artillery. Stood to. Gas became afterwards at 5.30 AM sufficient alarm to make all wear water. Bombardment died down about 7 AM. Work proceeded as normal afterwards. Similar scenes occurred as KINGSWAY. On H.Q. at RENNINGHELST the violent bombardment was heard at 5.30 AM and gas appeared about 6 AM. Gas was sufficiently strong to make one cough distinctly unpleasant. As one stood to - receiving an order to do so half an hour later. Battalion was headquarters including transport within the hour. Received orders to stand down about 11AM. Casualties 1 O.R. wounded.	JM
	20/12/15 to 28/12/15	Work as VOORMEZEELE + KINGSWAY and in Camp. Code of movements was used during this period. Casualties NIL.	JM
	29/12/15	Draft of 400R. joined Battalion from No 5 Infantry 2 Battalion. Casualties NIL.	JM

Army Form C. 2118.

WAR DIARY
or
INTELLIGENCE SUMMARY.
(Erase heading not required.)

Instructions regarding War Diaries and Intelligence Summaries are contained in F.S. Regs., Part II. and the Staff Manual respectively. Title pages will be prepared in manuscript.

Hour, Date, Place	Summary of Events and Information	Remarks and references to Appendices
RENNINGHELST. 30/12/15.	Woke as usual. Casualties NIL. Major Crosfield returned from leave & took over command of 2nd SUFFOLK REGIMENT.	am
" 31/12/15.	Woke as usual. Casualties 1 O.R. wounded.	am am

www.ingramcontent.com/pod-product-compliance
Lightning Source LLC
Chambersburg PA
CBHW080836010526
44114CB00017B/2321